PENELOPE'S DAUGHTERS

PENELOPE'S DAUGHTERS

A feminist perspective of the myth of Penelope in
Annie Leclerc's *Toi, Pénélope*,
Margaret Atwood's *The Penelopiad*
and Silvana La Spina's *Penelope*

Barbara Dell'Abate-Çelebi

Zea Books: Lincoln, Nebraska
2016

ISBN 978-1-60962-083-7 paperback
ISBN 978-1-60962-084-4 electronic book

Composed in Georgia and Lithos types by Paul Royster.

Zea Books are published by the
University of Nebraska–Lincoln Libraries.

Digital ebook edition (pdf) available at
http://digitalcommons.unl.edu

Print edition can be ordered from
http://www.lulu.com/spotlight/unllib

UNL does not discriminate based upon any protected status.
Please see go.unl.edu/nondiscrimination

Nebraska
UNIVERSITY OF
Lincoln

Per Ümit,
sonsuza dek

CONTENTS

FOREWORD

In the introductory part of this book Dr. Barbara Dell'Abate-Çelebi traces the changing perceptions of Penelope from the 5th century BC to the 20th century. We learn how Penelope's image alternated from that of an adulteress to a faithful spouse awaiting the return of a lost husband and lover. The book attributes the changes in attitude and ways of representation of Penelope to the then current political and social *status quo*.

In a style that addresses both the professional scholar and the beginner in literary theory, chapter one traces the emergence, growth and development of the feminist movement from its inception around the early 19th century to the postmodern era. We learn, for example, that Mary Wollstonecraft, Mary Shelley's mother, was described by a later generation feminist critic as a "hyena in petticoats" and a "philosophical wanton." We also learn that some feminist scholars view the sexual relation as a beating by the penis or a symbolic form of male aggression. The discussion invokes an array of influential female scholars who shaped the feminist movements in the western world, including Simone de Beauvoir, Betty Friedan, Kate Millett, Mary Ellmann, Elaine Showalter, Sandra Gilbert, and many more. Literary and philosophical movements that influenced feminist thinking are dealt with and elucidated too. Structural theories, we learn, such as formalism, new criticism, and most linguistic-based readings of texts are opposed by the various feminist movements as they have alienated the text from its cultural and historical signification.

Chapter two provides a succinct and interesting introduction to the historical and mythical origins of Homer and his composition. With scholarly precision, the author documents the writings of various critics who shed light on Homer, his work and his world. Ulysses gains his mythical reputation, the author tells us, because of his refusal to accept mortality at the expense of denying recognition of the human condition. The chapter also examines how Penelope moved from the marginal position assigned by earlier critics to occupy a central position in the epic as judged by postmodernist interpreters. The chapter refers to seminal scholars such as Marie Madelaine Mactoux, Marylin Arthur-Katz, Nancy Felson-Rubin, Ioanna Papadopolou-Belmehdi, and Adriana Cavarero, among others whose perceptions of Penelope are similarly insightful and provoking.

Chapter three compares the original Penelope with the Penelope of *Toi, Pénélope* by Annie Leclerc. The analysis of the texts is a *tour de force* through two different mind sets: one is Homeric and the other is contemporary. In a critical reading of the two Penelopes' social and psychological situatedness, Dr. Dell'Abate Celebi argues that memory and oblivion are among the motives of modern Penelope's attachment to her absent spouse.

Chapter four examines *The Penelopiad* by Margaret Atwood. We learn that Atwood's career not only involves writing about "power politics" between lovers but also gives voice to silenced and marginalized females in mythical and other narratives. With this in mind, the chapter animates an altogether new Penelope who is very different from her Homeric namesake. Is the new Penelope wicked, faithful, treacherous, dangerous, and subversive? Answers lie in the way Penelope is analyzed in this chapter.

Penelope by Silvana La Spina is the subject of the fifth and last chapter of the book. Penelope is viewed from a modern Italian feminist perspective as a victim of institutionalized violence against women. We see a Penelope vocalizing the humiliation and violence inflicted upon women in the name of social values and norms. The argument in the chapter is informative, exciting, and inspiring.

Throughout, the text is infused with French and Italian quotations that add a touch of lyrical sweetness to the reading. For those who cannot read French and Italian or infer the meaning from the context, English translation is provided in the endnotes.

Prof. Dr. Visam Mansur
Head of the English Language and Literature Department
Beykent University, Istanbul

PREFACE

This book has many souls and multiple sources of inspiration. The original idea dates back to 2007 when I was asked to speak of the literary character of Penelope in a course dedicated to the *Odyssey* within the program of Italian Literature at the Université Libre de Bruxelles (ULB). I was just completing my Ph.D. thesis on Italian feminist writers and certainly, I thought, Penelope did not re-enter within classical feminist or proto-feminist figures.

As I remembered her from my readings of the *Odyssey* in high school and university she was utterly at the antipodes of it, rather a passive and subordinated character, secondary to the super-hero Ulysses. However I had quite a lot to discover. I started my research in the ULB library where I came across mainly with French sources (re-elaborated in the second chapter dedicated to the myth of Penelope) centering mainly on the idea drawn from Ioanna Papadopoulou-Belmehdi's re-interpretation of Penelope as the central character of the *Odyssey*, the one who allows with her memory the return of Ulysses to Ithaca.

In the following years my teaching and researches switched to English and Italian literatures focusing mainly on women writing. Reading and teaching feminist literary criticism in its Anglo-American, French and Italian declinations broadened my horizons and became a focal point and an anchorage in my researches. I have learnt to realize that feminism, in all its forms, cannot be separated from issues of power and politics. Feminism within literature aims to show one more time that there is no neutral perspective in literature, there are no universals on which to base our interpretations, there is no one 'Canon' but many 'canons'.

Feminism is certainly sharing with post-modernism and post-structuralism this distrust for certainties and universals but its focus on women makes the difference. Anglo-American critics, with their pragmatic approach, highlighted since the 1970s the importance of looking back for the forgotten women writers to recreate a tradition deleted by time. This work has been done also by French and Italian critics who have started to question the centrality of man in philosophy, the 'One' in opposition to woman, the 'Other'. Both the Anglo-American and the Franco-Italian feminist theories are daughters of their respective cultures and histories and their development and international popularity is the result of different ways of positioning and channeling feminist thought.

The Anglo-American formula has been certainly the winner on the international arena. With the institutionalization and academisation of feminism, the creation of women's studies departments since early 1970s, feminist literary criticism has been the object of elaboration and re-elaboration by critics, mainly but not only women, working solely on issues related to women and whose professional careers were based on original and sophisticated researches. This has given life to an incredibly rich and challenging atmosphere within the Anglophone world which has no link any more with political, activist feminism but has inserted feminist criticism as a sophisticated instrument within literary criticism.

The same cannot be said for French and Italian feminist criticisms. In both cases the universities with their long and established traditions have been much slower in accepting regular courses in women's studies, though leaving the initiative to the particulars. So we find centers of excellence in feminist theory in France or Italy, headed by groups of critics interested in a specific aspect of feminism: history, philosophy, anthropology, mythology, etc. As research is certainly based on individual excellence but cannot exist without adequate funding, it is quite natural that it is the Anglo-American model which has spread globally, and it is nowadays the basis of any research within women's literature. This also explains the relatively longer space I dedicated in the first chapter to the Anglo-American in respect to the French and Italian literary criticisms, as the articulation and quantitative data of the first have no equivalent within the French and Italian homonyms. It is also interesting to notice that 'French Feminism' is a North-American neologism as are 'French Theory' and 'Post-structuralism'. These 'labels' have all been created in the 1970s within North-American universities where French critics as Derrida, Foucault, Lacan, Cixous, Irigaray started to be translated and assimilated and where their being French gave a kind of 'exotic' taste to a quite complex philosophical thought deriving from Continental Europe's philosophy.

My interest in the figure of Penelope is thus strictly linked and substantiated by theories and sources made available through feminist studies and criticism. As the book is mainly targeted to students and general readers interested in feminist literary studies and women's literature, without necessarily a previous knowledge of the subject, the first chapter offers a brief overview of feminist literary criticism from 1970s onward within

the Anglophone world, in France and Italy and moreover provides a con-
cise introduction to proto-feminist writings in the three languages. This is
followed by the second chapter centering on the figure of Penelope in the
Odyssey and on its modern re-interpretations looking at the theme of Penelope diachronically with particular reference to the issue of "re-vision"
as highlighted by Adrienne Rich[1] as a revision of the past aimed at changing the future.

The second part of the book focuses on the analysis of three contemporary novels centering on the figure of Penelope, written by women belonging to different countries and written in three different languages: *Toi, Pénélope* by Annie Leclerc in French, *The Penelopiad* by Margaret Atwood in
English and *Penelope* by Silvana La Spina in Italian. Though different in style
the three novels are united by the centrality given to the figure of Penelope
who is not only the protagonist but also the focalizer of the narration, so recalling to us her version of the events. The novels have not been officially
branded as feminist as the respective authors, except for Annie Leclerc, refuse any type of label. However it seems clear by simply reading them that
they are daughters of a wave of feminist revisionism within literature that
by giving for the first time voice to women characters grants them a new life
and makes them not only objects but subjects of the writings.

As a last point I need to explain my decision to write this book in English.
This was not a straightforward and self-evident choice as most of my original
bibliographical sources were in French and my first drafts in Italian. However the decision to choose English has been driven by the fact that both the
Italian (*Penelope*) and the French (*Toi, Pénélope*) novels do not dispose of
an English translation while the English one (*The Penelopiad)* can be read
in both French and Italian translations (and in further 26 languages!). Likewise, the majority of the French and Italian references I consulted do not
have official English translations to date and by citing them here, supported
by my own translations, would offer an opportunity to readers not trained
in Italian or French to be exposed to otherwise not easily accessible texts.

I strongly believe that in a world where English has gained the status of
undisputed *lingua franca*, it is important for speakers of languages other
than English to activate personally in facilitating the circulation of ideas
especially utilizing texts whose translations are not available. The issue of
translating or reading from the original language is certainly an old issue
in comparative literature and my aim here is not to argue for any of the two
positions. Nor do I intend to enter in polemics in relation to the issue of

---

1. Adrienne Rich, "When We Dead Awaken: Writing as Re-Vision" in *College English* vol.
34, no.1 (1972): 18-30.

"center" and "periphery" within literary studies and its connection to the market of translations. I simply believe that one's own national literature (as history, sociology, philosophy etc.) can be better understood by being aware of other countries' experiences. Only by enlarging our horizons, looking at our individual literary history within a broader context of affinities, differences and reciprocal influences we can be able to become better readers and critics within our own national language specific domain.

A NOTE ON THE TRANSLATION OF FRENCH AND ITALIAN TEXTS:

The following texts do not have an English translation to date. As a consequence the translations to English provided in this book are mine:

Claudel, Paul. *Œevres en prose*, (Paris: Gallimard, Biblioteque de la Pleiade, 1965).

Citati, Pietro. *La lumière de la nuit*, trad. Tristan Macé et Brigitte Pérol, (Paris: Gallimard, 1999).

Delebecque, Eduard. *Construction de l'Odyssée*, (Paris: Les Belles Lettres, 1980).

La Spina, Silvana. *Penelope*, (Milano: La Tartaruga, 1998).

Leclerc, Annie. *Toi, Pénélope*, (Aries: Actes Sud, 2001).

Lévêque, Pierre. *L'Aventure grecque,* (Paris: Armand Colin, 1964). Pierre Brunel Homere

Loraux, Nicole. *Les experiences de Tiresias. Le feminin et l'homme grec*, (Paris: Gallimard, 1989).

———. *Les mères en deuil*, (Paris: Seuil, 1990).

Mactoux, Marie Madeleine. *Penelope. Legende et mythe* (Paris: Les Belles Lettres, 1975).

Papadopoulou-Belmehdi, Ioanna. *Le chant de Pénélope. Poétique du tissage féminin dans L'Odyssée*, (Paris: Belin, 1994).

Robert, Fernand. *Homère*, (Paris: Presses Universitaires de France, 1950).

Trousson, Raymond, *Thèmes et mythes. Questions de méthode*, (Bruxelles: Editions de l'Université de Bruxelles, 1981).

Vernant, Jean-Pierre. *Mythe et pensée chez les Grecs. Études de psychologie historique,*

(Paris: Maspero, 1965).

———. "Mythologie et citoyennete" in *Democratie, citoyennete, et heritage greco-romain*, Pierre Vidal-Naquet, Jean-Pierre Vernant, Jean-Paul Brisson, (Paris: Liris, 2004), 41-72.

Penelope:
The Myth of True Womanhood
Re-vised

When men are oppressed, it's tragedy.
When women are oppressed, it's tradition.

Bernadette Mosala

Who doesn't know Penelope? The shroud she weaves in the day while unravelling her work in the night, the long years spent waiting for the return of her spouse, the cunningly ingenious Ulysses. He departed twenty years earlier for the Trojan War leaving her alone in the kingdom of Ithaca to bring up their child, Telemachus, and to face the inevitable wooers. She represents in everyone's imagination the symbol of the quintessential faithful and wise spouse. We imagine her sitting next to the loom weaving, lost in her thoughts, looking for the memory of the love of her youth. But who is she really? This question is certainly delicate and with no certain and absolute answer.

Penelope, daughter of king Icarius of Sparta and cousin of the beautiful Helen of Troy, is a discreet but at the same time essential character of the *Odyssey*. She looks inactive and resigned while acting incessantly in the hope of gaining time. She pretends to accept the death of Ulysses but continues nevertheless to cry every day and night praying for his return. It is then not surprising that Penelope has inspired a great number of writers through the ages. Her enigmatic side has woken up the interest of artists and excited their imagination. We find her in all arts, in all times. The result is sometimes surprising, every time different. The character has followed the desires of the various authors and has evolved with time. Continuously interpreted, imagined, remodeled, Penelope has passed through the centuries to arrive up to us, often different from what she was.

Since Homer, the revisions and the personal interpretations of the authors have brought modifications to the theme of Penelope and to its characteristics. Very early on in the literary tradition the representation of Penelope tends to swing from one extreme to the other, from the pure incarnation of faithfulness to the worst of libertines. The ancients have even made of her a philosophical symbol[1] as she weaves and "analyses"[2] (unweaves) her shroud. Plato in the *Phaedo*[3] uses Penelope's unweaving of the fabric of her cloth as a metaphor for philosophy.

Homer's epoch and the one that followed are marked by important epic poems that give prominence to the glory of the Greek heroes. Ulysses takes up there a place of honour. Penelope is considered in some of these poems as only a vulgar lover or even an unfaithful woman, responsible for the death of her spouse. Only Anacreon in the sixth century B.C. praises her love for the faraway Ulysses. In the same way, in the archaic art the representation of Penelope is very faithful to the image transmitted by the poems: she is almost absent. Ulysses is not here the husband of Penelope but "le héros légendaire qui lutte contre les monstres".[4]

Starting from the fifth century B.C. Penelope is present more and more. Many authors don't see her only as the spouse of Ulysses. She starts becoming a legend for herself, her faithfulness is considered as a social virtue. She is even opposed to the trickery of Ulysses as a positive counterweight. Everyone agrees in qualifying Penelope as a virtuous woman and no writer dares to make of her a subject of comedy. In the same way the arts represent her as a suffering and melancholic heroine. We have to wait for the end of the fifth century, starting of the fourth century B.C. to see her becoming a subject of comedy. The arts then represent her relaxed in the presence of Ulysses, symbolising the outcome of the waiting. In the fourth century B.C. the theme recedes, disappearing completely for some decades. At the end of the fourth century B.C. the dualism of the character appears. From one side the philosophers and the writers see Penelope as a scandalous woman, on the other side the popular writers continue to represent (notably through the epitaphs) the virtuous and wise woman as she was described in the fifth century B.C.

1. Félix Buffière, *Les mythes d'Homère et la pensée grecque* (Paris: Les Belles Lettres, Collection d'études anciennes, 1956), 389-390.
2. The verb used in Old Greek is the first utilization in Western literature of the concept of 'analysis'. For the ancient Greeks the unweaving of the cloth was a metaphor for the analytic method used in philosophy.
3. Plato, *Phaedo*, tr. David Gallop (Oxford: Clarendon Press, 1975), 84a-b.
4. Marie Madeleine Mactoux, *Penelope. Legende et mythe* (Paris: Les Belles Lettres, 1975), 41. "the legendary hero who fights against the monsters". My translation.

Douris of Samos is the first to represent "Pan comme le fils de l'adultère de Penelope avec tous les prétendants".[5] The artistic representations allow us to understand that the scandalous Penelope participating in the banquets of the suitors will be dominant in the evoked dualism. The Etruscans, having an intense commerce with Greece, represent Penelope on their objects of art. The place of the woman in the Etruscan society was radically different from the one held in Greek society. They accepted without problems seeing Penelope participating in the banquets, a common thing among Etruscan women. In the same way, Penelope has, like many other women, known a painful separation: this fact is not rare in Etruria. Penelope is not by any means a model of wisdom or cunning. The Etruscans do not try to project in her their fears or hopes.

Starting from Cicerone and until Seneca, Penelope becomes a model of morality and fidelity. Ovid, the exiled writer, quotes Penelope many times. She is for him the symbol of love and fidelity. The Roman arts of the first century B.C. borrowed heavily from the classic Greek culture. The important place of Penelope in classic Greece, added to the equally important place of the woman under Republican Rome, make Penelope a character admired and respected for her numerous virtues and her wisdom. The arrival of Augustus in Rome coincides with an increase of corruption. Faithfulness and justice that were key values under the Republic disappear in Rome. The faithful Penelope allows the Romans to find an identity link with the *fides* that they have lost under the empire. So Sextus Propertius writes: "si fas est, omnes pariter pereatis avari, et quisquis fido praetulit arma toro!"[6]

During the first centuries of our era Penelope remains a model of marital faithfulness and wisdom. She is often mentioned on the epitaphs. Starting from the fifth century A.D. the legend rarefies and disappears, but evocations of the theme still subsist. In this period Penelope is seen as the wife of a hero to whom she has given proof of immense chastity. Traces can be found also in Egypt. The evocations of the theme are mainly anecdotal and popular. She is cleared of everything of which she had been previously reproached. The grammarian Servius first and then Philagyrius retain especially the non-Homeric aspects of Penelope. Servius hides behind the authority of Pindar[7] to speculate that Pan is the son Penelope had from

---

5. Mactoux, *Penelope. Legende et mythe,* 99. "Pan as the son of the adultery of Penelope with all the wooers".

6. *Elegies* III, 12, 4; Mactoux, *Penelope. Legende et mythe,* 130: "périsse quiconque préfère les armes à une couche fidèle". ("They should perish who prefer arms to a faithful spouse.")

7. Greek writer of the 5th century B.C.

Mercury. Up to that time two versions were circulating regarding the kinship of Pan: a son that Penelope had by laying with all the suitors or only with Hermes.

In the sixth and seventh century A.D. the subject of the birth of Pan is at the centre of the writings on Penelope. She is considered as a victim seduced "par la force"[8] by the suitors or by Hermes. Up to the ninth century there is a common intention to clear Penelope from adultery, even as the theme declines starting from the fifth century. The subject starts being treated in an anecdotal way till a "déclin total sensible dans la littérature comme dans l'art".[9] The study of Marie-Madeleine Mactoux lets us believe that only the character drawn by Homer has survived.

Arriving in the twentieth century, what has become of her in modern rewritings? How does this feminine figure differ today from the one in the Homeric text, and why? Over the past fifty years the figure of Penelope has gradually been re-discovered, and she has become the protagonist of various novels, short stories and poems in Western literature — showing the centrality of Penelope within the *Odyssey*. Works like Marie Madelaine Mactoux, *Penelope. Legende et mythe* (1975), Marylin Arthur-Katz, *Penelope's Renown. Meaning and Indeterminacy in the Odyssey* (1991), Nancy Felson-Rubin, *Regarding Penelope: From Character to Poetics* (1994), Ioanna Papadopolou-Belmehdi, *Le chant de Penelope* (1994), Barbara Clayton, *A Penelopean Poetics. Reweaving the Feminine in Homer's Odyssey* (2004) and Richard Heitman, *Taking her seriously. Penelope and the plot of Homer's Odyssey* (2005) refute the interpretation of Penelope as a passive character and underline the central role of Penelope within the narrative strategy of the *Odyssey,* making of her an essential and modifying agent of the plot.

One of the most interesting readings is done by the anthropologist of ancient Greece Papadopolou-Belmehdi who concentrates on the link between Penelope and her weaving (discussed in the second chapter of this book). According to this author, Penelope is a unique character compared to other women of the *Odyssey* because her weaving relates not only to a literary meaning but also to a metaphorical one. Penelope is weaving the shroud for Laertes but at the same time she is weaving her cunning, plotting trickeries. She is gaining precious time to enable Ulysses to come back.

While the literary meaning pushes her back to her domestic role and function, the metaphorical one projects her forward in the public space, the

---

8. Mactoux, *Penelope. Legende et mythe*, 186. "by force".

9. Mactoux, *Penelope. Legende et mythe*, 187. "noticeable total decline in literature as in the arts".

space of actions, of heroes, of men. The alleged passivity of the queen is so re-interpreted as a time of action, where what it seems is different from what it is in a continuous tension between being and appearing, thinking and talking: "entre l'être et le paraître, entre la pensée et la parole".[10] According to Papadopolou-Belmehdi, Penelope is an essential character of the *Odyssey*. Even if she has no direct influence on the action, she is the one who makes the action possible by keeping alive the memory of Ulysses.

She belongs to the different representations of memory as "le rôle poétique essential de Pénélope n'est pas d'incarner la fonction royale, la fidélité conjugale ou même la passivité féminine mais d'être une expression de la mémoire".[11] This faithfulness so praised in Penelope is linked to recollection and it is one of the consequences of her resilience in remembering her husband.

Though it gives the queen's standing a new meaning and place, and opens the way for a new centrality for Penelope within Ancient Greece and Homeric studies, the queen's identity still seems to be paralyzed, almost caged within her role of side character and faithful wife of Ulysses, where her faithfulness is "a stick used to beat other women with".[12] The historical tendency associates mythic and literary female characters with the feminine stereotypes of passivity, submission and subordination. Penelope as an archetypal literary woman has long served as a model of subservience and silence.

However this fixed model of femininity has begun to be denounced in the last two decades by contemporary writers directly or indirectly related to feminism and feminist theories. Penelope has become the central character of a series of rewrites aiming to provide new representations of female subjectivities that break stereotypical molds and emphasize autonomy. Among these works, three of the best in terms of critical reception are Silvana La Spina, *Penelope* (1998), Annie Leclerc, *Toi Pénélope* (2001) and Margaret Atwood, *The Penelopiad* (2005); these will be analyzed in more detail in the second part of this book. Around these novels – representative of three different national literatures – exists a rich bibliography, in various languages, of texts that share the same desire to re-write the myth

---

10. Ioanna Papadopoulou-Belmehdi, *Le chant de Pénélope. Poétique du tissage féminin dans L'Odyssée*, (Paris: Belin, 1994), 170. "Between being and appearing, between thought and word".

11. Mactoux, *Penelope. Legende et mythe*, 171. "The essential poetic role of Penelope is not to embody the royal function, the faithfulness in marriage or even the feminine passivity but of being an expression of memory".

12. Margaret Atwood, *The Penelopiad. The Myth of Penelope and Odysseus*, (Edinburgh: Canongate, 2005), 2.

of Penelope[13] by suggesting that Penelope is an amalgam of her past identity as well as those she constructs for herself. This follows Estella Lauter's argument in *Women as Mythmakers*,[14] according to which myths are not replaced or invalidated but only transformed and modified over time.

Feminist criticism has played an important role in this re-vision of the past within the field of literary history. One of its milestones can be dated back to Adrienne Rich's famous 1972 essay on re-vision, where the young critic regarded "re-vision" as "an act of survival" consisting of "looking back", "seeing with fresh eyes", "entering an old text from a new critical direction".[15] Re-vision within feminist literary criticism has become a critical term in the last decades of the twentieth century and a key concept for feminist literary critics. Many scholars have started revisiting the texts of the past, offering new perspectives and interpretations in order to create new scenarios for women's lives and open the future to new possibilities.[16]

These studies aim to identify sources of oppression rooted within a gendered division of society and denounce the presumed 'naturalness' of this division, rescuing women from the confines of domesticity. In the same way also myths have become subjects of revision, their alleged timeless truthfulness has been denounced, while a creative surge has been injected into literary criticism by looking for "the other side of the story".[17] As highlighted by Peter Widdowson, "re-vision" as intended by feminist literary critics "could also be achieved by the creative act of 're-writing' past fictional texts in order to defamiliarize them and the ways in which they have been conventionally read within the cultural structures of patriarchal and imperial/colonial dominance".[18] In his classification of re-visionary novels, Widdowson touches

13. Among the most interesting can be mentioned Luigi Malerba, *Itaca per sempre,* (Milano: Mondadori,1997); Bianca Tarozzi, "Variazioni sul tema di Penelope" in *Nessuno vince il leone: variazioni e racconti in versi,* (Venice: Arsenale, 1989); Stefano Benni, *Achille piè veloce,* (Milano: Feltrinelli, 2003); Giorgio Manganelli, "Di Circe e di Penelope", in *Ti ucciderò mia capitale,* (Milano: Adelphi, 2011); Carmen Estévez ed., *Ni Ariadnas ni Penélopes: Quince escritoras espanolas para el siglo veintiuno,* (Madrid: Castalia, 2002); Angela Vallvey, *Los estados carenciales*, (Barcelona: Destino, 2002).

14. Estella Lauter, *Women as Mythmakers. Poetry and Visual Art by Twentieth-Century Women,* (Bloomington: Indiana UP, 1984).

15. Adrienne Rich, "When We Dead Awaken: Writing as Re-Vision" in *College English,* vol. 34, no.1, (1972): 18-30, 18.

16. See Judith Fetterly, *The Resisting Reader. A Feminist Approach to American Fiction,* (Bloomington: Indiana University Press, 1978), xx.

17. Molly Hite, *The Other Side of the Story: Structures and Strategies of Contemporary Feminist Narrative.* (Ithaca, NY: Cornell University Press, 1989).

18. Peter Widdowson, "Writing back: Contemporary Re-Visionary Fiction", *Textual Practice,* vol. 20, no.3, (2006): 491-507, 497.

upon feminist and/or postcolonial texts affirming that they demand that

> past texts' complicity in oppression – either as subliminally in-
> scribed within them or as an effect of their place and function as ca-
> nonic icons in cultural politics – be revised and re-visioned as part
> of the process of restoring a voice, a history and an identity to those
> hitherto exploited, marginalized and silenced by dominant inter-
> ests and ideologies.[19]

Fiction has been central to feminist literary criticism since its beginning (see chapter 1 of this book) for its strong interrelationship with ideology. In 1985 Rachel Blau DuPlessis proposed that "narrative may function on a small scale the way the ideology functions on a large scale – as a 'system of representations by which we imagine the world as it is' ".[20] Linda Anderson, in her introduction to her 1990 collection of essays *Plotting Change*, argued that "the stories women inherit from culture are powerfully oppressive and part of that oppression lies in their unitary character, their repression of al-ternative stories, other possibilities, hidden or secret scripts".[21]

In the same way Molly Hites in her 1989 work[22] noticed that a number of stories do not get told because they are crossed out by literary conven-tions that are always ideologically charged. She praises a number of writers, among them Atwood, Rhys, and Lessing, for articulating in their novels the "other side of a culturally mandated story, exposing the limits it inscribes in the process of affirming a dominant ideology".[23] These critics aimed to show that the novel may be part of a hegemonic intention, but at the same time its form is sufficiently flexible to allow for new patterns and new pos-sibilities, thereby acting as an agent of change. This potential for change is certainly a task within feminism and feminist novels. In the words of Gayle Greene: "We may term a novel 'feminist' for its analysis of gender as so-cially constructed and its sense that what has been constructed may be re-constructed – for its understanding that change is possible and that narra-tive can play a part in it."[24]

19. Widdowson, "Writing back: Contemporary Re-Visionary Fiction", 505-6.
20. Rachel Blau DuPlessis, *Writing Beyond the Ending: Narrative Strategies of Twenti-eth-Century Women Writers*, (Bloomington: Indiana University Press, 1985), 3.
21. Linda Anderson, *Plotting Change: Contemporary Women's Fiction*, (London: Ed-ward Arnold, 1990), vii.
22. Molly Hite, *The Other Side of the Story: Structures and Strategies of Contemporary Feminist Narrative*, (Ithaca, N.Y.: Cornell University Press, 1989).
23. Hite, *The Other Side of the Story*, 4.
24. Gayle Greene, *Changing the Story: Feminist Fiction and the Tradition*, (Blooming-ton: Indiana University Press, 1991), 2.

In the rewrites of Penelope's story, the utilization of a feminist perspective was inevitable. The celebrated patience of the queen hides a cunning that goes well beyond Ulysses' renowned cleverness. Her wit and ingenuity are well documented by Homer, as her nightly unravelling of the shroud she has been weaving during the day, postpones for three years her choice of a new spouse. However she shows fully her superiority in wit and self-control in the last and less-remembered part of the poem, when after Ulysses' manslaughter of the suitors and the full recognition of the hero by all other servants and family, she declines to acknowledge him as her husband and asks for his bed — built to incorporate a living olive tree — to be taken out of their bedroom. Only after Ulysses' imprecations on the impossibility of displacing it, does she embrace him as her husband.

We, readers of today (and I guess especially women readers) wonder how could so smart a woman not recognize her husband immediately, even if disguised as a beggar? And even more, was she really so passive and cold-tempered as described, or was she just playing a role, according to what was expected from her? And if so, who was she really? As a myth of the origin the figure of Penelope is not like any other fictional female character. Her faithfulness and patience have become traditionally connected to a gendered distinction of sexes.

A re-vision of the figure of Penelope in feminist terms was not only inevitable but also necessary. The French feminist Hélène Cixous in a classic of feminist criticism from 1981 asked what would happen if the myths that sustain the patriarchal order were to be demystified and claimed: "Then all the stories would have to be told differently, the future would be incalculable, the historical forces would, will, change hands, bodies; another thinking as yet not thinkable will transform the functioning of society".[25] After more than thirty years from these words we have to accept unwillingly that "the functioning of society" has not been drastically transformed by this "thinking as yet not thinkable". Moreover, in the late 1980s postfeminist fictions seemed, in the words of Gayle Green "profoundly depressing" and "no longer envision(ing) new possibilities".[26]

It is certainly true that feminist novel writing in general has deeply changed in the last twenty years and has been moving in new political territories. However, as affirmed by Deborah Rosenfelt, postfeminist novels did not refute feminism's insights about male domination and women's oppression, but they

25. Hélène Cixous, "Sorties", trans. Ann Liddle, in *New French Feminisms: An Anthology*, ed. Elaine Marks and Isabelle de Coutivron, (New York: Schocken, 1981), 90-98, 93.

26. Gayle Green, *Changing the Story: Feminist Fiction and the Tradition*, (Bloomington: Indiana University Press, 1991), 193.

simply deemed them "insufficient" to account for the "diversity of women's experiences or naively optimistic about the possibilities for change".[27]

This hopelessness in a possibility of change certainly is shared by French and Italian feminist philosophers, according to whom no change is possible without an in-depth revolution of the socio-symbolic structures on which the system rests. Luce Irigary in France and Adriana Cavarero and Luisa Muraro in Italy constitute the more popular representatives of the feminist "Thought of Sexual Difference", re-elaborated and popularized internationally by Rosi Braidotti and Teresa de Lauretis. The Italian feminism of sexual difference is of particular interest in the creation of a new model of womanhood as it rejects equality — considered as emulation of masculine models — and demands that the specificity of being a woman be translated into social reality. Equality entails the erasure of one's sexed body, making it an irrelevant particular.

However for Italian feminist philosophers, relations of difference and asymmetry that characterize women's lives should be incorporated into social and political realities.[28] In this perspective the aim of feminism is not liberation or equality, but the attainment of individual freedom that can be found through the modification of oneself. This modification cannot be obtained in isolation, but rather through actions that establish a collective sense of self and create a new symbolic order in the name of the mother. The heart of Italian feminist thought is the challenge to established norms deeply rooted within the socio-symbolic order in which we live and the coming-into-being of a female subjectivity to stand next to the dominant masculine/neuter/universal subjectivity without being forcibly assimilated into it.

The representations of womanhood within revisionist novels in contemporary women's literature play an important role in this regard, as they help to challenge the traditional definition of femininity while re-building and consolidating new definitions that include new possibilities. So the Penelopes we are going to meet reflect modern but also dissimilar ways of being a woman, wife or mother. Freed from the traditional prohibition to speak, Penelope can express herself freely. All three novels rely in fact on a first person feminine voice that substitutes for the Homeric narrator. The three

27. Deborah Rosenfelt, "Feminism, 'Post-feminism', and Contemporary Women's Fiction", in Florence Howe, ed., *Tradition and the Talents of Women* (Urbana: University of Illinois Press, 1991), 268-91, 270.

28. See Luisa Muraro, "The Passion of Feminine Difference beyond Equality", in Graziella Parati and Rebecca West, eds., *Italian Feminist Theory and Practice. Equality and Sexual Difference*, (Madison, Teaneck: Fairleigh Dickinson University Press, 2002), 77-87, 79.

texts belie a univocal reading of Penelope's multiple and conflicting roles in the *Odyssey*, but they do, however, shed light on her agency in the epic plot and give voice to the queen's desires.

Penelope is fundamentally the same woman of the *Odyssey* but these new literary rewritings have been able to exploit the full range of her character. After reading them it will certainly be more difficult to continue to associate Penelope with the archetype of abandoned, faithful, submissive, passive wife. Her classic figure, re-interpreted in contemporary novels, is permeated with new and more complex representations of feminine diversity that, by subverting the roles attested by the canon, break with stereotypes and pursue autonomy.

PART I

FEMINIST LITERARY CRITICISM AND THE THEME OF PENELOPE

CHAPTER 1

FEMINIST LITERARY CRITICISM AND WOMEN'S WRITING: AN OVERVIEW.

> Feminism is not simply about rejecting power, but about transforming the existing power structures – and, in the process, transforming the very concept of power itself. To be 'against' power is not to abolish it in a fine, post-1968 libertarian gesture, but to hand it over to somebody else.
>
> Toril Moi

One of the main goals of feminism within literary criticism has been to point out that interpretative strategies are learned, historically determined, and therefore necessarily gender-inflected.[1] Throughout the twentieth century and until the late 1970s, formalism, structuralism, and new criticism — with their emphasis on a neutral, objective, descriptive approach to texts — have proclaimed and spread the illusion that literary theory could be a place impermeable to sexual politics, to gender bias and where the text – and not the author – speaks directly to a likewise neutral, ungendered, and objective reader.

All we needed, as readers, was just a good acquaintance with a few technical tools that could allow anyone to dissect the text and decipher its embedded meanings. Likewise, narratology, the theory and systematic study

---

1. See Annette Kolodny, "A Map for Rereading: Or, Gender and the Interpretation of Literary Texts", *New Literary History* 11, no. 3, On Narrative and Narratives: II (Spring 1980): 451-467.

of narrative hatched from French structuralism in the late 1960s, has seen its genesis within the field of linguistics and has adopted the same approach and terminology utilized in the analysis of language systems. Its foundations are laid in the synchronic and atemporal nature of structuralist analysis, and as a consequence its methods are alien from any subjective, idyosincratic judgement of value or ideological/political standing.

However the study of novels written by women, as a specific field of literary criticism, is a relatively recent phenomenon compared to the preponderant place given the analysis of canonical texts, mostly written by male writers. This new interest in writings by women coincided not casually with the resurgence of second wave feminism in the late 1960s and 1970s in North American universities and was rapidly followed by the majority of European countries and mostly in France, Italy, Germany, and Northern European countries — adapting its focus in each in relation to the special characteristics of the originating country. The pragmatic and sociological approach of Anglo-American criticism found a philosophical, linguistic and historical counterbalance in the French, Italian, and German critics.

The origin of modern feminist thought can be dated to 1792, year of the publication in London, in the years of the French Revolution, of *A Vindication of the Rights of Woman* by Mary Wollstonecraft. It is important to remember that one year earlier, in France, Marie Olympe de Gouges had published the *Declaration of the Rights of Woman and the Female Citizen* (1791) to ask for an acknowledgement of woman's rights, not recognized after the French Revolution. Olympe de Gouges was a public intellectual, as was Wollstonecraft, and a 'femme de lettre' who was strongly concerned with the issue of equality for women. She was unjustly accused of being a royalist and guillotined in November 1793.

Wollstonecraft was in Paris during the French Revolution and was deeply influenced by its new ideals of equality, liberty, and brotherhood and critical of the lack of recognition given to women in the aftermath. In *A Vindication of the Rights of Woman* the author proclaims the need for women to have a revolution in the ways they live, so that by reforming themselves they could reform the world. In the words of Gilbert and Gubar, the book "presents the first fully elaborated feminist criticism of misogynist images of women in literature as well as the first sustained argument for female political, economic, and legal equality".[2]

At that time the ideas of Wollstonecraft seemed subversive, as the image of woman followed the traditional ideal of mother and wife. The writer

2. Sandra M. Gilbert and Susan Gubar eds., *The Norton Anthology of Literature by Women. The Traditions in English*, vol. 1, 3rd ed. (New York: W. W. Norton, 2007), 370.

Horace Walpole called her "a hyena in petticoats" and a "philosophical wanton".[3] Wollstonecraft (1759-1797) became infamous for her life, considered scandalous according to the moral norms of the time. From her relation with William Godwin, in 1797, she had a daughter – the future Mary Shelley, wife of the Romantic poet Percy Bysshe Shelley, author of *Frankenstein* (1819). Wollstonecraft contracted puerperal fever following the birth of her daughter and died a few days after.

In Mary Wollstonecraft we have one of the first middle-class figures, a writer and theoretician who affirmed that the oppression which women undergo is not a fact of nature but of education, that it depends in other words on the organization of society and its patriarchal basis. It is to enlightened men and to educated women that she addresses her book. She believes in the possibility of a change in society, especially in morality, if to women were given in concrete the "natural" and so "universal" rights, without distinctions of sex, that in the previous century philosophers and theoreticians had elaborated. These rights would substitute for the traditional beliefs (from Moses onward), according to which the inferior condition of women had been justified as the relation between sexes set by God.

According to Wollstonecraft, if progressive and revolutionary men wanted a better society, this could be realized only if women were given the kind of education and cultural formation to which men only had access. Wollstonecraft does not speak yet of woman suffrage, an issue that will be at the center of women's pleas starting from the second part of the nineteenth century. The stress for the moment is on 'education', but with a larger meaning within which re-enters a necessary 'reform' that women first of all need to operate on themselves to break the image of the role fixed and imposed on them by men, a role often accepted and 'performed' by themselves. The rights of women as rational and autonomous human being are, for Wollstonecraft, to be conquered by women themselves from one side and, from the other, obtained through the initiative of the most progressive political men.

The issue of education and of the 'biological' or 'constructed' nature of gender became a major issue within the feminisms of the twentieth century. Its seeds started bore the first fruits during the Enlightenment and in the late eighteenth centuries with women like Wollstonecraft. However, the basis of these theories can be traced back to Humanism and to an extension of the concept that one's intellect was not predetermined by one's birth or class, to include gender as well.

3. Gilbert and Gubar eds., *The Norton Anthology of Literature by Women*, 257.

The humanist debate about woman's nature spread mainly in France under the name of *"Querelle des femmes"* ("quarrel about women") and in Italy, known as *"Questione femminile"*, and occasioned, as Gerda Lerner has noted, the first discussions in Western literature about gender as a social construct.[4] The *querelle* was initiated by the most prominent early European feminist, the fifteenth century writer Christine de Pizan, an Italian writer who moved with her parents to France as an infant. In 1405 Christine wrote the dialogue *Le Livre de la Cité des Dames (The Book of the City of Ladies)* which was a response to two highly influential misogynist texts, Jean de Meun's continuation of *Roman de la Rose (Quarrel of the Rose*, ca.1276) and Boccaccio's *De Claris Mulieribus (Concerning Famous Women*, 1361).

De Pizan's book reformulated the lives of ancient women as portrayed in the *De Claris Mulieribus* – for which Boccaccio had drawn on Livy, Ovid, Tacitus, Suetonius, Pliny, Valerius Maximus, and Hyginus, among other classical authors – and her dialogue represents, in effect, a revision of the classical tradition. Besides producing this fervent affirmation of the rights and achievements of women, the widowed Christine wrote a number of other books and became the first 'man of letters' to support herself (along with three children) by her pen. She is also considered the first "(proto)feminist literary critic" as with her *Epistle of the God of Love* (1399) she is the first woman writer to critically comment from a woman's perspective on a work written by a man, in this case *Le Roman de la Rose*. No other woman of letters of her time can be said to have had a professional literary career comparable to Christine. Moreover, unlike the independent *bourgeoise* Christine, most writers of the Middle Ages and Renaissance frequently articulated conventionally submissive attitudes towards women's place, in the cultural scheme.

Female 'men of letters' such as Christine are certainly rare until the seventeenth and eighteeenth century. In Europe in general, women writings of the origins have been associated with women belonging to religious orders or to the aristocracy, the only groups of women that had an access to education and the ability to read and write. In the Middle Ages, writing by women was almost exclusively limited to nuns, such as Julian of Norwich (1342-c.1416) and Mergery Kempe (1373-1439) in England, Chiara d'Assisi (1194-1253), Angela di Foligno (1248-1309) and Caterina da Siena (1347-1380) in Italy, and Hildegarde de Bingen (1098-1179) in Germany.

An interesting and not very well known phenomenon that spread in the Flemish regions, Belgium and Germany between the thirteenth and

---

4. Quoted in Rinaldina Russell, ed., *The Feminist Encyclopedia of Italian Literature*, (Westport, Connecticut: Greenwood Press, 1997), 270.

fourteenth century is the *beguinage*. The beguines were women who abandoned their houses and lived together in groups of women only, refusing a married life. They were not nuns but dedicated their lives to God and wrote about their spiritual experiences. They were mostly widows or women with no husbands, who had to defend themselves against the dangers faced by single women of the time or against accusations of witchcraft. So they decided to live in small communities, recognized by the city in which they lived, helping each other and writing. They anticipated the mystic movement of the Spanish Barocco by giving importance to the individual character of meditation, which would later be taken up by Martin Luther and St. Ignazio of Loyola.

Although they were following a life of meditation, they had a freedom that was not allowed to other women. They created a new form of society that was based on the thematic of the garden. The garden of the soul, as the Garden of Eden, allows the soul to exist. Many among them devoted their life to writing mostly lyrical poems dedicated to God or autobiographies using Augustinian style. They were among the first writers to use vernacular languages instead of Latin in dealing with spiritual matters. Among them we can count Mechthild of Magdeburg (1212-1282) who wrote in middle-low German, Beatrice of Nazareth (1200-1268) in middle-Dutch, Hadewijch of Brabant in Flemish, and Marguerite Porete – burned as a witch in 1310 – in Old French.

Along with the mystic beguines, but at the other end of the respectability spectrum, we have another group of women writers. This time we move to Italy, more precisely to Venice, and this group belongs to the courtesans living within the *Serenissima*. In the sixteenth century Venice was the center of commerce of spices, salt, and clothes, and beautiful women were considered a precious good for its economy. In 1509 were documented in Venice 11,165 women who practiced the job of 'courtesan'. Courtesans were not merely prostitutes; some were able to climb the social ladder and become recognized poets and intellectuals, enjoying a particular freedom and being known as 'cortigiane oneste' (honest courtesans).

Among them the most famous are Veronica Franco (1546-1591) and Gaspara Stampa (1523-1554), 'cortigiane onorate' who during their lifetimes published a great number of poems and an epistolary. They also organized concerts in their houses where intellectuals and artists were invited. Courtesans would never be fully accepted within the "donne oneste," but they have left an important testimony of the presence of women writers in sixteenth century Italy. Next to courtesans we need to remember other famous poetesses of the time as Veronica Gambara (1485-1550), Vittoria Colonna (1490-1547), Tullia D'Aragona (1510-1556), Chiara Matraini (1515-1604), Laura Terracina (1519-1577), Isabella Di Morra (1520-1546), Laura Battiferri

Ammannati (1523-1589), Olympia Morata (1526-1555), Moderata Fonte (1555-1592), Isabella Andreini (1562-1604), Lucrezia Marinella (1571-1653); all these represent a generation of women intellectuals recognized publicly within the new laic literature as models of "donna nuova".[5]

When we consider novel writing, women have been playing an important role since this new literary form took its first steps. Aphra Behn' *Oroonooko* (1688), considered by many critics the first English novel, sets the start of popular prose fictions produced by women. Behn was a dramatist and professional writer, belonging to the middle-class, who died in pain and poverty within one year of the publication of her best known novel. Quickly forgotten after her death, she was brought back to life by Virginia Woolf in her *A room of One's Own,* where she affirms: "All women together ought to let flowers fall upon the tomb of Aphra Behn [...] for it was she who earned them the right to speak their minds."[6]

If Apra Behn can be regarded as the first English novel writer we should not forget that ten years earlier, in France, Mme de la Fayette had published anonymously *La Princesse de Clèves* (1678), a best seller of the time and one of the founding text of modern psychological novel. For the first time, in fact, this novel explores the interiority of its characters, enters in their intimate thoughts and leads us in a world of ambiguity and hesitations. The plot of the novel, with the main female character sacrificing her true love for M. de Nemours to abide by a promise made to her dying husband, has given rise to many debates among the critics of the time.

The most famous are certainly the comments of Stendhal who in *De l'amour* criticized the decision of the Princesse de Clèves to confess her platonic love for De Namour to her husband and concluded, quite sagaciously: "Pour les femmes, le courage moral est toujours employé contre leur bonheur".[7]

The extensive and early involvement of high middle class and aristocratic French women in literature should not be a surprise. In the seventeenth and eighteenth century the literary salons (*salons litteraire*) continued to characterize the French intellectual scene and remained a typical French phenomenon that later spread to neighboring countries such as Italy.

Aristocratic, well-educated women organize receptions, inviting the most popular writers, politicians and artists of the time into their houses, where

5. Marina Zancan, *Il doppio itinerario della scrittura. La donna nella tradizione letteraria italiana*, (Torino: Einaudi, 1998), 48. "new woman".

6. Virginia Woolf, "A Room of One's Own", in *Selected Works of Virginia Woolf*, (Ware, Hertfordshire: Wordsworth, 2005), 604.

7. Stendhal, *De l'amour*, (Paris: 1822), ch. xxix. "For women the moral courage is always employed against their happiness." My translation.

political, philosophical, artistic and literary issues are informally discussed. For women the aim of these salons is not to enter in concurrence with men, but to endorse the talents of the best among them. Thinking and writing is, in fact, still considered a man's privilege and the women writers of the time publish their works anonymously to avoid being ridiculed or accused of being 'femmes savantes', as satirized by Moliere's homonym comedy (1672). Moreover the novel is just taking its first steps on the literary scene and is considered among the less prestigious of literary genres, and so adaptable to be utilized by women. Writers like Mme de Tencin (1682-1749), Mme de Graffigny (1695-1758), Louise D'Epinay (1726-1783), Mme Riccoboni (1714-1792), Isabelle de Charrière (1740-1805) will publish anonymously some of the most popular novels of their time, to be uniformly forgotten in the following centuries.

With Mme De Staël (1766-1817) we have the first recognized woman intellectual, novelist, literary critic and pioneer — with *On Germany* (1810) — of comparative literature. We need to arrive at the nineteenth century to have the first full acknowledgement of women writers as main agents on the literary scene, both in France[8] (George Sand), and England[9] (Jane Austen, the Brontës, George Eliot). Italy will follow suit eventually, but we wait until the last twenty years of the nineteenth century to see the entrance of middle-class women writers on the Italian literary scene.

Among the most important Italian writers of that time we remember Marchesa Colombi, Neera, Jolanda, Contessa Lara, Matilde Serao and the first feminist Italian writer Sibilla Aleramo with her novel *Una donna (1906)*. Most of these writers worked as journalists before starting their professional careers as writers, as did George Sand in France and George Eliot in England. Their novels have as main characters women of the middle and working classes who are in most cases victims of injustices or trying to fight for their rights. The thematics range from difficulties in work contexts (Marchesa Colombi, *In risaia* (1878) and Beatrice Speraz, *La fabbrica* (1908), to prostitution (Emma, *Una fra tante*, 1878), the loneliness of spinsters (Neera, *Teresa*, 1886), divorce (Anna Franchi, *Avanti il divorzio*, 1902), maternity (Sibilla Aleramo, *Una donna*, 1906) to set marriages (Marchesa Colombi, *Un matrimonio in provincia*, 1885).[10]

8. See Christine Planté, *La petite soeur de Balzac. Essai sur la femme auteur*, (Paris : Seuil, 1989).

9. See Gilbert and Gubar, *The Norton Anthology of Literature by Women*.

10. See Barbara Dell'Abate (Çelebi), *L'alieno dentro. Percorso semiotico alle origini del romanzo femminista italiano*, (Bruxelles: Peter Lang, 2011), 47-72.

Love and the difficult relation with men are at the heart of every novel, as the whole universe for women at the end of the nineteenth century turns around family and man. For this reason, these novels have been initially and wrongly labelled as sentimental, while when read attentively, they have all the characteristics of acts of social denunciation. Most of the writers belong to the middle class, however, and do intend not to ignite open revolts but to keep a quite conservative outlook as intellectuals. Starting in the 1960s, these novels have been rediscovered and republished, opening the way in Italy for specific studies that could help to establish a tradition of women's writings.

The development of studies of specific national traditions of women's writing owes much to feminism and feminist literary criticism. Its pioneers are Virginia Woolf in England and Simone de Beauvoir in France. Their texts, however, were not followed immediately by others: with the First and Second World Wars, women's claims were relegated to a secondary position; and with suffrage obtained by women in most European countries after 1945, the first wave feminism is considered concluded. We need to reach the 1960s to see the resurgence of claims for equal rights by women. This new surge of feminism is known as the second wave feminism and will give rise to a specific field of studies dedicated solely to the analysis of literature. This new impetus given to the study of writings by women will definitely open a new door and will allow one to see with new eyes the history of literature and its canons.

Anglo-American Feminist Literary Criticism

Within the Anglo-American tradition, foregrounding works by writers like Kate Millet, Mary Ellmann, Ellen Moers, Elaine Showalter, Sandra Gilber and Susan Gubar opened the way to a series of studies on women in literature. In the early works by Kate Millet (*Sexual Politics*, 1970) and Mary Ellman (*Thinking about women*, 1968), stereotypes of women in male writers' fictions were detected and the foundations of the so-called 'images of women' criticism were laid.

In the mid-1970s with Ellen Moers (*Literary Women*, 1976), Elaine Showalter (*A literature of their own*, 1977) and Sandra Gilbert and Susan Guber (*The madwoman in the attic*, 1979) the analysis does not focus solely on women as characters within novels, as it had previously. Rather, investigating for the singularity, and at the same time the continuity, of a tradition of women writers, these critics started to look for clues signaling a woman's tradition that could connect among them the works of Western women writers. This tradition, as underlined by Elaine Showalter, is not to be found in a specific notion of "female imagination" but rather in the "still-evolving relationships between writers and their society".[11] There is not in fact a clear continuity of female writings; however, patterns and recurrent concerns do emerge.

In analyzing the development of British women fiction, Showalter proposes the now-classical distinction in three stages following the historical and syncronical development of British novel: the Feminine, the Feminist, and the Female phase. The Feminine – from 1840 to 1880 – is a period of imitation of prevalent tradition; the Feminist – from 1880 to 1920 – covers a period of protest; and the Female – from 1920 to the present – a time of self-discovery.

It is important to highlight that, except for Mary Ellman, a journalist and literary critic, all the writers listed above belonged to — and most of them are still active within — the academic world. The cited texts by Kate Millet and Elaine Showalter were the published versions of their doctoral theses, while the works of Ellen Moers, Sandra Gilbert and Susan Gubar were inspired by the courses in women literature they were offering within the newly born field of women's studies. The increase in interest in literature about and by women saw its light, in fact, within the resurgence of the important political force of feminism in the late 1960s and early 1970s in the United States.

The impulse came from activist and civil rights movements involved initially in protests against the war in Vietnam. The link between civil rights and feminist writers is not new. From Christine de Pizan to Mary Wollstonecraft and Elisabeth Cady Stanton, the issue of equal rights and women's rights have always been strictly entangled. However the resurgence of an organized movement of women as a political force in the world, after the organized campaign for the vote in the late eighteenth and beginning of the twentieth century, dates back to 1963 with the publication of *The Feminine Mystique* by the American journalist Betty Friedan.

Betty Friedan, *The Feminine Mystique* (1963)

In the first chapter of her book, entitled "The problem that has no name", Friedan analyses the discrepancies between the reality faced by American women of that time and the image to which they were trying to conform — what the author calls the "feminine mystique". Through a series of interviews with middle-class housewives living in the American suburbs, there arises a schizophrenic split between a supposed "true feminine fulfillment as wife

---

11. Elaine Showalter, *A Literature of Their Own: British Women Novelists from Brontë to Lessing* (Princeton, New Jersey: Princeton University Press, 1977), 15.

and mother"[12] as depicted by media and "a sense of dissatisfaction, a yearning that women suffered".[13] The author realizes that this "problem that has no name" is shared by countless American housewives caged in comfortable houses but condemned for life to a spiritual death. These women, dedicated completely to their husbands and children, tend to lose their sense of self-identity over time and to suffer generally from symptoms of more or less evident states of depression.

After a well-informed and deep analysis of the different contexts within which this dissatisfaction takes place (health, psychological, sexual problems) and a strong critique of the Freudian theory of women's penis envy, in the final chapter "A new life plan for women", Friedan admits that there is no easy solution. For women — left alone and without any recognition by doctors, sociologists, politicians, or media of the reality of the problem — the solution is extremely hard. Only through a fulfilling, paid job could women develop their full potential. However this means "saying no to the feminine mystique and sustain[ing] the discipline and effort that any professional commitment requires".[14]

This return of women to education needs to be supported by a wide national program through a general re-organization of the courses offered at universities and by policies that allow the return of women to education. Moreover, to avoid women wasting their university degree, educators "must see to it that women make a lifetime commitment (call it a 'life plan', a 'vocation', a 'life purpose' [...] to a field of thought, to work of serious importance to society. They must expect the girl as the boy to take some field seriously enough to want to pursue it for life".[15]

For Friedan, women have to be aware of the "trap" of a feminine mystique that is made up of a series of clichés, and they need to start to compete with men for jobs and positions in the real world. "A girl should not expect special privileges because of her sex, but neither should she 'adjust' to prejudice and discrimination. She must learn to compete then, not as a woman, but as a human being."[16] Friedan's book sanctioned the starting of the so-called "second wave feminism".[17] Following its publication,

12. Betty Friedan, *The Feminine Mystique*, (New York: W. W. Norton, 1963),16.

13. Friedan, *The Feminine Mystique,* 13.

14. Friedan, *The Feminine Mystique,* 304.

15. Friedan, *The Feminine Mystique,* 320.

16. Friedan, *The Feminine Mystique,* 328.

17. The 'first wave'" feminism developed in the late 19th and early 20th century and was centered in the struggle for gaining the suffrage. It is generally best represented by the feminist texts by Virginia Woolf and Simone de Beauvoir.

the writer continued her feminist activism and co-founded the National Organization for Women (NOW) to fight sex discrimination in all fields of life, and her organization is still active internationally today. The new women's movement did not seem particularly interested in feminist literary criticism until the late 1960s. The cultural/political struggle of feminism, aiming to highlight and put to an end women's discrimination, was initially concentrated on political activism. Within this context it is not a coincidence that one of the first and certainly the most popular text of feminist literary criticism of the late 1960s originated at the interception of sex and politics.

Kate Millett, *Sexual Politics* (1970)

Published in 1970, *Sexual Politics*, is considered nowadays the manifesto of the second wave feminism within the field of literary criticism. As a best-selling doctoral thesis, the book contributed to narrowing the gap between institutional and non-institutional feminist criticism and showed a new direction within literary criticism.

Challenging the premises of New Criticism and its limitation to a formal, close-reading, self-referential analysis, *Sexual Politics* took back, as an essential part of the literary analysis, the historical and cultural contexts of the work; it aimed to reveal the patriarchal ideology hidden behind the representation of men and women. According to Kate Millet, in literature, as in a mirror of society, the ruling sex seeks to maintain and extend his power over the subordinated sex. Power and domination are at the core of man-woman relation and the sexual act is, according to Millet "a frequently neglected political aspect".[18]

The first chapter in fact analyses literary descriptions of sexual intercourse in novels by Henry Miller, Norman Mailer, and Jean Genet — writers that Millet will further analyze in the third and last part of the book, "Literary Reflections", together with works by D.H. Lawrence. By her analysis it appears clear that sexual roles and sexuality are not a matter of biology but of social construction. To be 'masculine' or 'feminine' is not a direct correspondence to being 'male' or 'female' as revealed by the analysis of homosexual relations in Jean Genet, that "mimics with brutal frankness the bourgeois heterosexual society".[19] Within the ideology of virility the Masculine is active, strong, brutal and holds the power over the Feminine that is weak, passive and submissive.

18. Kate Millet, *Sexual Politics*, (New York: Doubleday, 1969), xi.
19. Millet, *Sexual Politics*, 19.

As explained in the second chapter "Theory of Sexual Politics", the relation between the sexes is based on the continuous oppression of the weaker sex through social authority and economic forces. On a path similar to the one followed by Simone de Beauvoir in *Le deuxième sexe* (1949), Kate Millet looks for ideological, biological, sociological, economic, educational, anthropological, religious, and psychological reasons that have justified in the eyes of men and women the inferiority status of women as a category.

All these theories, issued and perpetuated within a patriarchal vision of society, have been internalized by women, and they constitute, for Millet, a system of power that passes itself as natural. In the second part of the book she analyses the historical development of the feminist movement from 1830-1930, "the sexual revolution", with its development in the Western world and from 1930-60, "the counterrevolution", with the forces of reaction re-establishing the subordination of women. Within this context a long chapter, "The reaction in ideology. Freud and the influence of psychoanalysis thought", is dedicated to the influence of Freud in ratifying traditional roles.

The anti-feminism of Freud, based primarily on the penis-envy theory, has offered a vision of women as haunted from childhood by a sexual inferiority, the lack of a "penis". This lack would justify the "three corollaries of feminine psychology: passivity, masochism and narcissism, so that each was dependent upon, or related to, penis envy".[20] With the third and last chapter, "The Literary Reflection", Millet, in a continuation of the first chapter, aims to show how the politics of power and domination are enacted in the novels by Lawrence, Miller, Mailer, and Genet.

By analyzing almost exclusively the sexual scenes described in the novels, Millet reads the sexual act as man's weapon of power and confirmation of his supremacy on women, both condescending to men's will and depending on it for their happiness. In D. H. Lawrence's novels *Lady Chatterley's Lover*, *Sons and Lovers*, *The Rainbow,* and *Women in Love*, Millet traces the author's hostility and negative attitude towards women. In Millet's view, Lawrence's novels mount a negative campaign against the modern woman, with the Lawrentian hero setting for himself the mission to subjugate, through the sexual act, the woman in question.

In Miller's case, the formula is even simpler: women are just sexual objects, to be used and discarded as "sanitary facilities – Kleenex or toilet paper".[21] Millet confutes the popular image of Miller as a liberated man writing freely about sex, and on the contrary she finds him "a compendium of

20. Millet, *Sexual Politics,* 179.
21. Millet, *Sexual Politics,* 296.

American sexual neuroses"[22] while transposing in his novels his own personal, economic failures, and sublimating it by sex: "the only approved avenues of masculine achievement were confined to money or sex. [...] If he can't make money, he can make women."[23]

By using women as a commodity, Miller could enjoy the success he could not get through money. His novels are, in Millet's view, a simple transposition of the author's experiences or fantasies. Intimacy and love are completely excluded from Miller's novels and the sexual act is reduced to a "biological event between organs."[24] Millet's main thesis is that Miller, far from being a writer of "free love", shows a neurotic hostility towards women, and in using and abusing them, confirms men's political use of sex as an instrument of power and domination over women.

In the chapter dedicated to Norman Mailer, Millet highlights the links, present in Mailer's novels, between violence and sexuality that are "so inextricably mixed that the 'desire to kill' is a phrase truly aphrodisiac".[25] Just like Lawrence, Mailer believes in a natural, primitive stage of men and women relation and, as Lawrence, he is anxious that civilization "will bury the primitive" with the danger that "they will extinguish the animal in us". Within this "logic of virility",[26] violence is an innate psychological trait in male, while there is "an intrinsic relation between homosexuality and evil"[27] where the feminine is the negative and destabilizing element.

In the last chapter, dedicated to Jean Genet, Millet analyzes the representation of homosexual relations in some of Genet's novels, highlighting how the passive/feminine and dominant/masculine roles and politics are kept within homosexual relations, so representing in Jean Paul Sartre's words "'femininity without women', an abstraction, a state of mind".[28] These roles are kept, according to Genet, in the relations of whites and blacks, colonialists and colonized, so deepening this psychology of oppression and showing how women, black, colonials are all "prisoners of definitions imposed on them by others".[29]

Millet's book has certainly some revolutionary aspects: it breaks with the literary, apolitical criticism of the time, as intended within New

22. Millet, *Sexual Politics*, 295.
23. Millet, *Sexual Politics*, 298.
24. Millet, *Sexual Politics*, 300.
25. Millet, *Sexual Politics*, 319.
26. Millet, *Sexual Politics*, 330.
27. Millet, *Sexual Politics*, 334.
28. Millet, *Sexual Politics*, 353.
29. Millet, *Sexual Politics*, 354.

Criticism and centers its analysis on men's clear affirmation of a presupposed natural superiority over women that is made explicit in the description of the sexual act; the literary and the political become in Millet's text integral parts of the same metanarrative of domination. Moreover Millet destabilizes the biological, natural distinction associating maleness/masculinity/activity vs. femaleness/ femininity/ passivity by showing how masculinity and femininity are politically constructed fields, applicable to any power relation. Another original point is her focus on sex as a political instrument of power.

Love and romanticism are completely absent in the books of the authors she choses to analyze, while the male perspective of the sexual act shows the characters guided by an animal instinct than by feelings. On the negative side, Millet's book has been criticized by Toril Moi[30] for omitting to recognize her debts to previous feminist writers, such as Simone de Beauvoir or Mary Ellmann, who have treated similar arguments. Moreover, Millet's choice of writers is limited to a very distinct group of novelists, for whom we acquire a distaste and from whom she induces a universal theory of domination. The same kind of harsh criticism would certainly be difficult in cases of more 'sensitive' writers or women writers. This monolithic view seems quite impartial, and in its limitedness does not give way to any possible revolt by women, completely subjugated within the patriarchal culture. Despite its limitations *Sexual Politics* remains a breaking point within literary criticism, opening a new direction of studies of literature with gender in mind.

Mary Ellmann, *Thinking about women* (1968)

Two years earlier, in 1968, Mary Ellmann, a freelance journalist and literary critic, had published *Thinking about Women*, a book dealing with literary criticism within a gender perspective. Unlike Kate Millet, Ellmann does not intend to deal with the theory of domination within patriarchy nor with its political and historical aspects, but concentrates instead on women as *words*, as explained in her preface.[31]

In her first chapter, "Sexual Analogy", Ellmann deconstructs the basic principle of sexual difference based on strength in men and childbearing in women. She affirms that although modern society is no longer based solely on these biological characteristics, men and women are still thought

---

30. Toril Moi, *Sexual/Textual Politics*: Feminist Literary Theory, (New York: Methuen, 1985), 24.

31. Moi, *Sexual/Textual Politics*, xv.

of in relation to their bodies and sexual characteristics. So the "hunter is always male, the prey female"[32] and in arts and literature "the woman's function is to inspire the man, whereupon he proceeds to develop and eventually to produce his completed work".[33] Ellmann gives plenty of examples in this direction as expressed by social scientists, writers, psychologists, religious texts, all rigorously following a stereotyped vision of femininity and masculinity.

Her thesis is fully developed in the second chapter, "Phallic criticism": texts written by women are judged differently from texts by men because the critics and readers cannot read texts neutrally but automatically apply to them the stereotypes of femininity and masculinity. As explained by Ellmann: "Books by women are treated as though they themselves were women, and criticism embarks, at its happiest, upon an intellectual measuring of busts and hips."[34] To be woman and to be feminine is the common stereotype that Ellmann intends to deconstruct. In doing this she utilizes a particular weapon: irony. Her style is, in fact, very different from Millet's. While in *Sexual Politics* Millet aims to shock her readers by highlighting the passive and degrading position of women in society through the descriptions of sexual acts from men's perspective, Ellmann masques her critique under a lighter, sardonic tone that makes the reader laugh but at the same time reflect on the harsh reality behind her irony.

So, for example, within her discussion on the negative connotation given by men writers to the term 'feminine', commenting on the study of Woodrow Wilson by Sigmund Freud and William Bullit, she states: "At one heated point, Clemenceau calls Wilson feminine, Wilson calls Clemenceau feminine, Wilson calls Clemenceau feminine, then both Freud and Bullitt call Wilson feminine again. The word means that all four men thoroughly dislike each other."[35] The use of this ironic stance makes the text an easier reading for a general public though highlighting through parodies and contrasts a serious problem within literary criticism, a field still and strongly in the hands of male critics.

Ellmann uses the term 'phallic' criticism not only to place the literary criticism by men under one umbrella, but also to expose the limits of a criticism structurally founded on a biological essentialism. Intellectual faculties are associated with sexual ones, and women's presupposed sexual

---

32. Mary Ellmann, *Thinking about women*, (New York: MacMillan, 1968), 8-9.

33. Ellmann, *Thinking about women*, 16.

34. Ellmann, *Thinking about women*, 29.

35. Ellmann, *Thinking about women*, 38; Sigmund Freud & William Bullitt, *Thomas Woodrow Wilson, Twenty-Eighth President of the United States: A psychological study* (Boston, 1966).

inferiority becomes in a synecdochical manner the synonym of an incapability of writing as men do. If a woman should show this capability, then it would be a sign of a 'masculine mind', where masculine has a specific virile, i.e. positive, connotation missing in its feminine counterpart. Ellmann writes: "Mary McCarthy has been complimented [...] on her 'masculine mind' while, through the ages, poor Virgil has never been complimented on his 'effeminacy' (Western criticism begins with this same tedious distinction – between manly Homer and womanish Virgil)."[36] Phallic criticism is discussed further in the third section of the book through the analysis of various stereotypes of feminine characters. Ellmann distinguishes nine stereotypes (formlessness, passivity, instability, confinement, piety, materiality, spirituality, irrationality, and compliance) and two "incorrigible figures" (the Shrew and the Witch). In the last chapter "Responses", Ellmann deals with the way in which women writers have exploited, debated, avoided and transcended the opinions on womanhood that surround them. Ellmann's book, though less popular and incisive than Millet's *Sexual Politics,* has contributed to demonstrate that the concepts of masculinity and femininity are social constructs which refer to no real essence in the world. Ellmann's main thesis is that writing is not gendered and that it is not possible to differentiate a text written by a man or by a woman; it depends on the writer's personality, experience and personal style and not on his/her sexual orientation. This issue will be central to the forthcoming feminist debate, especially within French feminist criticism, centered on language and related to the search of an *écriture féminine*.

Ellmann's attack on the biases of literary criticism based on the sex of the author has opened another important direction of studies, but it has not avoided having her text labeled as essentially feminine for her preponderant use of irony. In fact, according to Patricia Spacks: "The woman critic demonstrates how feminine charm can combat masculine forcefulness",[37] invoking the same essentialistic vision of masculine and feminine that Ellmann had tried to deconstruct.

Susan Koppelman Cornillon, *Images of women in fiction. Feminist perspectives* (1972)

Along with Millet's book, *Thinking about women* belongs to a first group of literary criticism that centered mostly on male writers' description

---

36. Ellmann, *Thinking about women,* 42.
37. Patricia Meyer Spacks, *The Female Imagination. A Literary and Psychological Investigation of Women's Writing*, (London: Allen & Unwin, 1976), 26.

of women and aimed to denounce the general stereotypes characterizing women mainly within novels. This first branch of feminist criticism has been denominated 'Images of Women' criticism, and it has generated a great number of works, both in response to the spread of feminism in society and the creation of new courses in women's studies within American colleges and universities.

One of the most representative texts of the time is *Images of women in fiction. Feminist perspectives* edited by Susan Koppelman Cornillon and published in 1973. The preface acknowledges that the book is a consequence of the increased need for textbooks for the "over eight hundred new courses in women's studies in the past few years," as "People – both women and men – are beginning to see literature in new perspectives (many of which have been) opened up by the Women's Liberation Movement."[38] The twenty-one essays of this book (nineteen written by women, two by men) aim to construct a new way of reading and understanding fiction through the analysis of female roles.

The book is divided in four sections: "Women as Heroine", "The Invisible Woman", "The Woman as Hero", and "Feminist Aesthetics". The first three sections analyze respectively stereotypes of women in fictions, the roles women play, and women as whole persons. The last section looks at critical methodologies utilized within feminist literary analysis. Most of the analyzed novels belong to nineteenth and twentieth century English and American literature and are written by both male and female authors. The main criticism in the twenty-one essays is of the creation within the analyzed novels of "unreal" female characters, "false" images of women that do not conform, according to the writers, to the reality of things.

According to Joanna Russ in the first section of the book, we cannot find real women within literature but only "images" of them. "They exist only in relation to the protagonist (who is male). Moreover, look at them carefully and you will see that they do not really exist at all — at their best they are depictions of the social roles women are supposed to play and often do play, but they are public roles and not the private women."[39]

Along the same lines, the essays by Kathleen Conway McGrath, Susan Gorsky, and Charles Blinderman look at stereotyped visions of angelic and demonic women in *Charlotte Temple* by Susan Rowson, in English women's

---

38. Susan Koppelman Cornillon, ed., *Images of Women in Fiction. Feminist Perspectives*, (Ohio: Bowling Green University Popular Press, 1972), ix.

39. Joanna Russ,"What can a Heroine Do? Or Why Women Can't Write", in Susan Koppelman Cornillon, *Images of Women in Fiction. Feminist Perspectives*, (Ohio: Bowling Green University Popular Press, 1972), 3-20, 5.

novels between 1840 and 1920, and in Anthony Trollope's novels. The essay by Joanna Russ about women in science fiction, or rather images of women in science fiction, arrives at similar conclusions; in the writer's words: "the title I chose for this essay was 'The image of women in Science Fiction'. I hesitated between that and 'Women in science fiction' but if I had chosen the latter, there would have been very little to say. There are plenty of images of women in science fiction. There are hardly any women."[40]

The second section entitled "The invisible woman" starts with an essay by Tillie Olsen, "Silences: when writers don't write" that would be republished in 1978 as part of her famous book *Silences*.[41] In this foregrounding essay, following inspiration by Woolf's *A room of one's own*, Olsen focuses on the issue of literary creativity and its basic material needs — time, space, family obligations — as major factors influencing a writer. After looking at male writers' periods of 'silences' in their creative production, as in the difficulties experienced by Kafka, Rilke, Hemingway etc., Olsen looks at women writers living in the nineteenth and twentieth century. She highlights the fact that marriage, children and generally looking after a family did not and do not leave women time for literary creativity. As a consequence she notes that many famous women writers were not married, married late, or did not have children. She concludes her essay by recalling her autobiographical experience and her difficulties as writer and as mother of three children. The ensuing essays in this section deal with the description of women characters as 'Others' in respect to men, highlighting how female characters depicted in novels are not portrayed as fully developed complete human beings, but rather are presented only in romantic or sexual contexts or have fixed and culturally accepted connotations. Novels by various American and English authors – Joyce Carol Oates, Doris Lessing, James Fenimore Cooper, Henry James, and others – are here considered.

The third section "The Woman as Hero" investigates fictions in which women are portrayed as "whole people or as people in the process of creating or discovering their wholeness".[42] The analysis covers neo-feminist novels (Ellen Morgan), *The Bostonians* and *The Odd women* (Nan Bauer Maglin), *To the lighthouse* (Judith Little) and the novels by May Sarton (Dawn Holt Anderson). In the fourth and last section, "Feminist Aesthetics", the focus

---

40. Russ,"What can a Heroine Do? Or Why Women Can't Write", 91.

41. Tillie Olsen, "Silences: When Writers Don't Write" in Susan Koppelman Cornillon, *Images of Women in Fiction. Feminist Perspectives*, (Ohio: Bowling Green University Popular Press, 1973), 97-112. Republished in *Silences*, (New York: Delacorte Press/Seymour Lawrence, 1978).

42. Koppelman Cornillon, ed., *Images of Women in Fiction*, xi.

is on literary criticism and the political nature of any critical discourse. According to the authors, reading literature cannot be considered a neutral and objective activity, especially for women reading about women. The discovery of a female hero by a woman can initiate a process of identification in terms of her own experience and make her "more intolerant of the discrimination against women and more dedicated to working against it".[43]

In fact, in the words of Nancy Burr Evans, "after encountering women hero uncannily similar to ourselves a number of times, we finally have to act. Women's literature felt and learned can effect social change."[44] Literature has a precise social task and can help to change the perception of women's role within society. In this direction feminist criticism has a central role; according to the essay by Marcia R. Lieberman "Feminist criticism can expose and overturn the double standard that is manifested in literature and criticism. [...] We must establish and at the same time defend feminist criticism, not only to correct literary distortions but also to expose the sources of covert bias, and to free women from the unchallenged assumptions that limit their lives."[45]

This collection of essays had the principal merit of shifting literary criticism away from the neutrality of New Criticism, which invoked a value-free type of criticism, to the subjective and specific position of the feminist critic, with an awareness of the social and cultural factors influencing both writers and critics in their description and analysis of male and female characters. The binary distinction between male and female roles is disentangled from masculine and feminine natural characteristics; and the existence of a universal positioning, external from a male or female perspective, is rejected. In the essays both sexes are criticized for the creation of unreal female characters, stereotypes of men's imagination, more than real characters, while the drawing of reality is considered the highest goal of literature. In this respect many of the essays' female authors refer to themselves, to their lives and to their personal experiences, thus highlighting the female perspective and positioning of the critic in respect to the texts analyzed.

The use of autobiography by the critic clearly locates the subject of the enunciation within a female reality. The weakness of this approach is in the difficulty of delimiting a female reality. Political, historical and sociological factors need to be taken into account as female reality is far from monolithic.

---

43. Nancy Burr Evans, "Women Writers for Women," in Koppelman Cornillon, ed., *Images of Women in Fiction*, 311.

44. Koppelman Cornillon, ed., *Images of Women in Fiction*, 312.

45. Koppelman Cornillon, ed., *Images of Women in Fiction*, 337.

Moreover, regarding the subjective perspective of the critic, as highlighted by Toril Moi, "it is difficult to believe that we can ever fully be aware of our own perspective".[46] In the inclusion of autobiographical elements the main difficulty lies in deciding which are the 'relevant' details to include without risk of becoming a "more or less unwilling exhibitionist rather than a partisan of egalitarian criticism".[47] Despite its weaknesses and its outdated approach, this text remains important today as one of the best representatives of a feminist shift in literary criticism and of a new need for re-reading the classics from a woman's perspective.

Starting about 1975 the interest of critics began to focus exclusively on texts written by women. With *Literary Women* (1976) by Ellen Moers, *A literature of their own* (1977) by Elaine Showalter, and *The Madwoman in the attic* (1979) by Sandra Gilbert and Sandra Gubar, feminist literary criticism entered a second phase and started investigating women's representations of the world. This approach has subsequently become dominant within Anglo-American feminist criticism. In the first texts by Moers and Showalter, a geneaology of women writers is searched for, lesser-known women writers are rediscovered and brought back to life, and the relation between women's lives and their works is investigated. With Gilbert and Gubar, the issue of literary creativity and writer's anxiety are re-elaborated in a psychoanalytic context. The main contribution of these texts, however, is their basic belief that society and not biology shapes women's different perception of the world.

Ellen Moers, *Literary Women* (1976)

Literary Women by Ellen Moers was among the first scholarly feminist texts of the mid-1970s to argue the existence of a female literary tradition, describing the history of women's literature as an "undercurrent, rapid and powerful".[48] The book is divided in two parts: "History and Tradition" and "Heroinism". The first part lays out an interesting and well-researched survey of literature by women in the late eighteenth and nineteenth century in England, America and France. From George Sand, Charlotte and Emily Brontë to Harriet Beecher Stowe, Harriet Martineu, Mme de Staël and Mrs Gaskell, Moers follows the lives and comments on the texts of the major women writers of the time.

46. Moi, *Sexual/Textual Politics*, 44.
47. Moi, *Sexual/Textual Politics*, 44.
48. Ellen Moers, *Literary Women*, Reprinted, (London: The Women's Press, 1986). 1st ed. New York: Doubleday, 1976, 42.

Her history of women's literature strongly interwines personal events and literary texts, providing interesting biographical details of women writers' lives. Relations among women writers are highlighted in the text: George Sand's and Charlotte Brontë's positive comments on *Uncle Tom's Cabin* by Beecher Stowe, George Eliot reading aloud the novels by Jane Austen under the advice of George Henry Lewes, the influence of Sand's *La petite Fadette* on Eliot's *The Mill on the Floss*. Moers' intent is to show her readers the existence of a tradition of women writers, reading each other and influencing each other's texts. So Moers argues "Jane Austen achieved the classical perfection of her fiction because there was a mass of women's novels, excellent, fair, and wretched, for her to study and improve upon."[49] And "There is one page in *Emma* which, when I read it, makes me picture George Eliot bending over Austen's novel and planning her own."[50]

Moers does not believe in the existence of a typical feminine writing or style: "There is no single female style in literature, though in every country and every period it has been wrongly believed that a female style exists."[51] However by reading each other they were recognizing an echo of their own voice: "Each of these gifted writers had her distinctive style; none imitated the others. But their sense of encountering in another woman's voice what they believed was the sound of their own is, I think, something special to literary women."[52]

In the fourth section of the first part entitled "Money, the Job, and Little Women: Female Realism", Moers anticipates an aspect of women novels that will be considered again by future critics: the issue of money within sentimental novels. According to Moers, the novels by Austen, Gaskell, Eliot etc. are strongly realistic in their description of money and job issues. Although they are novels on "marriageableness"[53], Austen's works, for example, are extremely realistic in matters of money; marriage is considered not simply in its sentimental aspects but as the greatest investment in a woman's future. So her deep interest in money issues was "the result of her deep concern with the quality of women's life in marriage".[54]

Moers also looks at American women writers Louisa May Alcott, Margaret Fuller and Harriet Beecher Stowe, all of whom had a strong realistic vision of money and work, since their writings were the main support for their families. Moers refers within this context to the transcendental philosophy

49. Moers, *Literary Women*, 44.
50. Moers, *Literary Women*, 51.
51. Moers, *Literary Women*, 63.
52. Moers, *Literary Women*, 66.
53. Moers, *Literary Women*, 77.
54. Moers, *Literary Women*, 71.

popular in America in the mid-19th century as a rejection by many intellectuals of the puritan work ethic of the founding fathers: "Transcendental improvidence we now know to have been a source of much literary industry on the part of American women. The father, brother, or husband who could not or would not work, and left the entire or major support of a large household to his womenfolk, was responsible for the writing of many best sellers by American women, and a few masterworks."[55]

In the last section of the first part entitled "Female Gothic", Moers introduces the concept of female gothic novels such as *Frankenstein* and *Wuthering Heights*. Mary Shelley's book is considered by Moers as a woman's "birth myth"[56]. While male writers look at birth as the conclusion of a path leading to happiness, *Frankenstein* deals with the rejection of the newborn baby by the mother: "*Frankenstein* seems to be distinctly a woman's mythmaking on the subject of birth precisely because its emphasis is not upon what precedes birth, not upon birth itself, but upon what follows birth: the trauma of the afterbirth."[57]

Moers analyses the life of Mary Shelley, her early pregnancies, the loss of two newborn children and the death of many family members. Despite its richness of information and details concerning the writers and their works, Moers' text cannot be considered more than a "pioneer work"[58] within feminist criticism. Her direct link between the life of the authors, mostly sentimentalized and abounding with circumstantial details, and the works they wrote seems to originate from an implicit vision of women's literature as exceptional and associated to extraordinary women only. Moreover, she affirms her belief in a neutral registration of events where "the literary women themselves [...] have done the organizing of the book – their concerns, their language"[59] that today sounds naïve after the ideas that spread in the early 1980s on the non-neutrality of language and Foucauldian researches on the relativity of truth that have implied the inseparability of the thing in itself from the discourse within which it is entangled.

Elaine Showalter, *A Literature of Their Own* (1977)

A more mature and influential text is *A Literature of Their Own* by Elaine Showalter, published one year after Moers' book. It inaugurated a new path

---

55. Moers, *Literary Women*, 85.
56. Moers, *Literary Women*, 92.
57. Moers, *Literary Women*, 93.
58. Moi, *Sexual/Textual Politics*, 54-55.
59. Moers, *Literary Women*, xii.

within Feminist Literary Criticism, one concentrating on the minor, forgotten women writers who need to be re-discovered to enable the tracing of a women writers' tradition. Showalter underlines the difficulty of each generation of women writers who had to "rediscover the past anew"[60] and sets out to investigate forgotten British women novels from the mid-19th to the mid-20th century.

The result is an interesting, well-documented book that goes further than the Austen, Brontës, Eliot and Woolf figures and reveals a rich underground of minor women novelists who can testify according to Showalter a female tradition within English literature characterized by "our imaginative continuum, the recurrence of certain patterns, themes, problems and images from generation to generation".[61]

An important issue in Showalter's book is the "phenomenon of the transience of female literary figure"[62] already highlighted by Germaine Greer[63] in 1974. According to Showalter, like any subculture, such as black, Jewish, Canadian etc., the development of female literature went through three major phases: imitation, protest, and self-discovery that correspond to her now famous division in Feminine, Feminist, and Female. After a general introduction Showalter dedicates the first five chapters to feminine novelists, two more chapters to feminist ones, and the last three to female and contemporary women novelists.

Two interesting chapters are chapter three "The Double Critical Standard and the Feminine Novel" and chapter nine "The Female Aesthetic". Chapter three is dedicated to the issue of nineteenth century negative criticism and its impact on women writers' difficulty in being recognized as belonging to 'serious' literature. It shows clearly and with plenty of evidence the general prejudice toward the inferiority of women's novels, in comparison with with men's, on the basis of their being byproducts of a female body, reputedly inferior in strength and intelligence, and lacking in experience. The chapter highlights the difficulty of women writers' texts achieving acceptance within the literary canon of the time, and thus their absence from literary history.

As shown by Showalter, this is due not to the lack of quality in women's works but to a biased gendered perception of quality that discriminated *a priori* against the novels by women. Consequently, the use of male pseudonyms becomes a natural defense from such discriminated criticism,

60. Showalter, *A literature of their own*, 11-12.

61. Showalter, *A literature of their own*, 11.

62. Showalter, *A literature of their own*, 11.

63. Germaine Greer, "Flying Pigs and Double Standards", *Times Literary Supplement*, (July 26, 1974): 784-787, 784.

but does not defend women from an internalized negative self-perception of their work and a sense of guilt in allocating time to writing that will accompany women well into the twentieth century. The chapter "Female Aesthetic" is centered on Dorothy Richardson, a writer recognized as the pioneer of the stream of consciousness technique, who opened the way to the modernist novel followed by authors like Virginia Woolf and James Joyce. The chapter plays a strong tribute to Richardson and to her sequence of thirteen novels titled *Pilgrimage*.

Showalter clearly shows that Richardson's modernism cannot be separated from her perception of "women's art as both qualitatively different and superior [to men's]"[64] while at the same time denouncing women writers' difficulty in being accepted as free beings. Through her autobiographic work she shows the high price she had to pay for her freedom. Richardson, anticipating French feminist critics, denounced the difficulty of women who have to use a language that does not belong to them and who have to go down to a lower level: "Women are disadvantaged – not as deprived subculture forced to use the dominant tongue, but as a superior race forced to operate on a lower level."[65]

Richardson's work is seen by Showalter in direct opposition to the literary tradition of her time, as represented by the novels of H. G. Wells, with whom Richardson had a difficult sentimental relationship that finished shortly before she set herself to writing her first novel. All her work is however defined by Showalter as "the anti-Wellsian novel",[66] and she adds "though male artists too have had to struggle against the influence of famous predecessors, only in rare cases have those celebrities been their lovers"[67].

Showalter's work shows its weaknesses in the lack of an explicit theoretical framework and in a more or less assumed belief that "a text should reflect the writer's experience, and that the more authentic the experience is felt to be by the reader, the more valuable the text"[68]. Her clear preference for realistic novels deters Showalter from appreciating the modernist work of Virginia Wolf, accused of being unable to "produce really committed feminist work"[69] and to accept images of women that are not rooted in realistic representations of characters. Despite these criticisms Showalter's work remains an important step forward in the construction of a

64. Showalter, A literature of their own, 259.
65. Showalter, *A literature of their own,* 259.
66. Showalter, *A literature of their own,* 253.
67. Showalter, *A literature of their own,* 253.
68. Toril Moi, *Sexual/Textual Politics,* 4.
69. Toril Moi, *Sexual/Textual Politics,* 3.

feminist literary criticism to which the author will further contribute with article like "Towards a Feminist Poetics" (1979) and "Feminist Criticism in the Wilderness" (1981).

Sandra Gilbert and Susan Gubar, *The Madwoman in the Attic* (1979)

In 1979 *The Madwoman in the Attic* by Susan Gubar and Sandra Gilbert appeared. Like Showalter, Gilbert and Gubar were young academicians in the late 1970s working in the new field of women's studies that was starting to spread in American universities. As affirmed in the preface to their first edition "the book began with a course in literature by women that we taught together at Indiana University in the fall of 1974".[70] While pursuing this new branch of feminist criticism, Gilbert and Gubar acknowledge following in the footsteps and researches of Moers and Showalter, whom they recognize as having "so skillfully traced the overall history of this community [Victorian women novelists], [that] we have been able to focus closely on a number of nineteenth-century texts we consider crucial to that history".[71] Their massive volume of about 700 pages, subtitled "The woman writer and the nineteenth-century literary imagination", focuses on major women writers of the nineteenth century: Jane Austen, Mary Shelley, the Brontës, George Eliot, Elizabeth Barrett Browning, Christina Rossetti, and Emily Dickinson. These are analyzed according to recurrent patterns and images of anxiety, obsessive diseases, enclosure and madness.

The book by Gilbert and Gubar opened new directions for studies, but it is interesting that the negative criticisms have played a larger role than the positive ones towards provoking a deep re-evaluation of the field. Though scrupulously researched and written, the *Madwoman in the Attic* has been accused by its detractors of being essentially a book centered on middle-class, white writers, focusing on biography and offering "selective analysis and exaggeration".[72] The two authors commenting on these criticisms have justified their work in the introduction of the second edition published in 2000: "We were being accused of sins that in those early days we knew not of – essentialism, racism, heterosexism, phallologocentrism."[73]

---

70. Gilbert Sandra M. and Susan Gubar, *The Madwoman in the Attic. The Woman Writer and the Nineteenth-Century Literary Imagination*, 2nd ed. (Yale: Yale University Press, 2000), 1st ed. Yale University, 1976, xi.

71. Gilbert and Gubar, *The Madwoman in the Attic*, xii.

72. Danielle Russell, "Revisiting the Attic. Recognizing the Shared Spaces of *Jane Eyre* and *Beloved*", in Federico, Annette R. ed., *Gilbert and Gubar's The Madwoman in the Attic After Thirty Years*, (Missouri: University of Missouri Press, 2009), *127-148*,128.

73. Gilbert and Gubar, *The Madwoman in the Attic*, xxiv- xxv.

It will be in particular the article by Gayatri Chakravorty Spivak "Three Women's Texts and a Critique of Imperialism" published in *Critical Inquiry* in 1985 that will align the version of feminism promoted by Gilbert and Gubar – and in particular the reading of Jane Eyre's Bertha as "Jane's dark double" – with imperialist practices, and that will give a fresh impetus to the new postcolonial perspective within feminist literary studies.

Despite its detractors and its detected weaknesses, the publication of *The Madwoman in the Attic* brought feminist literary criticism to a new maturity and helped establish new parameters within this new territory. The aim of the authors was not only to provide an analysis of major and minor novels within a patriarchal society but also to "understand the dynamics of female literary response to male literary assertion and coercion",[74] analyzing the situation of the woman writer under patriarchy.

Building on Harold Bloom's "anxiety of influence", Gilbert and Guber affirm that the female poet suffers from "anxiety of authorship", "a radical fear that she cannot create, that because she can never become a 'precursor' the act of writing will isolate or destroy her".[75] If the author is defined as male, then, they ask, how can women take the pen? The answer they give, through the analysis of Victorian women novelists, is that women writers of the time repudiated patriarchal prescriptions but at the same time conformed to patriarchal literary standards. The voice of these women authors is "duplicitous" and expresses itself through the "paradigmatic polarities of angel and monster"[76] famously represented by the madwoman of the title, the 'mad double' that is the common factor in all novels analyzed in the book.

More than thirty years after its publication *The Madwoman in the Attic* still keeps its place as a critical forerunner work of feminist literary criticism because of its search for a common methodology in the analysis of literature by women, a methodology that relies strongly on the analysis of the unconscious, both of the author and of the character. But developing in these same years is a hidden universe that will take central stage in the years to come and that is already central within French feminist criticism.

The 1980s

By the eighties new changes started taking place, led by minority groups like black, lesbian and gay, Chicana etc. who could not recognize themselves

---

74. Gilbert and Gubar, *The Madwoman in the Attic*, xii.
75. Gilbert and Gubar, *The Madwoman in the Attic*, 49.
76. Gilbert and Gubar, *The Madwoman in the Attic*, 76.

in the stereotyped white, middle class representation of woman and who aimed to affirm the need for a new epistemology within feminist studies. At the same time French feminist texts began to be translated into English, and French psychoanalysis and deconstructive theories entered American academia. To the first and second phase of feminist criticism, denominated respectively "critique" (images of women criticism) and "gynocritics" (the recovery of a female literary tradition) by Elaine Showalter follows a third phase called by Susan Gubar "engendering of differences",[77] characterized in the words of Gubar by "bringing gender to bear upon other differences: sexual and racial differences primarly, but also economic, religious, and regional distinctions".[78]

For Gloria Anzaldúa, the precursor of borderlands identity, the borderland – which she renames "entremundos" or "nepantla" (the in-between space) – is made of apparently fixed categories that by intersecting with each other "begin to erode creating shifts in consciousness and opportunities for change".[79] The mixture of races, the "racial, ideological, cultural and biological cross pollinization" gives way to "a new mestizia consciousness, una conciencia de mujer".[80] This new 'borderlands' consciousness is characterized by a "movement away from set patterns and goals and towards a more whole perspective, one that includes rather than excludes".[81] The ones living in the thresholds, called by Anzaldúa the "nepantleras", are the mediators, the "in betweeners", "those who facilitate passages between worlds". By being a mediator herself, Anzaldúa is aware of running the risks of rejection, misunderstanding, alienation. However she refuses to deny her many identities and she locates herself simultaneously in multiple worlds.[82]

Following Gloria Anzaldúa's steps, a new generation of critics associated to academic disciplines such as feminism, Chicana/o studies, or queer theory have argued for a feminist revision of border studies. One of the most interesting figures uniting theory with social and personal experience is Sonia Saldívar-Hull, a "chicanoist",[83] interested in the exploration of different

77. Susan Gubar, "What Ails Feminist Criticism?", *Critical Inquiry*, vol. 24, no. 1 (Summer, 1998): 878-902, 884.

78. Gubar, "What Ails Feminist Criticism?", 884.

79. AnaLouise Keating ed., *EntreMundos/Among Worlds: New Perpectives on Gloria E. Anzaldúa*, (New York: Palgrave Macmillan, 2005), 1.

80. Gloria Evangelina Anzaldúa, *Borderlands/La Frontera: The New Mestiza*, (San Francisco: Spinsters/Aunt Lute, 1987), 77.

81. Anzaldúa, *Borderlands/La Frontera: The New Mestiza*, 79.

82. Keating ed., *EntreMundos/Among Worlds: New Perpectives on Gloria E. Anzaldúa*, 3.

83. Sonia Saldívar-Hull, *Feminism on the Border: Chicana Gender Politics and Literature*, (California: The University of California Press, 2000), viii.

sides of Chicana feminism as mestizia, intersectionality and collective identity. In *Feminism on the Border: Chicana Gender politics and Literature*
(2000) she interposes literary analysis of works by Gloria Anzaldúa, Sandra
Cisneros and Helena Maria Viramontes with the recollection of her own life
events, mapping her development as a Chicano feminist writer and positioning herself within the same borderline identity (Chicano/American, Span-
ish/English, Third world feminism/Euro-US white feminism) of the writers
she discusses. Moreover, in the first part of her book, by providing detailed
information on the works of other Chicano-feminist writers, Saldívar-Hull
clearly intends to lay down the foundation of a Chicana-Latina feminist genealogy, or "political familia" extending across the America[84] through the
"articulation of political solidarity"[85] which, according to the author, lies at
the very heart of feminism on the border.

In the course of the seventies and eighties feminist literary criticism developed quickly but still did not reach as full a recognition as other branches
of criticism. In 1980 Annette Kolodny denounced the difficulties encountered
by feminist critics in being recognized as such. Despite many accomplish-
ments, she affirmed, feminist literary critics "have been forced to negotiate
a minefield. The very energy and diversity of our enterprise have rendered
us vulnerable to attack on the grounds that we lack both definition and coherence."[86] The issue at stake was the institutionalization of feminist literary criticism, and that could not take place without a deep revision of the
criteria surrounding the canonization of literary works.

As Kolodny affirms in her article "For insofar as literature is itself a social institution, so, too reading is a highly socialized – or learned – activity."[87] Feminist literary criticism needs to find new methods and criteria
to shift the conventions that surround the esthetic judgements of a literary text. However, according to Kolodny "feminist literary criticism appears woefully deficient in system, and painfully lacking in program".[88] The
search for a theoretical basis continued throughout the 1980s as the aca-
demization of feminism prompted a search for more elaborated and complex theories that could allow for a full acceptance of feminist criticism by
the literary academy.

---

84. Saldívar-Hull, *Feminism on the Border*, 127.

85. Saldívar-Hull, *Feminism on the Border*, 54.

86. Annette Kolodny, "Dancing through the Minefield: Some Observations on the Theory,
   Practice and Politics of a Feminist Literary Criticism", *Feminist Studies*, vol. 6, no. 1
   (Spring 1989): 1-20, 6.

87. Kolodny, "Dancing through the Minefield", 11.

88. Kolodny, "Dancing through the Minefield", 17.

As recalled by Jane Gallop: "Theory included a feminist component, although it also dismissed feminist criticism that was not properly theoretical".[89] African American,[90] Chicano,[91] lesbian[92] and postcolonial[93] scholars started to make their voice heard and attacked any generalizing, abstract appeal to "woman", recurring in some cases to the sophisticated concepts coming from French psychoanalysis, deconstruction and poststructuralism.

Since the 1990s

In the course of the 1990s feminist criticism entered a fourth phase, characterized by a questioning of the same category 'woman' that is dismantled on the one hand by African-American and postcolonial thinkers and on the other by poststructuralists. The most often cited critic, who embodies

89. Jane Gallop, *Around 1981: Academic Feminist Literary Theory*, (New York/London: Routledge, 1992), 6.

90. See Audre Lorde, *Sister Outsider* (New York: Trumansburg, 1984); bell hooks, *Ain't I a Woman: Black Women and Feminism* (Boston, 1981); Barbara Smith, "Toward a Black Feminist Criticism", *The New Feminist Criticism: Essays on Women, Literature, and Theory*, ed. Elaine Showalter (New York. 1985); Michele Wallace, "For Whom the Bell Tolls: Why America Can't Deal with Black Feminist Intellectuals", *Voice Literary Supplement*, no. 140 (Nov. 1995); Toni Cade Bambara ed., *The Black Woman: An Anthology* (New York, 1970); Barbara Christian, *Black Women Novelists: The Development of a Tradition, 1892-1976* (Westport, Conn: Greenwood, 1980); Alice Walker, *In Search of Our Mothers' Gardens* (New York: Harcourt, 1983).

91. See Gloria Anzaldúa and Cherríe Moraga eds, *This Bridge Called my Back: Writings by Radical Women of Color*, (New York, 1981); Saldivar-Hull Sonia, *Feminism on the Border: Chicana Gender Politics and Literature* (Berkley: University of California Press, 2000); Gloria Anzaldua, *Borderlands/La Frontera: The New Mestiza* (San Francisco: Spinsters/Aunt Lute, 1987); AnaLouise Keating ed., *EntreMundos/Among Worlds: New Perpectives on Gloria E. Anzaldúa*, (New York: Palgrave Macmillan, 2005).

92. See Adrienne Rich, "When We Dead Awaken: Writing as Re-Vision", *On Lies, Secrets and Silence: Selected Prose, 1966-1978* (New York, 1979); Diana Fuss ed., *Inside/Out: Lesbian Theories, Gay Theories*, (New York, 1991); Margaret Cruik-shank, ed., *Lesbian Studies: Present and Future* (Old Westbury, New York: Feminist Press, 1982); Lillian Faderman, *Surpassing the Love of Men: Romantic Friendship and Love between Women from Renaissance to the Present* (New York: Morrow, 1981); Catherine R. Stimpson, "Zero Degree Deviancy: The Lesbian Novel in English", *Critical Inquiry, no.* 8 (Winter 1981).

93. See Chandra Talpade Mohanty, "Under Western Eyes: Feminist Scholarship and Colonial Discourses", in *Contemporary Postcolonial Theory: A Reader*, ed. Padmini Mongia (London, 1996); Hazel V. Carby, "White Woman Listen! Black Feminism and the Boundaries of Sisterhood," in *The Empire Strikes Back: Race and Racism in 70s Britain*, ed. Centre for Contemporary Cultural Studies (London, 1982); Sara Suleri, "Woman Skin Deep: Feminism and the Postcolonial Condition," *Critical Inquiry, no.* 18 (Summer 1992); Sarah Harasym ed., *The Post-Colonial Critic: Interviews, Strategies, Dialogues* (New York, 1990).

this new attention to racial identity politics combined with poststructuralist methodologies, is Gayatri Chakravorty Spivak, who came to prominence
with her provocative 1985 article on *Jane Eyre*, cited earlier, that according
to Erin O'Connor "may be understood as a primal scene of postcolonial reading, the place where many of the guiding assumptions and logical premises
of postcolonial thinking about Victorian fiction were born".[94]

However, one of the most prominent poststructuralist thinkers of the
nineties is Judith Butler who considers gender as performance and aims to
demonstrate that sex, as much as gender, is made to seem natural through
regulatory practices that set in place the "heterosexualization of desire".[95]

In her main texts, *Gender Troubles* (1990) and *Bodies that matter*
(1996), Butler affirms her theory of sex and gender as performances. Identity for Butler is not something fix, immutable but is suspended in the multiple occasions of change. Her theory refuses a fixed concept of gender, affirming the impossibility of any political action. This makes her position in
respect to feminism critical, as she considers the system of heterosexuality
only one of the possibilities and she restates that there cannot be a sexual
hierarchy since gender is by its own nature unstable. Despite the philosophical sophistication of Butler's argument, her work has had, in the words of
Susan Gubar, the consequence "to divorce feminist speculations from literary texts or to subordinate those texts to the epistemological, ideological,
economic, and political issues that supplanted literary history and aesthetic
evaluation as the topics of writing about women".[96]

Equally influential been Donna Haraway, who by rejecting biologism introduces the figure of the cybor, announcing a world beyond gender, what
Haraway herself calls "a postgender world".[97] Both Butler and Haraway try
to debiologize gender roles, following a trend persisting well into the second
millennium, which sees a transformation of women's studies into gender
studies and queer studies, so embracing lesbian, gay and transgender issues.
Moreover in the English speaking world feminist/gender theory has further
become more abstract, contemplative and analytical in style. Its main issues
are nowadays sexuality, personal identity, symbolism and difference, and its
main points of reference are French philosophers such as Michel Foucault

94. Erin O' Connor, "Preface for a Postcolonial Criticism", *Victorian Studies* 45, no.2,
   (Winter 2002): 217-46.

95. Judith Butler, *Gender Trouble: Feminism and the Subversion of Identity* (London:
   Routledge, 1990), 17.

96. Susan Gubar, "What Ails Feminist Criticism?", 896.

97. Donna Haraway, "A Manifesto for Cyborgs: Science, Technology, and Socialist Feminism in the 1980s," in *Feminism/Postmodernism*, ed. Linda J. Nicholson (New York,
   1990), 192.

and Jacques Derrida. In the last decades the intersections of post-structuralism, queer studies and transgender studies have offered new space and a new arena in which Anglo-American feminist studies have been reconfigured and productively re-theorized.

French Feminist Literary Criticism

Feminist literary criticism in France has been characterized since its twentieth century origin by a strong connection with Continental philosophy. Its first theoretician was the existentialist philosopher and novelist Simone de Beauvoir, author of the 1949 now-canonical feminist text, *The Second Sex*.[98] Interestingly, *The Second Sex* had not been planned by Beauvoir as an intentionally feminist critical work nor did the author aim to expose through her work any sort of discrimination that she had suffered as a woman working within a discipline, philosophy, strongly rooted in masculine thought.

On the opposite, when she wrote her book De Beauvoir was an affirmed and successful philosopher and novelist, free from any discrimination related to her gender. She had obtained her aggregation in philosophy when only twenty-one years old, second only in the national ranking to Jean-Paul Sartre, and after leaving her job as high-school teacher, she had dedicated her life fully to writing, sharing the freedom of other left-wing male intellectuals of her time. In 1949 Simone de Beauvoir did not consider herself a feminist but an existentialist philosopher who, as such, followed the principle that "existence precedes essence" and utilized the Hegelian concept of the Other to explain women's oppression.

In fact her work is deeply rooted within the existentialist thought that prevailed from the 1930s to the 1950s in French intellectual milieu before the advent of structuralism. De Beauvoir refuses any notion of a female nature or essence. Her famous statement "One is not born a woman but becomes one" summons her idea of a 'construction' of femininity in opposition to a 'natural', essentially biological way of being a woman. De Beauvoir does not believe in the need of a struggle by a feminist movement but envisages the possibility of reaching the equality between man and woman through the advent of socialism. She will change her opinion following the May '68 movement.

In 1972 she will declare for the first time to be a feminist, linking her name to radical feminism, without however repudiating socialism. The link between socialism and feminism will be a characteristic of the French

98. Simone De Beauvoir, *Le deuxième sexe* (Paris: Gallimard, 1949).

neo-feminism that, starting from May 1968, is dominated by various shades of Marxism. French Feminism as a political movement develops in the course of the 1970s similarly to the American one. However in relation to feminist criticism, French neo-feminism shows from the beginning a stronger intermingling of politics and psychanalysis that, together with the recourse to philosophy, gave readers not familiar with the European philosophical tradition and psychoanalytical theory (i.e. Anglo-American critics) an initial "feeling of utter obscurity".[99]

French neo-feminist theory is not a homogeneous corpus of thoughts but is characterized by many, fragmented trends. However, what has been called 'French Feminism' in the English-speaking world is its more philosophical branch represented by academics as Hélène Cixous, Luce Irigaray and Julia Kristeva. In early 1980s the works of these scholars became available to American readers through translations[100] and entered the field of women's studies primarily through departments of French and Comparative Literature. As affirmed by the American feminist critic Elaine Showalter:

> They [French feminists] saw post-Saussurean linguistics, psycho-analysis, semiotics, and deconstruction as the most powerful means of understanding the production of sexual difference in language, reading, and writing [...] and following the work by Jacques Derrida, Jacques Lacan, Hélène Cixous, Luce Irigaray and Julia Kristeva, Franco-American feminist critics focused on what Alice Jardine calls 'gynesis': the exploration of the textual consequences and representations of 'the feminine' in Western thought.[101]

French feminism has since become the dual pole of Anglo-American feminism, and already by 1988 the critic Nancy Miller refers to the relation between the two movements as "the old Franco-American game of binary oppositions (theory and empiricism, indifference and identity)".[102]

As clearly synthetized by Elaine Marks, "American feminists emphasize the oppression of woman as sexual identity, while French feminists investigate the repression of woman as difference and alterity in the signifying

---

99. Toril Moi ed., *French Feminist Thought: A Reader* (Oxford: Blackwell, 1987), 5.

100. From 1980s, with the publication of the anthology *New French Feminisms. An Anthology,* Elaine Marks and Isabelle de Courtivron eds., (Amherst: University of Massachusetts Press, 1980), French feminist theory starts entering the Anglo-American arena and by mid-80s most of French feminist critical texts are translated into English.

101. Elaine Showalter, "A Criticism of Our Own: Autonomy and Assimilation in Afro-American and Feminist Literary Theory" in Sandra Kemp & Judith Squires eds., *Feminisms*, (Oxford-New York: Oxford University Press, 1997), 58-69, 65-66.

102. Nancy Miller, *Subject to Change*, (New York: Columbia University Press, 1988), 17.

practices of the West".[103] The three strongest female voices in French feminism Cixous, Kristeva and Irigaray argue in fact that women's repression is embedded in the foundations of the *logos* and not merely in the economic, political and social structures. According to them what we perceive as reality is the manifestation of the symbolic order as constituted by men. So only by exposing this phallogocentrism can we try to transform the reality in which we live.

One of the methods utilized by French critics is Derridian deconstruction, in which the principles of identity and resemblance are shaken in the name of a revaluation of heterogeneity, multiplicity and difference. Difference is not defined in reference to the masculine norm but is thought as other, not bounded by any system or structure. That is why the established discourse is rejected as essentially male, since it is the existing language. This absolute difference is not posited within the norms but against and outside the norms. This explains the limits that according to French feminist critics are encompassed in achieving a mere socio-economic equality.

The issue at stake is not only the question of woman but a broader change that would involve society as a whole, the existing values or discourses, its truth imposed as the only Truth. As affirmed by Annie Leclerc "They invented the whole sexuality while silencing ours. If we invent ours, they will have to rethink their own."[104] By deconstructing the binary logic of masculine/feminine a new field of signification will open wide, breaking the stability of accepted knowledge by recognizing the "free play" of the signifier, as described by Derrida.[105] For this French critic *différance* – with an 'a' instead of an 'e'– can be translated into English as both "difference" and "deferral". For Derrida "meaning is never truly present but constructed through the potentially endless process of referring to other absent signifiers".[106] There is no 'transcendental signified' but a continuous process of referring to signifiers that are absent and can be continually retrieved.

The analysis of a text within this perspective is not simply the search for the binary oppositions it encloses but an affirmation of the pleasures of open-ended textuality. So, following Derrida's notion of *differance*, Cixous' concept of *écriture féminine* or *feminine writing* aims to oppose the

103. Alice Jardin "Prelude: The Future of Difference" in *The Future of Difference,* Hester Eisenstein and Alice Jardine, eds., (New Brunswick, NJ: Rutgers University Press, 1980), xxvi.

104. Annie Leclerc, *Parole de femme*, (Paris: Grasset, 1974), 42.

105. Jacques Derrida, "Structure, Sign and Play" in *Writing and Difference*, trans. Alan Bass, (London: Routledge, 2005), 278-294, 278.

106. Moi, *Sexual/Textual Politics*, 106.

phallogocentric logic of binary opposition and opens the text to the exploration of new lands strictly connected with woman's repressed unconscious.
For Cixous woman must write herself: "To write and thus to forge for herself
the antilogos weapon. To become at will the taker and initiator, for her own
right, in every symbolic system, in every political process."[107]

The *écriture féminine* becomes then the occasion for women to articulate
the unspoken unconscious, free of cultural constrains, and the forbidden aspects of female sexuality: "Let her speak of her pleasure [*sa jouissance*], and
God knows that she has enough to say, in such a way that she manages to
unblock both female and male sexuality, and to 'dephallocentrize' the body,
deliver man from his phallus."[108] Cixous takes further the old opposition
between masculine and feminine and affirms her strong belief in the inher-
ently *bisexual* nature of all human beings. This bisexuality is multiple, vari-
able and ever-changing and "doesn't annul differences, but stirs them up,
pursues them, increases them".[109] She is against the use of the terms 'masculine' and 'feminine' and warns against confusing the sex of the author with
the 'sex' of the writing produced. So texts written by men – as in the case of
Jean Genet or Shakespeare's *Cleopatra* – can be qualified as feminine or bisexual according to the articulations of sexuality and desire within the literary text itself and not according to the author's biology.

Following a parallel path, Luce Irigaray carries on a feminist deconstruction of the Western *logos* examining the strategies that have reduced woman
to man's opposite, his Other, his negative or specular-image.[110] For Irigaray
the patriarchal discourse situates woman outside representation: "She is absence, negativity, the Dark Continent, or at best a lesser man."[111] However
woman ought not to try to become the equal to man and should avoid falling into the essentialist trap:

> They must not pretend to rival them by constructing a logic of the
> feminine [...]. They must, through repetition-interpretation [...] –
> as lack, default, or as mime and inverted reproduction of the sub-
> ject – show that on the feminine side it is possible to exceed and dis-
> turb this logic.[112]

107. Hélène Cixous, "The Laugh of the Medusa", trans. Keith Cohen, Paula Cohen, *Signs*
    1 (Summer 1976): 880.
108. Domna C. Stanton "Language and Revolution: The Franco-American Dis-Connec-
    tion", in *The Future of Difference*, 77.
109. Cixous, *The Laugh of the Medusa*, 254.
110. Luce Irigaray, *Speculum of the Other Woman*, trans. Gillian C. Gill (Ithaca, N.Y., 1985).
111. Moi, *Sexual/Textual Politics*, 133-4.
112. Luce Irigaray, *This Sex Which Is Not One*, trans. Catherine Porter and Carolyn Burke
    (Ithaca, N.Y., 1985), 75-6.

Irigaray, as does Cixous, also believes in a specific woman's language, which she calls 'le parler femme' or 'womanspeak', that emerges spontaneously when women speak together. This style "resists and explodes all firmly established forms, figures, ideas, concepts".[113] Other French writers as Monique Wittig, Marguerite Duras, Chantal Chawaf, Emma Santos, Nicole Brossard, Madeleine Gagnon and feminist critics as Michele Montrelay and Xaviere Gauthier have tried to formulate aesthetic principles on feminine writing defined as open, nonlinear, fluid, attempting to 'speak the body' i.e. the unconscious. Irigaray, like the other critics, refuses to specify the content of femininity, as this would repeat patriarchal imperatives that tell what women are and must be. The focus of French neo-feminism on language anticipates a postmodern/poststructuralist inclination to move from 'the real world' towards the study of how meaning is constituted in a culture. In this direction Julia Kristeva affirms that there can be no essential female difference in language; whatever may seem to be specific to women's texts in a specific period may be the effect of prevailing ideologies imposing themes and stylistic effects on women writers. As she affirms in an interview: "There is nothing in either past or recent publications by women that permits us to claim that a specifically female writing exists."[114] And she specifies:

> In books written by women, we can eventually discern certain stylistic and thematic elements, on the basis of which we can then try to isolate a relationship to writing that is peculiar to women. But in speaking of these characteristics, for the moment I find it difficult to say if they are produced by something specific to women, by socio-cultural marginality, or more simply by one particular structure (for example hysteria) promoted by present market conditions from among the whole range of potential female qualities.[115]

For Kristeva an analysis of isolated sentences will not lead to any conclusion, as the same structures can be found in male writers. The only way to have interesting results is to look at the whole text, at its ideological, political, psychoanalytical articulations, its relations with society and with other texts. To explain this, Kristeva has coined the concept of *intertextuality* to indicate how various systems of signs are transposed into others. Moreover, Kristeva recognizes within language a heterogeneous, disruptive dimension that she postulates as the female principle.

113. Irigaray, *This Sex Which Is Not One*, 76.
114. Julia Kristeva "Talking about *Polylogue*" in *French Feminist Thought. A reader*, Toril Moi (Oxford: Blackwell, 1987), 111.
115. Kristeva "Talking about Polylogue", 112.

Drawing on Lacan's distinction between the Imaginary and the Symbolic Order, Kristeva distinguishes two phases: the *semiotic (le semiothique* – different from *la semiotique* i.e. 'semiotics') and the *symbolic*. The *semiotic* precedes the imposition of the *symbolic* – the *logos*, the law of the father – and represents the preverbal locus when the child is bound up with the mother's body. This first phase, the *semiotic*, the female modality, has been consistently repressed by the *logos* and represents an essential negativity. This *semiotic negativity* has been expressed by avant-garde male writers and represents for women a sort of inspiration for "the development of new forms of discourse harmonious with the women's cause as (an) activity of subversion".[116]

Italian Feminist Literary Criticism

Italian feminist thought is characterized by specific cultural and historical elements.[117] Philosophy, psychoanalysis, semiotics, language studies, and leftist politics have all had an influence and are clearly detectable as fundamental elements though at different stages of development. In the 1970s Italy's feminism formed a highly politicized movement under the umbrella of the Left, and in particular of the Italian Communist Party, which was the largest in the Western world. This first wave of feminism, with its left-wing allies, was convinced that it could overthrow patriarchal institutions, including parliament as well as the family. By the end of the decade, however, the leftist parties entered a deep crisis, discredited by extreme-left terrorism, and feminists dissociated themselves from their former allies, becoming increasingly divorced from party politics.

It is important to emphasize that, though generally linked to left wing ideologies, the feminist movement has been characterized since its origins by two distinct souls: a 'separatist' and an 'activist' or 'political' one; the first denominated neo-feminism and formed by independent and extra-parliamentary women, and the second more strictly related to the UDI (Unione Donne Italiane), the feminist group born from the Communist party in 1944 and separating from it in 1982. Despite tensions within ranks, all the feminist groups collaborated throughout the seventies in lobbying the government

---

116. Domna C. Stanton "Language and Revolution: The Franco-American Dis-Connection", 75.

117. See Barbara Dell'Abate-Çelebi, "Italian Feminist Thought at the Periphery of the Empire", *LITERA, Journal of Western Languages and Literatures*, vol. 22, no. 1 (2009): 17-35.

for adoption of progressive legislation for women, such as the protection of working women (1972), equal rights in the family (1975), equal wages with men (1977), and the rights of divorce (1970) and abortion (1978). The campaign to reform the old law on rape has witnessed, since 1980s, an even stronger collaboration between political feminists and neofeminists that in 1996, after more than fifteen years of lobbying, has finally borne fruits.[118]

Since the 1980s, in coincidence with a more stable domestic political background in the Italian society, the feminist movements, no longer united by clearly defined political objectives, have undergone a substantial process of revision and reevaluation. Feminism, in general, has shifted from its position of marginal and subversive ideology towards more theoretical contexts related to the development of women as individuals mainly through philosophy and psychoanalysis.

From this process two main schools of thought have emerged: one derived by 'separatism', committed to sexual difference and motivated by the desire to inject all facets of life with a feminist perspective; and a second, closer to leftist political parties, that seeks a mediation with the mainstream. The first group is mainly represented by the *Libreria delle donne* and *Diotima* groups and by leading feminist figures such as the philosophers and scholars Luisa Muraro, Adriana Cavarero and the journalist Ida Dominijanni — interested almost exclusively in the theory and practice of sexual difference. The second group is headed by the feminist magazine *Noidonne* and its literary supplement *Legendaria* and by famous feminist journalists Miriam Mafai, Anna Maria Crispino, Monica Lanfranco, and Tiziana Bartolini, and is committed instead to researching all subjects related to women.

Polemics over separatism have characterized the dialogue between the two factions, and Miriam Mafai, former editor of *Noidonne* has accused separatist feminists of being less open-minded than men.[119] The feminist theory, elaborated by the Diotima group mainly within a philosophical and psychoanalytical framework, has also been criticized by non-academic feminists for its obscurity and elitism of language that have alienated many readers. Despite these criticisms, the 'separatist' feminists have reached in the last twenty years a recognized, prominent position in the cultural landscape of Italian feminism by developing a fully original and unitary construction to which all Italian feminists now tend to refer.

---

118. The old law declared rape a crime 'against public morality' while the new law, approved by Italian Parliament in February 1996, reclassified rape as a crime 'against the person'.

119. See Isabella Bertoletti, "Feminist Theory: Italy" in *The Feminist Encyclopedia of Italian literature*, Rinaldina Russell ed., (Westport-Connecticut, London: Greenwood Press): 113-116.

To understand the theory of sexual difference we need to start from its basic concept: 'difference'. While Anglo-American feminisms and Italian feminist activists have focused mainly on 'equality', intended in a libertarian and equalitarian sense, the feminists of *Diotima* and of the *Libreria delle donne* have since the 1980s placed their emphasis on 'differences', the notion that equality between men and women, or among women, must not erase individuality or multiplicity of perspectives. Adriana Cavarero, along with Luisa Muraro one of the founder members of *Diotima*, affirms that Western philosophical thought is not neutral and universal but rather the thought of the male subject. She stresses the rethinking of sexual difference within a dual conceptualization of being in a female and in a male subject in opposition to the 'One' that has characterized Western thought. In the words of Luisa Muraro such difference "is not one culturally constructed from biology and imposed as gender but rather a difference in symbolization, a different production of reference and meaning out of a particular embodied knowledge".[120] Hence, Muraro's elaboration of thought takes as its project the establishment of a new feminine genealogy or *collocazione simbolica* (symbolic placement), the research of a new reference and tradition within which to situate woman. She re-elaborates the psychoanalytic thesis of Jacques Lacan, which underlines the implications for the human subject of being born into a symbolic order that pre-exists the subject and gives him its identity.

For this 'symbolic order of the father' Muraro substitutes the 'symbolic order of the mother' (*L'ordine simbolico della madre*[121]), which is the capacity to keep together body and words, experience and language, that women learn in their primary relation with the mother. It is a revolutionary order, since the mother-daughter relation has been cancelled in the patriarchal order. Learning to practice this order in the adult life, substituting the opposition towards the mother with the gratitude to her and to the other women that continue her work, opens the space and the possibility to express female experiences otherwise negated by the conformation to the male norms and power.

Muraro's work puts at its center not the maternal in its ethical or psychological capacities, but the relation with the mother as a symbolic form, able to generate social forms leading to a linguistic mediation more than to law. For Muraro, women have lost their originality as a consequence of the relation with men. They have internalized men's needs and lost their female

120. Milan Women's Bookstore Collective, *Sexual Difference: A Theory of Social-Symbolic Practice,* trans. Teresa de Lauretis and Patricia Cicogna, *(Bloomington: Indiana University Press, 1990),* 27.

121. Luisa Muraro, *L'ordine simbolico della madre,* (Roma: Editori Riuniti, 1991).

origin. The new order can allow a rediscovery of the deeper maternal/feminine unconscious layer that can be joined with the more superficial and rational conscious.

This position may sound essentialist to the Anglo-American feminists, but it is not perceived in the same way within the Italian context. Cavarero and Muraro as professional philosophers draw their discourses from philosophy and psychoanalysis. As academics belonging to Italian humanistic tradition, their references are to Greek and Latin mythology and German and French philosophy. They are not concerned with issues related to the distinction between 'sex' and 'gender' that has strongly characterized the Anglo-American feminist discourse; the Italian language has no distinction between the two words, and the term *sesso* (sex) is used to mean both. They follow neither the pragmatic route of gender identity nor that of social changes; they seek a deeper, structural analysis of the psychoanalytical and philosophical roots of women's difference. For the Italian theorists of sexual difference, in fact, to be woman is not simply a biological factor, as affirmed by essentialism, but it is also an experience of estrangement and separateness and it is strongly rooted in history. This is, moreover, not only limited to the personal sphere of women but it is also a highly political issue. To affirm a difference rooted in the symbolic order means affirming something more than equality to the male subject, as the two subjects, different from each other, have to be accepted both as partial and as fundamental to the new order. Within this theory difference means 'duality', and it is on this duality that the universe needs to be reshaped by a deep modification of all structures at all levels — symbolic, institutional and economic.

However, difference does not only characterize the man/woman relation but also relations among and between women. In this context Muraro argues for the theorization and practice of 'entrustment' and 'disparity' that both derive from a new understanding of 'authority', distinguished from male authoritarianism and hierarchy but read in the frame of the mother/daughter relationship. It is, in fact, through the recognition that all women are not equal that one woman may entrust herself to another, taking that other, authoritative woman as her frame of reference and symbolic mediation with the world.

For Chiara Zamboni, another philosopher of *Diotima*, authority becomes "a bridge, a mediation, between two women"[122] and it is clearly distinct from 'power' as intended within the framework of paternal authority. In the words of Susanna Scarparo: "The feminist intellectual is granted such authority by

122. Chiara Zamboni, 'Ordine simbolico e ordine sociale' in Diotima, *Oltre l'uguaglianza: le radici femminili dell'autorità*, (Napoli: Liguori, 1995), 40.

the person with whom she forms a relationship, but she does not assume that authority a priori. This understanding of authority is markedly distinct from power, particularly institutional power."[123] As we have seen, the reconstructed relation with the mother, intended in a metaphorical and philosophical approach, becomes the basis of a new symbolic order where the woman does not have to sacrifice her symbolic origins to accede to language and to the paternal law. The research for a female subjectivity, or *pensiero sessuato* (sexed thought) in the words of Cavarero, is also stated by the postmodernist feminist critic Rosi Braidotti, who considers the philosophy of sexual difference:

> a necessary political gesture. As a collective political, social, theoretical, movement we must found a female *cogito*. We authorize for ourselves the statement: 'I/woman/ think/as/woman and therefore I am'. *What* I am, as a woman, is another matter, located at a more individual level. Let us not confuse the individual with the subject. We can all agree on the affirmation of a female subjectivity. 'We', movement of liberation of each woman's 'I', of all those women who recognize themselves in the statement 'I/woman am'.[124]

The theory of sexual difference has had powerful repercussions on the issue of language and on the way in which the female "sexed thought" could be expressed by the medium of the existing language created by men within a patriarchal system. Feminist studies within the field of linguistics, semiotics and literature have dealt with this issue not by trying to create a new female language, as in the French feminism, but by a re-reading of literary, philosophical, mythological, psychoanalytic discourses. This occurs not within a male, neuter perspective but by using the female subjectivity as the new measure of research.[125] This allows new freedom within the field of research. without subordination or identification with the codified knowledge, but rather with the intellectual attitude of an itinerary subjectivity in

123. Susanna Scarparo, "Feminist Intellectuals as Public Figures in Contemporary Italy", Australian Feminist Studies 19, no. 44 (July 2004): 2001-2012, 208.

124. Braidotti Rosi, "Commento alla relazione di Adriana Cavarero" in Cristina Marcuzzo and Anna Rossi Doria (eds), *La ricerca delle donne. Studi femministi in Italia,*(Torino: Rosenberg & Sellier) 188-202, quoted in Paola Bono and Sandra Kemp, eds. *Italian Feminist Thought. A Reader*, (Oxford: Basil Blackwell, 1991), 17.

125. Among the most important studies in this field: Elisabetta Rasy, *La lingua della nutrice. Percorsi e tracce dell'espressione femminile*, (Roma: Edizioni delle donne, 1978); Patrizia Magli (ed), *Le donne e i segni: scrittura, linguaggio, identità nel segno della differenza femminile*, (Ancona: Il lavoro editoriale, 1988); Patrizia Violi, *L'infinito singolare. Considerazioni sulla differenza sessuale del linguaggio*, (Verona: Essedue edizioni, 1986).

transition between places, experiences, roles and languages — an attitude that Rosi Braidotti has assimilated to the image of the 'nomad'. She identifies, in fact, an interrelationship between female identity, feminist subjectivity, and "the radical epistemology of nomadic transitions from a perspective of positive sexual difference".[126]

The new female subjectivity as a nomadic concept does not observe disciplinary boundaries and "has relinquished all idea, desire, or nostalgia for fixity"[127] as the nomad is a "form of political resistance to hegemonic and exclusionary views of subjectivity".[128] Braidotti's theory of sexual difference represents a further development from Diotima's thought at the intersection between feminism and postmodernism/post-structuralism. Following the path of Diotima's theorists, Braidotti also intends to work with the body as "a point of overlapping between the physical, the symbolic and the sociological."[129] For her, locating subjectivity in the body is not an essentialist position but, on the contrary, it is radically anti-essentialist because it forces subjective specificity, multiplicity and complexity within multiple discourses and physical positions. However, she is mindful of the question of how deeply subjectivity can be rooted in embodiment and sexual difference before it slips into nostalgia or moralism.

Italian feminist thought has suffered from relatively low international diffusion and visibility. It is clearly not a highly accessible theory for international grass-roots feminists or for a wider, popular audience. Its natural rooting in Continental philosophy and psychoanalysis creates, in fact, both linguistic and content barriers for non-academic feminists. This difficulty is further accentuated with regard to the Anglo-American audience, with its more pragmatic and less philosophical approach to feminism and general unfamiliarity with Continental philosophy, unlike in Germany, France and Italy where it represents a common subject of study since secondary school.

Moreover it is important to underline that the 'thought of sexual difference' in the words of Cavarero is born as the "*philosophical* systematization of the concepts and categories of the feminist theoretical speculations carried on by the feminist movement in Italy"[130] (my emphasis). Therefore the theory of difference, is basically a 'philosophical' theory laid down by

126. Rosi Braidotti. *Nomadic Subjects: Embodiment and Sexual Difference in Contemporary Feminist Theory*, (New York: Columbia University Press, 1994), 149.

127. Rosi Braidotti, *Nomadic Subjects*, 22.

128. Rosi Braidotti, *Nomadic Subjects*, 23.

129. Rosi Braidotti, *Nomadic Subjects*, 4.

130. Adriana Cavarero, "The Need for a Sexed Thought" in P. Bono and S. Kemp , eds., *Italian Feminist Thought. A reader*, 181-185, 181.

professional women philosophers working within the academia in a period of no institutionalization of feminism in Italy and, as we have previously underlined, does not represent Italian feminism as a whole but it is its more philosophical, elitist, separatist branch. As a natural consequence, it has been exported abroad in the nineties by two academics, Teresa De Lauretis and Rosi Braidotti, and because of its specialist nature it has maintained a marginal role with respect to the larger culture while finding resonance only among feminist academia and intellectuals.

The close relation bonding French and Italian feminist thought is due in particular to the debt that the Italian theory of sexual difference has in respect to the Belgian-French philosopher, linguist and psychoanalyst Luce Irigaray. She has been in fact one of the main points of reference for Italian feminist thought, and all her works have been translated in Italian by *Libreria delle donne* of Milan within one year of their original publications. Luisa Muraro and Adriana Cavarero, as well as other major Italian theorists of difference, have been deeply influenced by these works and by the ideas of Irigaray, who has also been actively engaged in the feminist movement in Italy and has participated in several initiatives to implement a respect for sexual difference on a cultural and, in her most recent work, governmental level.

Italian feminist thought has suffered the effects of the same sorts of criticism levelled against French feminist theory. The main criticisms are linked to the issue of essentialism: Italian feminist thought is generally accused of accepting the thesis of a fundamental difference between men and women rooted in biology. As the British feminist researcher Helen Haste has pointed out, however, the major issue is not its claim of biological determinism but rather its claim that there can be a "universal female experience" and that under this invoked universalism it has ignored "the diversity and plurality of female experiences and perspectives".[131]

In fact Anglo-American feminist theoretical production has engaged, since the nineties, with issues of class, race, culture and sexuality, leading to an eclipse of the importance of sexual difference and the emergence of a plurality of identities, and thus diluting the centrality of male/female divide. Black, lesbian and migrant feminisms are nowadays important realities and major theoretical and political issues within the Anglo-American feminism, but their specific problems are not confronted by the Italian theory of sexual difference, and this is certainly a strong limit to its 'exportability'.

---

131. Helen Haste, "Sexual Metaphors and Current Feminisms" in Anna Bull, Hanna Diamond and Rosalind Marsh eds., *Feminisms and Women's Movements in Contemporary Europe*, (New York: St. Martin's Press, 2000), 21-34.

Further, as noted by the critic Carol Lazzaro-Weis,[132] this limitation is exacerbated in the eyes of American feminists by the strong tie that Italian theorists of difference appear to have with the more radical separatist and essentialist factions of early American feminism, writers such as Mary Daly, Adrienne Rich and Shulamith Firestone, who have been superseded by other stages of American feminist criticism. Their definition of sexual difference – the different nature of women's experience, history, tradition and culture from that of men – had been, in fact, swept away by internal criticism from women of color, lesbians and Jewish women who felt marginalized by this emphasis. It is this critique, aiming at unmasking the essentialist bias of mainstream feminism of the seventies and eighties, that eventually produced the shift in Anglo-American feminism from the label "Women's" to the label "Gender" in feminist studies.

It is important, when drawing similarities, to take into account the specific historical, cultural, social backgrounds that have led to the creation of national feminisms. In this context separatism and essential female difference have to be considered primarily strategic responses to the specific situations Italian feminism has had to contend with as it developed within its own tradition. However it is not a static and immutable position but a direct response to external stimuli that a fast-changing reality strongly influences and directs. In the last ten years new elements have concurred in modifying Italian feminism's social basis as a result of a complex, cross-cultural pattern of thoughts and ideologies. These and many more new questions have begun to be discussed by Italian feminists in the last ten years, and this constant work-in-progress is deeply affecting and influencing the nature of Italian feminism that, as affirmed by Parati and West "as itself a site of dialogue and difference, if not conflict, is anything but monolithic".[133]

132. Carol Lazzaro-Weis, "The Concept of Difference in Italian Feminist Thought: Mothers, Daughters, Heretics", in Graziella Parati, Rebecca J. West, *Italian Feminist Theory and Practice: Equality and Sexual Difference*, (Madison, Teaneck: Fairleigh Dickinson University Press, 2002), 31-49.

133. Graziella Parati, Rebecca J. West, *Italian Feminist Theory and Practice: Equality and Sexual Difference*, (Madison, Teaneck: Fairleigh Dickinson University Press, 2002), 16.

CHAPTER 2

THE THEME OF PENELOPE AT THE ORIGIN

Those without power cannot always afford to be honest.
Sandra Gilbert and Susan Gubar

Penelope symbolizes in our imagination the model of faithfulness. She is praised for her legendary forbearance in waiting for her spouse for almost twenty years. Her first literary appearance can be traced back to the *Odyssey*. The famous epic poem by Homer is the source of many interrogations and is the center of various studies. Philology, anthropology, psychoanalysis are some of the disciplines that have dealt with this subject. The *Odyssey* has generated many opposite interpretations and remains the object of many theories.

The two epic poems by Homer, the *Iliad* and the *Odyssey*, stand at the origin of Greek literature and constitute the first works of Western literature. However we cannot consider the author as inventor of the epic subject, since it is clear that the events narrated are anterior to the composition of the two poems. We find in Homer the traces of an older, oral tradition. By grouping together some epic poems he has created the most complex and organic form of epic saga, deriving from an oral tradition dating back to many centuries. Other writers have treated the same subject, but only the genius of Homer has been able to fix it in the form that we know nowadays. This singular capability has made of the author the founder of the theme of Penelope. According to Raymond Trousson: "Le fondateur n'est pas nécessairement celui qui a traité le thème le premier, c'est celui qui lui a donné sa forme la plus fameuse, qui l'a inséré dans le patrimoine culturel universel."[1]

---

1. Raymond Trousson, *Thèmes et mythes. Questions de méthode*, (Bruxelles: Editions de l'Université de Bruxelles, 1981), 98. "The founder is not necessarily the one who has treated the theme as first, but the one that has given to it its most famous form, that has inserted it in the universal cultural patrimony." My translation.

The *Odyssey* by Homer

The identity of the author of the two epic poems is still debated. Since the eighteenth century the existence of Homer has been questioned by the Ancients in their "querelle"[2] with the Moderns, continuing in the twentieth century under the name of 'Homeric Question'. The questions arise around the historical existence of Homer and the authorship of the two poems. Is he the only author of the famous *Odyssey*? Are there distinct authors for each of the two poems? Are they the productions of a group of poets? He is considered by some critics the author of only some episodes, with the remaining parts written by other poets of less literary value. These questions have not yet found a unique answer. For Paul Claudel, the *Iliad* "comme sa sœur l'*Odyssée*, reste ce qu'elle a été pour les siècles antiques, l'œuvre d'un seul homme appelé Homère".[3] On the other side, Pietro Citati speaks of the "premier Homère" and the "second Homère" and even imagines a sort of dialogue between them.[4]

Fernard Robert[5] asks at the end of his book on Homer the question "Un poète, ou deux poètes?" Although he is persuaded that both the *Iliad* and the *Odyssey* have received their definitive structure in the aristocratic Milesian (from the town of Miletus in Asia Minor) circle, he does not judge it necessary that the two poems are products of the same author. He recognizes, however, an unquestionable relation between the poets, a sort of Homer senior and Homer junior, where the senior was able to transmit to the junior "les recettes plus subtiles de son art".[6] Following this reasoning, the critic dates the *Iliad* to the eighth century while the *Odyssey* is presumably posterior to 734 or even 708 B.C. The general opinion agrees with the critic, dating both poems at the end of the ninth or eighth century, with the *Iliad* preceding the *Odyssey* by some decades.

Both questions related to the author of the poems and to the date of birth of Homer raise doubts in relation to a unique author or a group of poets. Another French critic, Gérard Lambin,[7] has made the hypothesis that the

2. "dispute".

3. Paul Claudel, *Œevres en prose*, (Paris: Gallimard, Biblioteque de la Pleiade, 1965). "like her sister the *Odyssey*, remains what has been for the ancient centuries, the work of a single man called Homer". My translation.

4. Pietro Citati, *La lumière de la nuit*, trad. Tristan Macé et Brigitte Pérol, (Paris: Gallimard, 1999). "First Homer", "Second Homer". My translation.

5. Fernand Robert, *Homère*, (Paris: Presses Universitaires de France, 1950). "One poet, or two poets?" My translation.

6. Fernand Robert, *Homère*, "the more suble recepits of his art".

7. Gérard Lambin, *Homère le compagnon*, (Paris: CNRS, 1995).

authors are in reality a group whose collective name would be Homer as to-day the name Nicolas Bourbaki refers to a group of French mathematicians.

Another characteristic feature of the legendary figure of the poet inspired by the Muses is his blindness. Homer is most likely a pseudonym; *homeros* in fact can be translated in Aeolian as 'blind'. The tradition holds that he was deprived of sight, like Tiresias the diviner of the town of Thebes inter-rogated by Ulysses in Book XI of the *Odyssey*. Poets and diviners had sim-ilar characteristics in Ancient Greece, as they both had the capability to see beyond appearances. As affirmed by Jean-Pierre Vernant: "Devin, poète et sage ont en commun une faculté exceptionnelle de voyance au delà des ap-parences sensibles; ils possèdent une sorte d'extra-sens qui leur ouvre l'ac-cès à un monde normalement interdit aux mortels."[8] With the progressive institution of temples in his honor, Homer became an almost-religious fig-ure, and worship was rendered to him. We find this in Athens and Alexan-dria, as witnessed by the sanctuary placed within the Museum which shel-tered the famous Library.

In relation to the geographic situation, it is difficult to localize with preci-sion the native region of Homer. Seven towns contended the paternity. These were: Smyrne, Rhodes, Colophon, Salamine, Chios, Argos and Athens. It is easy to observe that they are located both in Greece and in Asia Minor (the modern Turkey). The complex issue of Homer's motherland reflects the var-ious languages used by the poet. All the families of Greek dialects are mixed in the language utilized by Homer. As observed by Pierre Lévêque "une al-liance unique de formes dialectales empruntées essentiellement à l'ionien, mais aussi à l'éolien et a l'arcadien".[9] The composition of the poem has thus taken place in the Ionian world where many immigrants, casted out of their land by Dorian invasions, loved to hear the singing of the achievements of the glorious Achaeans.[10] According to the poet Pindar (sixth century B.C.) Homer would be "à la fois de Chios et de Smyrne",[11] since his language is a melange of Aeolian and Ionian (especially oriental Ionian). So Homer would

---

8. Jean-Pierre Vernant, *Mythe et pensée chez les Grecs. Études de psychologie historique*, (Paris : Maspero, 1965), 386. "The diviner, the poet and the wise man have in com-mon an exceptional capability of clairvoyance beyond sensible appearance; they have a sort of extra sense that gives them access to a world normally forbidden to living be-ings". My translation.

9. Pierre Lévêque, *L'Aventure grecque*, (Paris: Armand Colin, 1964). "A unique alliance of dialectal forms based essentially on Ionian, but also on Eolien and Arcadian". My translation.

10. Pierre Brunel, *Homère. VIII siècle av.J.-C.*, (Paris: SEM, 2009), 35.

11. Brunel, *Homère, VIII siècle av.J.-C.*, 21. "both from Chios and from Smyrne". My translation.

be a native of Smyrne (Izmir) who had lived in Chios, two cities where Ionians and Aeolians coexisted. Following the indication of Pindar, recent Hellenists have agreed that the first towns to claim Homer's paternity (Chios, Smyrne, Colophon and Cumes) correspond to the particularities of the language that he utilizes.

However we should not think that the geography of the places described by Homer is a true description of the Mediterranean, of its rivers or islands. This was certainly the illusion of Victor Bérard[12] when, at the beginning of the twentieth century, he tried to find, for each place cited by Ulysses, some points of anchorage in the real world. This approach was based mainly on the archaeological discoveries of late nineteenth century led by the coming to light of the ruins of the ancient town of Troy located by the German archaeologist Heinrich Schliemann in Hissarlık (Anatolia, modern Turkey). Following his excavations, nine levels, corresponding to different historical periods, were identified together with a rich treasure called by Schliemann "Priam's treasure" that was revealed in 1873.

Historians today believe that the Trojan War was really fought, though probably it did not have the importance the epic poems grant to it. It was most likely a military expedition led towards the end of the thirteenth century B.C. by some Mycenaean towns to conquer the town of Troy whose geographical location on the Dardanelles Strait was considered highly strategic. At the origin of the conflict were economic reasons, transposed by Homer into mythical and legendary ones.[13] As described by Pietro Citati,[14] the Mediterranean in the Homeric version has become something of a vast prison and the heroes of the *Odyssey* are victims of a long imprisonment in the heart of it.

In relation to the text of the poems, it is important to remember that their first recording dates to 560 B.C. by the will of Peisistratos, 'tyrant' (i.e. non-elected chief) of Athens, who decided to establish an official edition of the two epics. In Athens the Homeric poems were recited during the celebration of the religious festival of the Great Panathenaia.[15] The division of both poems in 24 books, following the Greek alphabet, can be dated back to the third and second century B.C. by Alexandrine scholars, while the first printed edition appeared almost two millennia later, in 1488 in Florence.[16]

12. Victor Berard, *L'Odyssée d'Homère, étude et analyse*, (Paris: Mellottée, 1934).

13. See Eva Cantarella, *Storie di dei ed eroi*, (Milano: Mondadori Scuola, 2010), 33-34.

14. Citati, *La lumière de la nuit*, 1999.

15. Brunel, *Homère, VIII siècle av.J.-C.*, 118.

16. Bernardus Nerlius and Demetrius Chalcondyles, eds., Homerus, *Editio Princeps* (Homer, Works), (Florence, Italy: 1488), Greek.

Despite the doubts related to the paternity of Homer, the *Odyssey* is considered here in its wholeness. Whether the whole work is legitimate or not is not important within this study. The total of the poem is the work of a Greek poet, mythic or not, a convenor poet, a Mediterranean poet. The focus is here on the first appearance of the theme of Penelope in Western literature. It is under this form that the theme has inspired writers throughout the centuries and is transmitted to us.

Structure

The *Odyssey* is an epic poem of about 26,000 verses, divided into 24 books. It narrates the story of the return of Greek Odysseus (Ulysses for the Latins) to his homeland, Ithaca, after the end of the Trojan War. The poem belongs to the narrative genre of *nóstoi* (in Greek 'returns') that included various poems relative to the adventures of the Greek heroes during their return home from Troy. The narration does not follow chronologically the adventures of the protagonist but concentrates mainly on the last part of his return to Ithaca, the last days of his staying with the nymph Calypso up to his reunion with Penelope.

As well documented by Eduard Delebecque in his detailed study on the structure of the poem: "l'action proprement dite [...] se developpe sur quarante jours et quarante nuits". [17] Apart from these forty days, narrated by the poet in third person, the adventures of the ten previous years by sea are recounted in a long *flashback* tale by Ulysses himself (Books IX-XII). The structure of the poem is thus quite elaborate. Three sections can be distinguished: the "Telemachy" (Books I-IV) narrating the travel of Telemachus, the son of Ulysses, who advised by the goddess Athena leaves Ithaca to look for news concerning his father; "The tale of Ulysses" (Books V-XII), anterior in time, that comprises the "grand conte",[18] the narration by Ulysses himself to the Phaecians (Books IX-XII); and "The return to Ithaca and the revenge of Ulysses" (Books XIII-XXIV), narrating in third person the arrival of Ulysses in Ithaca and the massacre of the suitors of Penelope who had occupied his mansion.

17. Eduard Delebecque, *Construction de l'Odyssée*, (Paris : Les Belles Lettres, 1980), 4. "the action covers forty days and forty nights". My translation.
18. Delebecque, *Construction de l'Odyssée*, 141. "Le conte le plus important, ou 'grand conte', est l'histoire faite par Ulysse de sa vie agitée depuis son départ de Troy, la guerre finie, just 'à son arrivée chez Calypso." (The most important tale, or 'main tale' is the story narrated by Ulysses of his turbulent life from his departure from Troy, at the end of the war, up to his arrival in Calypso's island).

Plot

Ulysses, having gone to participate in the war against Troy to rescue the beautiful Helen, has left his wife Penelope in charge of the kingdom of Ithaca. For many years she has been waiting for his return. The others, his war companions, have in the majority of cases returned home. Ulysses has not returned, and as he is considered dead, Penelope is vexed by marriage proposals. She is the key to access the throne left empty by the king's departure for war, and she is sought by the princes of the region. But she is still hoping and suffers for the absence of her husband beside her.

After years of adventures and wanderings, under the insistence of the goddess Athena, Zeus decides that it is time for Ulysses to return to his house. Despite the resentment of the sea-god Poseidon whose son Polyphemus, the cruel Cyclops, had been blinded by Ulysses, he finds his way back. In Ithaca Telemachus is informed by Athena that his father is coming back. Skeptical, he embarks on a trip looking for new evidence. While he is away the suitors begin to plot his death so as to force Penelope, without heirs, to choose a new spouse.

Arrived in Ithaca, Ulysses devises with Athena a plan to punish the suitors. Before leaving the island to inform Telemachus of the danger he is running, Athena gives the king the appearance of an old man. Under this appearance he enters in his house, resolved to regain possession of his goods and to take revenge of the suitors who have outraged his wife and sacked his house. His participation in the trial of the bow prompts a fight, and with the aid of his son, two faithful servants and the goddess Athena, he kills all of the suitors. After so many years, Penelope, still skeptical, takes some time to recognize the spouse of her youth, and she proposes one last trial before finally consenting to live in peace. It is to her that Ulysses will narrate his adventures, the journey of Ulysses, the *Odyssey*.

Commentary

The *Odyssey* is the story of the adventures of Ulysses/Odysseus, a solitary hero who wanders long years before finding his way home. His travel is both real and symbolic. Ithaca is a realistic place, a small community that will become a real town, a *pòlis,* as will Athens later on. The places, the customs, the relations among the characters are also credible and offer us important examples of daily life in the archaic Greek world. However the travel of Ulysses has been interpreted in the following centuries as a coming-of-age story, a story of individual formation in which the protagonist matures and becomes aware of his human condition. From this perspective, the *Odyssey* tells the story of the life-travel of each man, with the difficulties and obstacles that can be overcome only with the intelligence, wisdom and patience. To a portrait of its contemporary society the poem unites a number of fantastic elements that help to transmit precise moral values. In fact Ulysses' world is inhabited by monsters and bewilderments, towards which he has to confront by using his *mètis*, the ingenious intelligence, his courage and all the qualities that reveal the man. By celebrating the human condition, the *Odyssey* puts the accent on the moral preoccupations. It invites piety towards the gods, respect for religious rules and human laws. At the end the suitors are punished, the waiting of Penelope and the perseverance of the hero are rewarded.

The figure of Ulysses affirms the pre-eminence of intelligence over force. He embodies the new values that will make up the Greek man: ingenuity and curiosity. Nicole Loraux affirms that the king of Ithaca constitutes "le paradigme heroique du philosophe". And moreover, "de l'endurance et de la *métis* qui, dans l'Odyssée, constituent Ulysse, c'est [...] la première dimension que toujours choisit Platon en évoquant le héros homérique".[19] It is in fact a model to follow that is presented here by Homer. His tales aimed not simply to entertain and amuse but also to educate the hearers and improve the audience. Through the adventures of Ulysses, proposed as a model to follow, Homer suggested also how to behave in the society of the time, in relation with other men and with the gods. Even the most fantastic adventures shared this intention, as they presented examples of behaviors to be avoided or imitated.

Ulysses is in many aspects a new kind of hero, different from Achilles and from the other characters of the *Iliad*. He is a valorous warrior but his true arms are cunning, genius and intelligence. In many circumstances he saves himself by avoiding a sudden impulse and instead trusting reflection, wisdom and patience. Another of his notorious characteristics is curiosity, united with the desire to know and to experiment new situations. The hero never hesitates towards new adventures, although dangerous and painful. This will generate, in the following centuries, the myth of Ulysses as hero of intellectual boldness and knowledge. In Dante's *Inferno* Ulysses himself blames his death, if not his damnation, on "the burning wish / to know the world and have experience / of all man's vices, of all human worth"[20] and

---

19. Nicole Loraux, *Les experiences de Tiresias. Le feminin et l'homme grec*, (Paris: Gallimard, 1989), 205. "The heroic paradigm of the philosopher."; "Between endurance and the *métis* that, in the *Odyssey* represent Ulysses, it is [...] the first dimension that Plato always chooses in evoking the Homeric hero." My translation.

20. See Dante Alighieri, *La Divina Commedia, Vol. 1 Inferno*, ed. by Natalino Sapegno (Firenze: La Nuova Italia, 1955), XXVI, 97-99. "vincer potero dentro a me l'ardore /ch'i' ebbi a divenir del mondo esperto/e de li vizi umani e del valore".

for his continuous quest for "worth and knowledge"[21] as he recounts putting it to his men, a desire more powerful, in Ulysses' self-condemnation, than "sweetness of a son, reverence / for an aging father, [and] debt of love / owed to Penelope".[22] He recounts imploring his crew: "during this so brief vigil of our senses [i.e. life] / that is still reserved to us [before death], do not deny / yourself experience of what there is beyond, /beyond the sun, in the world they call unpeopled".[23] In Homer's poem, however, the greater desire of the hero is to return to his spouse and his house. To rejoin his dearest, he refuses the gift of immortality that the nymph Calypso is prepared to offer him. He prefers the human condition and decides to endure yet more sufferings. The wisdom of Ulysses is thus this acceptance of the human condition.

Penelope and the *Odyssey*

The *Odyssey* is the place of the first literary incarnation of the theme of Penelope. She appears also in the *Iliad* but she is only evoked there. There is an oral tradition previous to the poem composed by Homer, but we can only make suppositions on the existence of this tradition, which has long since disappeared. We have to rely on the *Odyssey* and consider it the representative model of the appearance of the spouse of Ulysses. We will utilize this poem to define the theme of Penelope at its origin.

In the many studies published on the *Odyssey* it is not normal to give great importance to Penelope as central character. So for example in the work by Edouard Delebecque on the structure of the *Odyssey* [24] she is hardly mentioned as the study is based exclusively on the events related to Ulysses and his son. Only in a later edition of the work [25] Delebecque dedicates a small section to Penelope, though outlining that "elle ne joue pas un role actif dans la construction de l'Odyssée. Elle n'est que la raison finale du retour."[26] Unlike the characters of Circe, Calypso and Nausica, who play capital roles

---

21. Alighieri, *La Divina Commedia*, XXVI, 120. "per seguir virtute e conoscenza".

22. Alighieri, *La Divina Commedia*, XXVI, 94-96. "né dolcezza di figlio, né la pieta/del vecchio padre, né 'l debito amore/lo qual dovea Penelopè far lieta".

23. Alighieri, *La Divina Commedia*, XXVI, 114-117. "a questa tanto picciola vigilia /d'i nostri sensi ch'è del rimanente /non vogliate negar l'esperïenza,/di retro al sol, del mondo sanza gente".

24. Eduard Delebecque, *Télémaque et la structure de l'Odyssée,* (Aix: Éditions Ophrys, 1958).

25. Delebecque, *Construction de l'Odyssée.*

26. Delebecque, *Construction de l'Odyssée*, 125-126. "She does not play an active role in the construction of the Odyssey. She is only the final reason of the return".

in the action and composition of the poem, the role that Homer has given to Penelope — according to the critic — is simply passive. She has the final task of characterizing the *Odyssey* as the poem of fidelity and trust: "Il reste qu'après la rencontre d'Ulysse avec deux amantes et une jeune fille a marier, c'est Penelope qui couronne une œuvre dont elle fait, avec la collaboration épisodique et inattendue d'Hélène repentie et pardonnée, le poème de la fidélité et de la confiance."[27]

In the same way, for another French critic, Pierre Brunel, "Penelope est célébré finalement comme un modèle de vertu. C'est la réduire que de ne la considérer que comme la femme d'Ulysse. Ou c'est à cause de cela qu'elle est pleinement elle-même."[28] This reductive view of Penelope, considered only as a symbol of faithfulness, chastity and patience, follows a stereotypical image that spread well into the twentieth century and that considered Penelope a minor and uninteresting character, not only by comparison to Ulysses but also to the other female characters of the poems. As affirmed by John Woodhouse in 1930s:

> Certainly Penelopeia does not in the world's imagination stand on a level with either Kirke or Kalypso, much less does she vie with 'Fayre Helen, floure of beauty excellent'. [...] For in truth nothing much could be made of the figure of Penelopeia in the Romance of the *Odyssey*, without disturbing the centre of gravity of the poem. The subject of the poem is the Man.[29]

This view has been strongly debated in the last decades, and a new approach to the analysis of the poem has shown the centrality of Penelope within the *Odyssey*. Works like Marie Madelaine Mactoux, *Penelope. Legende et mythe* (1975), Marylin Arthur-Katz, *Penelope's Renown. Meaning and Indeterminacy in the Odyssey* (1991), Nancy Felson-Rubin, *Regarding Penelope: From Character to Poetics* (1994), Ioanna Papadopolou-Belmehdi, *Le chant de Penelope* (1994) and Richard Heitman, *Taking her seriously. Penelope and the plot of Homer's Odyssey* (2005) refute this passive interpretation and emphasize the central role of Penelope within the

---

27. Delebecque, *Construction de l'Odyssée*, 126. "After the meeting of Ulysses with two lovers and a young maiden, it is Penelope who will set the end of a poem that she, together with the episodic and unexpected collaboration of Helen, repentant and forgiven, turns in the poem of faithfulness and trust".

28. Brunel, *Homère. VIII siècle av. J.-C.*, 106. "Penelope is celebrated as a model of virtue. It is reductive to consider her just as the wife of Ulysses. Or it is because of this that she is fully herself". My translation.

29. William John Woodhouse, *The composition of Homer's Odyssey*, (Oxford: Clarendon, 1930), 201-203.

narrative strategy of the poem, making her an essential and modifying agent of the plot. Moreover, two major contributions to the study of the myth of Penelope from Italian scholars, Adriana Cavarero's *In spite of Plato* (1990) and Monica Farnetti's *Non così per Penelope* (2007), offer a new feminist reading of this figure.

The character of the queen is the object of numerous interpretations because of apparent contradictions that are manifested all along the Homeric poem. While critics such as Marie-Madeleine Mactoux[30] have seen in Homer's Penelope a fragmented character, a figure of incoherence, more recent writers such as Ioanna Papadopoulou-Belmehdi have highlighted the issues related to the narrative construction of the poem: "Les contradictions à propos d'un même personnage sont dues à la forme 'dialoguée' de l'Odyssée, où l'on voit s'affronter non pas différentes versions du mythe mais des visions divergentes de la réalité."[31]

According to Papadopoulou-Belmehdi: "Toute une tradition de lecture en a fait un personnage fade et inactif, le plus souvent une figure de fidélité conjugale et parfois de lascivité démesurée, mais sans plus."[32] Ioanna Papadopoulou-Belmedhi gives us an explanation to his phenomenon. According to her:

> [...] la *mnêmê* [mémoire] d'Ulysse et de Pénélope ainsi que la *mnêsteia* [solicitation] constituent le pivot de l'*Odyssée*, même si le rôle de Pénélope est moins apparent car dessiné de façon codée. En effet, « la reine aux nombreux prétendants » ne génère pas seulement l'*éris* [discorde], elle est aussi figure poétique de la tension entre l'être et le paraître, entre la pensée et la parole, entre l'allusion et l'expression. Ce qui explique en partie l'approche érudite qui, jugeant l'importance du personnage selon sa participation à « l'action » ou la « décision » en fait une figure fade et subalterne.[33]

30. Marie-Madeleine Mactoux, "L'ambiguité de la legende homerique", in *Penelope. Legende et mythe*, (Paris: Les Belles Lettres, 1975), 5-28.

31. Ioanna Papadopoulou-Belmehdi, *Le chant de Pénélope. Poétique du tissage féminin dans L'Odyssée*, (Paris: Belin, 1994), 147. "The contradictions relating to a same character are due to the dialogic form of the *Odyssey*, where confronting each other are not different versions of the myth but different visions of reality." My translation.

32. Papadopoulou-Belmehdi, *Le chant de Pénélope*, 19. "A long reading tradition has made of her an inactive and fade character, the more often a figure of conjugal faithfulness and sometimes of immensurable lasciviousness, but no more..."

33. Papadopoulou-Belmehdi, *Le chant de Pénélope*, 169-170. "(...) la *mnêmê* (memory) of Ulysses and of Penelope as the *mnêsteia* (solicitation) constitute the pivot of the *Odyssey*, even if the role of Penelope is less apparent as designed in a coded way. In effect, the 'queen with many wooers' does not generate only the *eris* (discord), she is also a poetic figure of the tension between being and appearing, between thought and word,

Penelope is actually an essential character. She has no direct influence on the action but she is the one who makes it possible:

> Les personnages dominants de l'*Odyssée* sont ceux qui ont une forte affinité avec la mémoire infaillible: c'est ainsi qu'Ulysse atteint le statut de l'aède, c'est ainsi que dans sa dimension de memnêmenê « celle qui se souvient » Pénélope s'apparente en quelque sorte à la Muse de l'*Odyssée*, non seulement parce qu'elle inspire en Ulysse le désir du *nostos* (retour) mais aussi parce que la Muse est une expression métaphysique de la mémoire du poète épique. En effet, l'attitude de Pénélope en fait un personnage aussi solidaire du projet poétique odysséen que le héros du *nostos*.[34]

Faithfulness and patience return almost inevitably at the evocation of the theme of Penelope. Considering the twenty years during which Ulysses lives far from his spouse and the fact that in the meanwhile she does not re-marry, a number of authors bring forward the unique argument of the legendary faithfulness of Penelope. But the problem is more complex. It is certainly a question of faithfulness, but we should not forget that faithfulness was not a choice in the ancient Greek world, as it was obligatory for women not to be adulterous. Female infidelity was a highly reprehensible act while, on the contrary, male adultery was accepted by the social and cultural sphere.

From this perspective Penelope respects her duty and preserves her well-being. But here, the faithfulness of the queen is exaggerated and even excessive. Because in her case, by being the queen of a kingdom whose throne is vacant for years, it is her duty to take a new spouse and offer a new king to her people. Her refusal to re-marry is extreme in a society like Ithaca. We return to the starting problem: is it simply a problem of faithfulness? Why does Penelope refuse a marriage that everyone expects?

As framed by Papadopoulou-Belmehdi, the answer is subtler than the issue of marital loyalty. Penelope takes part in a project much more complex

---

between allusion and expression. This is what explains in part the erudite approach that, by judging the importance of the character according to its participation to the 'action' or the 'decision' makes of it a faded and subaltern figure."

34. Papadopoulou-Belmehdi, *Le Chant de Penelope.* 169-170. "The dominant characters in the *Odyssey* are those who have a strong affinity with the infallible memory: it is in this way that Ulysses reaches the status of *bard*, and in her role of *memnêmenê* (the one who remembers) Penelope resembles in some ways the Muse of the *Odyssey*, not only because the Muse is a metaphysic expression of the memory of the epic poet. In effect, the attitude of Penelope makes her a character as connected to the poetic project of the *Odyssey* as the hero of *nostos*."

than a hymn to marital faithfulness: she belongs to the different representations of memory: "Le rôle poétique essential de Pénélope n'est pas d'incarner la fonction royale, la fidélité conjugale ou même la passivité féminine mais d'être une expression de la mémoire."[35] Faithfulness then would be one of the consequences of her resilience in remembering her husband. The memory she displays is an element worth great consideration. For us, the faithfulness so admired in Penelope is linked to the heart and to recollection. Questions of adulterous desire or of her eventual temptation are secondary to the strength of her memory. While patience is another characteristic often associated to the theme of Penelope, her faithfulness must be linked to the issue of memory, of which it is the consequence.

Memory

Memory plays an essential role in the poem. Life, reputation, the home of the hero, royalty, justice and compensation depend on its strength. This explains the preponderant place of the bard, *l'aède*, in the *Odyssey*: it is his role to keep the memory of events. The relation of the poetic truth to the notion of destiny is a major trait of the text. In the Ithaca disfigured by the absence of Ulysses, Penelope thinks and acts in affinity with this principle. Against the pernicious story of the bard, she opposes her infallible memory. Remembrance has a fundamental place in the text of Homer. It is memory that, throughout the mediation of Penelope, allows Ulysses to take back his place at his return. During the twenty years of his absence, the throne of Ithaca remains vacant thanks to the infallible memory of his spouse. By refusing to marry again, Penelope preserves the royal power of her husband.

Penelope is also guarantor of Ulysses' honor. "Elle reste le seul personnage poétique à Ithaque qui s'obstine à associer la mémoire d'Ulysse au *kléos*."[36] According to Gregory Nagy: "Penelope is the key not only to the *nostos* but also to the *kleos* of Odysseus. [...] Odysseus gets the best *kleos* through his wife. Through Penelope, he has a genuine *nostos*, while Agamemnon gets a false one and Achilles, none at all."[37] During all the years of separation she is the guarantor of his status and reputation.

---

35. Papadopoulou-Belmehdi, *Le chant de Pénélope,* 171. "The essential poetic role of Penelope is not to embody the royal function, the faithfulness in marriage or even the feminine passivity but of being an expression of memory."

36. Papadopoulou-Belmehdi, *Le chant de Pénélope,* 73. "She remains the only poetic character in Ithaca who persists in associating the memory of Ulysses to *kleos*." (*Kleos* or epic glory).

37. Gregory Nagy, *The best of the Achaeans. Concepts of the Hero in Archaic Greek poetry,* (Baltimora: The Johns Hopkins University Press, 1999), 2nd Revised edition, 64.

Throughout the *Odyssey,* the different appearances of Penelope are marked by the issue of memory. Her first intervention is very emblematic. It is the episode of the refusal of the song during the feast of the suitors.[38] In this passage, Phémius, the royal bard, sings the story of the sad return of the Achaeans, cursed by the goddess Athena for their impiety at the siege of Troy. Penelope puts a stop to his song that recalls the non-glorious death of Ulysses, succumbed while returning back to his home. The content of the song is summarised by two verses pronounced by Telemachus when he rebukes his mother for her intervention against the bard: "Odysseus was not the only one to lose in Troy the day of his return: there many other warriors met their death."[39] Pietro Pucci says of Phemios, the bard, that he "forgets the truth".[40] Forced to sing for the necessity of survival, his aim is first of all to seduce his audience. The truthfulness of the song is not important. The fidelity to the story is recalled by Penelope. Her 'uninterrupted memory' of Ulysses contends with the singing of the bard. She holds the poetic truth:

> La transmission de la mémoire doit garantir la représentation véridique des exploits des héros et les valeurs du monde dans lequel ils vivent [...]. La poétique odysséenne situe le personnage de Penelope dans cet ordre héroïque de vérité, comme le montre sa toute première apparition épique, contre le chant de Phémios.[41]

In Ithaca she seems to be the only holder of the poetic Odyssean truth. She is the only one to oppose the singing of the bard who voices the dominant epic version on the island. And it is the great glory of the hero that she opposes to the sinister song of Phemius:

> You, Phemius, know many other deeds of men and gods – exploits that bring delight to mortals, acts that singers celebrate. Then, seated here among these suitors sing of such things – while they drink their wine in silence. But stop this dismal chant, for it consumes the heart within my breast, since I have been struck by a loss that cannot be forgotten. Indeed, such was the man for whom I

---

38. Homer, *Odyssey*, trans. Allen Mandelbaum, (New York: Bantam, 1991), Book I, 324-359.

39. Book I, 354-355.

40. Pietro Pucci, *Ulysse polutropos*, (Lille: Presses Universitaires du Septentrion, 1995), 270.

41. Papadopoulou-Belmehdi, *Le chant de Pénélope*, 197. "The transmission of the memory must guarantee the truthful representation of the exploits of the heros and the values of the world in which they live [...]. The Odyssean poem sets the character of Penelope in this heroic order of truth, as it is shown by her first appearance in the poem, against the song of Phemios."

grieve with endless memory, a man whose glory is known through
Hellas, Argos – all of Greece.[42]

According to Nicole Loraux "en tant qu'incarnation de la mémoire vé-
ridique, Pénélope tient dans [l'influence sur la version du *nostos* d'Ulysse]
un rôle unique et fragile".[43] Concerning the epic glory, there are some spec-
ifications to make in relation to the *Odyssey*. To gain the glory the warrior
must die on the field "la 'belle mort' [est] celle du citoyen-soldat tombé au
champ d'honneur. [...] [Il conquiert] du même coup la valeur et la gloire immortelle."[44] If he returns to his home once the enemy has been defeated and
he dies in peace among his friends, this is not enough. It is in the battle that
he has to die to guarantee for himself the epic glory.

Also, according to Papadopoulou-Belmehdi, the royal bard by invoking
the death of Troy "assimile Ulysse à la malédiction divine d'un *nostos* [re-
tour] douloureux et à une mort non glorieuse".[45] But the man who haunts the
memory of Penelope has another calibre: "sa gloire court a travers l'Hellade
et plane sur Argos".[46]

Meanwhile the project of Homer is different: The version of Phemios
"concurrence le projet même de l'Odyssée, qui fait du *nostos* d'Ulysse le su-
jet le plus digne de la gloire épique, se démarquant ainsi de la tradition des
retours maudits. La peine d'Ulysses est toujours pensée en méme temps
comme épreuve héroïque.[47] This clarification by Nicole Loraux accords with
the understanding of Jean-Pierre Vernant, who states the conditions according to which an action could be considered glorious: "Il faut qu'elle soit noble. Il faut qu'il y ait générosité, et qu'en même temps ce soit sa propre vie
qui soit mise en question à chaque moment."[48]

---

42. Book I, 336-344.
43. Papadopoulou-Belmehdi, *Le chant de Pénélope*, 68. "As embodiment of the remem-
    brance of truth Penelope has (within the influence on the version of *nostos* of Ulysses)
    a unique and fragile role."
44. Loraux, *Les experiences de Tiresias,* 77. "The 'deserved death' is that of the warrior-
    citizen dead in the honour field. [...] [He gains] at the same time the valor and the im-
    mortal glory."
45. Papadopoulou-Belmehdi, *Le chant de Pénélope*, 64, "Equates Ulysses to the divine
    curse of a sore *nostos* (return) and to a non-glorious death."
46. Papadopoulou-Belmehdi, *Le chant de Pénélope*, 64,"His glory runs through the Hel-
    lade and lands on Argos."
47. Loraux, *Les experiences de Tiresia,* 64. "Competes with the project of the *Odyssey,*
    that makes of the *nostos* (return) of Ulysses the worthiest subject of epic glory, dis-
    tancing itself also from the tradition of the cursed returns. The grief of Ulysses is al-
    ways thought at the same time as an heroic trial."
48. Jean-Pierre Vernant, "Mythologie et citoyenneté" in *Democratie, citoyennete, et he-
    ritage greco-romain*, Pierre Vidal-Naquet , Jean-Pierre Vernant, Jean-Paul Brisson,

Another important issue is the refusal of the marriage. Many passages are explicit on this point: Penelope refuses to choose a new spouse. Telemachus will say two times: "She'll not reject the hateful wedding or accept it."[49] The strong verb that Homer utilizes here suggests the high degree of repulsion that this marriage inspires in the queen: *stugeron*. "Car *stugeron* dans l'Odyssée qualifie la mort, les Erinyes, la monstruosité de Clytemnestre. Un mariage ne peut être odieux et désiré à la fois."[50]

Some authors, however, dispute this idea of the unequivocal refusal. Marie-Madeleleine Mactoux[51] belongs to the partisans of a Penelope who has the desire to marry again. She sees in her an image of an indecisive and mindless woman. By citing different episodes that she interprets as consistent with her hypothesis of a desire to marry, she explains the examples of the univocal behavior "par la présence au sein du récit de variantes mal amalgamées".[52] This means that there would be a Penelope at the origin who wishes to re-marry; but some versions in an oral tradition badly incorporated in the text spread doubts and lead some to think mistakenly that Penelope is opposed to re-marrying. This theory is founded on extrapolations difficult to verify and is reinforced by unconvincing interpretations.

It is clear that Penelope refuses this new "hateful marriage". Even those nearer to her, such as Telemachus who fears losing his estate and would not like to see his mother taking a new spouse, voices his strong opposition to the marriage. Penelope, moreover, cannot accept giving herself to a man who would be inferior to Ulysses. Papadopoulou-Belmehdi points out that "Pénélope se refuse à partager sa couche avec un être incarnant l'inversion des valeurs héroïques."[53] It is true that the attitude of the suitors is indecorous. They are particularly shameless in their behavior: they live in the palace just to force the queen to make her choice, they behave not as guests but as owners of the place. To delay as long as possible the day in which she will have to choose a new spouse, Penelope utilizes cunning under different forms. But when all her cunning is spent, she starts desiring death

---

(Paris: Liris, 2004), 41-72, 50. "It has to be noble. There has to be generosity, and at the same time his own life has to be put in question at any moment."

49. Book I, 209-210 and Book XVI, 126-127.

50. Papadopoulou-Belmehdi, *Le chant de Pénélope*, 53. "Because *stugeron* in the *Odyssey* qualifies death, the Erinyes, the monstrousity of Clytemnestre. A marriage cannot be hated and desired at the same time."

51. Mactoux, *Pénélope. Legende et mythe*, 9-12.

52. Mactoux, *Pénélope. Legende et mythe,* "by the presence within the story of versions badly fused".

53. Mactoux, *Pénélope. Legende et mythe*, 109. "Penelope refuses to share her bed with someone that embodies the opposite of the heroic values."

"comme seule protection possible contre le marriage abhorré".[54] She prays to the gods, and she asks that they give her a death similar to the daughters of Pandareus who died at the threshold of marriage:

> As the Olympians effaced those orphans, may they ruin me – or else permit the shafts of Artemis to strike and send me down below grim earth as I think on my lost Odysseus and am not compelled to please some lesser man.[55]

This prayer bears witness to the deep despair of Penelope: she contemplates all of the options to escape from a wedding that is imposed on her. According to Papadopoulou-Belmehdi the prayer of the queen "rappelle à quel point rapt et mariage ont tendance à se confondre à propos de Pénélope, à quel point l'union à laquelle on la conduit est forcée et irrégulière".[56]

To understand the comparison drawn by the author, we need to remember that Artemis punishes with death men who resort to abduction. Many consequences arise from Penelope's refusal. The first is plain: it is the presence of the young wooers who have their eyes on the hand of the queen. The kidnapping described in the passage of the prayer to Artemis represents the actions of the suitors. It is they who want to take her away from her house. It is for them, or at least, one of them, that Penelope will have to leave the palace. They remain there because the queen did not want to choose a new spouse.

They belong to the best families of the region and pass their time in endless banquets, giving proof of insolence and cowardice. They are many, but their number "n'est jamais indiqué avec précision [...] parce qu'Homère veut produire l'effet d'une masse".[57] And this crowd represents a danger. The suitors are not acceptable because their attitude is ill-mannered, especially towards Penelope and Telemachus. Edouard Delebecque reminds us that their death "est d'abord demandée, ou souhaitée [...] par tous les personnages sympathiques, et d'abord par Pénélope avant même qu'elle ne sache menacée la vie de son fils".[58]

---

54. Mactoux, *Pénélope. Legende et mythe*, 123. "as only protection against the loathed marriage".

55. Book XX, 77-81.

56. Papadopoulou-Belmehdi, *Le chant de Pénélope*, 125. "Reminds at which point abduction and marriage tend to get confused in relation to Penelope, up to which point the union to which she is lead is forced and irregular".

57. Delebecque, *Construction de l'Odyssée*, 49. "It is never indicated with precision [...] because Homer wants to produce the effect of a crowd".

58. Delebecque, *Construction de l'Odyssée,* 43. "is initially demanded, or hoped [...] by all the sympathetic characters, and first of all by Penelope even before she learns about the life threats facing his son".

They wish to take Penelope as spouse; but it is not the woman that they lust after but the function she represents, the kingship of Ithaca. This is the second consequence of Penelope's dissent from re-marriage: her refusal blocks the royal succession. In his meeting with the dead souls, Ulysses questions the shadow of his mother in relation to the situation and to the plans of his spouse. The deceased mother reassures him: "Indeed steadfast, within your house she stays. Her dreary nights and days are wept away. No one's usurped your kingship."[59]

The third consequence is the one that makes of Penelope a lonely being. The issue of loneliness will be developed in the next pages. This last consequence of her opposition is not the least important, as it is Ithaca itself that she immobilizes. By her persistance she gives proof:

> d'un refus suffisamment fort pour bloquer une société [...]. En se gardant d'entrer dans l'échange marital, elle réussit à rendre impossible toute solution de remplacement. Du coup, le blocage institutionnel se trouve doublé d'un blocage générationnel, d'une véritable pétrification autour d'un deuil conçu parfois comme démesuré.[60]

In Ithaca Penelope is the only one who remembers Ulysses. The remembrance of the hero relies only on her. When the queen declares that she cannot bear anymore the song of the royal bard Phemios, it is her personal truth that she is opposing to the expression of collective memory. It is her memory that she opposes to the general oblivion of the inhabitants of Ithaca. She is in some sense the muse of the *Odyssey*.

To the theme of remembrance corresponds its antithesis, oblivion. Everyone in Ithaca believes in the death of Ulysses, and it is in this sense that they have forgotten him. It is antithetic to remembrance because this last allows the *kleos* to exist while "l'oubli n'évoque pas le passage à l'immortalité mais à la mort".[61] The opposition between these two terms re-directs to the antagonism real/unreal. It seems that the recollection of events is the key to reality in Ithaca. By not believing in the return of the king, the people of

---

59. Book XI, 184-188.
60. Papadopoulou-Belmehdi, *Le chant de Pénélope*, 157. "of a refusal strong enough to block a society [...]. By avoiding the marriage exchange, she is able to make any alternative solution impossible. Suddenly, the institutional block is doubly impeded by a generational block, by a real petrification around a mourning sometimes considered excessive".
61. Papadopoulou-Belmehdi, *Le chant de Pénélope*, 177. "Oblivion does not suggest the transition to immortality but to death".

Ithaca live in the oblivion, in a world that is momentarily unreal because it does not conform to reality.

They live in a world where Ulysses will not return, where Penelope will take a new spouse, where the vanished hero cannot expect any glory. The figures deprived of memory evolve in a world at the margin of what it should be, unreal. For her part, the queen, due to the strength of her memory, is the only one with the key of the real world. But she does not share it with anyone because she is the only one who believes in the return of the king. It is from memory that depends the distinction between real and unreal.

As described by Papadopoulou-Belmehdi: "plus qu'une société sans chef, Ithaca est une société qui perd la mémoire, un lieu à l'écart du *kleos*".[62] For her refusal to marry, her preservation of the royal power, and her obstinacy in defending the honour of the hero, "Penelope is the key not only of the *nostos* (return) of Ulysses, but also of his *kleos* (glory)."[63] Papadopoulou-Belmehdi continues: "Pénélope devient le pivot du poème, celle dont l'esprit et les actes permettront au *nostos* de devenir *kléos*, en d'autres mots, celle qui permettra à Ulysse de regagner sa place."[64]

Penelope is divided between two forces that pull her in opposite directions. There is first of all the wish that Ulysses has expressed before his departure, according to which she should not leave the family home before Telemachus had reached his manhood:

> When I am far away be mindful of the welfare of my father and mother in this house — as you now are, but even more attentively. But when you see our son a bearded man, you can wed whom you would and leave your house.[65]

She might then leave now with another spouse, as that time is arrived. Through the words of one of the servants (Eurýnomë) the reader learns this: "Your deepest prayer to the undying gods has been – for years – to see him grown and bearded: now he is."[66] But her matchless memory and her attachment to Ulysses prevent it. This situation is the source of a deep remorse for the queen, as her refusal precludes Telemachus from taking his place as heir to the throne, and this pulls him away from her. Moreover, she

---

62. Papadopoulou-Belmehdi, *Le chant de Pénélope,* 70. "More than a society without a leader, Ithaca is a society that loses its memory, a place far away from the kleos".

63. Nagy, *The best of the Achaeans,* 63.

64. Papadopoulou-Belmehdi, *Le chant de Pénélope,* 73. "Penelope becomes the pivot of the poem, the one whose spirit and acts will allow the nostos to become *kleos*, in other words, the one who will enable Ulysses to regain his place."

65. Book XVIII, 264-270.

66. Book XVIII, 174-175.

could be the cause of the threat that weighs on the life of her son. In fact, during the absence of Telemachus, the suitors do plot his death, hoping that the disappearance of the son will hasten the decision of the mother in the choice of a new spouse. But even this danger is not enough to make her decide. It is here that appears the remorse: her tenacious memory leads her to see herself as a source of misfortune.

The infallible memory of Penelope is cumbersome for the people around her. It is also a source of isolation for the queen, who is not supported by anyone in her fight against oblivion. Her refusal to remarry places her in a conflictual situation: towards the suitors who have already waited years and have now discovered the subterfuge of the shroud; and towards her son who does not understand the obstinacy of his mother and does not wish to tolerate further the suitors ransacking his house. "Rien n'exprime mieux son isolement que l'attitude aggressive de Télémaque envers elle."[67]

Telemachus has such a hostile relationship with Penelope, source of all his ills, that in the *Odyssey* the story of Orestes is presented to him as a sort of model: when Agemennon went to war his wife Clytemnestra, mother of Orestes, gave in to the advances of Aegisthus. When Agamemnon returned from Troy, Clytemnestra and Aegisthus planned his death and that of his followers. In the *Odyssey* it is now the eight years since Orestes avenged his noble father by killing the two murderers, including his own mother.

The queen of Ithaca certainly cannot be compared to the mother of Orestes. The poem presents her as Clytemnestra's polar opposite. This comparison shows the very hostile attitude of Telemachus towards his mother who is however without fault. He will say to her: "Your heart is very cruel! Oh cruel mother."[68] Penelope's dilemma is heart-breaking, sinces she is conscious of acting against the will of her son. The relation of intense proximity that Penelope has with Ulysses makes no sense for Telemachus who has not met him. Moreover, by refusing to leave the palace of the king, Penelope prevents her son from enjoying the goods inherited from his father. To allow him to take his place as heir, she should return to her own father and resume the status of the daughter of Icarus.

By wishing the departure of his mother "Télémaque entend effacer tout lien entre sa mère et l'*oikos* [foyer] d'Ulysse pour déposséder le nouvel époux de tout accès à la fortune de son père."[69] There is as a consequence

---

67. Papadopoulou-Belmehdi, *Le chant de Pénélope*, 68. "Nothing expresses better her isolation than the aggressive attitude of Telemachus towards her."

68. Book XVIII, 97.

69. Papadopoulou-Belmehdi, *Le chant de Pénélope*, 157. "Telemachus intends to delete all links between his mother and the *oikos* (foyer) of Ulysses to prevent the new spouse any access to the goods of his father."

a seriously troubled relation between mother and son.[70] According to Papadopoulou-Belmehdi:

> L'agressivité de Telemaque fait partie d'un schéma plus large où l'on voit que chaque apparition de Pénélope crée des situations conflic-tuelles. Pourquoi le poéte tient-il à accentuer ainsi l'isolement de Pénélope au sein même de son *oikos* [foyer]? N'est-ce pas une fa-çon d'indiquer qu'à Ithaque, plus qu'un vide de pouvoir il y a un vide de mémoire ? En détachant l'entourage de Pénélope du mes-sage véridique de l'*Odyssée*, le poète insinue qu'à Ithaque la mé-moire d'Ulysse est sérieusement menacée.[71]

Penelope cannot forget the spouse of her youth. But no one listens to her. Her pain is therefore stronger, almost excessive, as it is the fruit "d'une femme dont la voix n'est pas entendue".[72] She has been suffering incessantly for twenty years, since the departure of her spouse, her heart cannot find a consolation. It is a huge pain that deprives her of happiness and does not leave her for a single moment. During the day the daily tasks allow her to appease the pain, but during the night the pain becomes unbearable. She reveals this pain during the visit of the foreigner just arrived in the palace, who is actually Ulysses disguised as beggar:

> [...] my sorrow has no bounds: by day I find release in grief and mourning as I tend to household tasks, my women's work, my own; but when night falls and sleep takes all, I lie upon my bed with my afflicted heart, besieged by tears so stubborn and so sharp that, even as I mourn, tear me apart.[73]

Her attachment to Ulysses seems even to go beyond her.[74] It is so heavy that she does not want to live anymore. In a section she invokes Artemis. She has dreamt of Ulysses, he looked like the day he left for Troy:

70. Papadopoulou-Belmehdi, *Le chant de Pénélope*, 140.
71. Papadopoulou-Belmehdi, *Le chant de Pénélope*, 70. "The aggressiveness of Telema-chus is part of a larger scheme where we see that each appearance of Penelope creates some conflicting situations. Why the poet means to emphasize the isolation of Penel-ope at the heart of his *oikos* ("house" and "household")? Isn't it a way to indicate that in Ithaca, more than a vacuum of power there is a lack of memory? Detaching the en-tourage of Penelope from the truthful message of the *Odyssey*, the poet insinuates that in Ithaca the memory of Ulysses is seriously threatened."
72. Papadopoulou-Belmehdi, *Le chant de Pénélope*, 159. "of a woman whose voice is not heard".
73. Book XIX, 511-517.
74. Papadopoulou-Belmehdi, *Le chant de Pénélope*, 136-137.

Grief still is bearable if one must weep with troubled heart by day
but then can sleep by night, a sleep that can enfold the lids and bring
forgetfulness of all that is – the good, the evil. I instead must live
with the malicious dreams a god inflicts: this very night beside me
lay a man who wore the likeness of Odysseus when he sailed away
with the Achæan ranks; my heart was glad; mistaking it as fact, I
thought it was no dream.[75]

The night spreads forgetfulness on men but does not give her any break.
According to Nicole Loraux it is her "chagrin incommensurable"[76] that brings
her bad dreams. She considers death as a means of being again next to her
spouse and avoiding the remarriage. Actually "pour se fixer dans le statut
d'épouse d'Ulysse, Pénélope n'a qu'un seul choix: mourir".[77]

Penelope is a heroine but not in the same sense as we consider Ulysses
a hero. Heroism is not appropriate for the feminine characters of epic poems as it is associated to military exploits, to death on the battlefield or, as
in the *Odyssey*, to dangerous adventures lived with success. Woman does
not go to fight in a war and so she cannot acquire the *kleos* of the warrior. However there is a theory that associates Penelope to another honor,
not less esteemed. Her virtues, her wisdom, her remembrance give her the
glory. The glory of overcoming many years of tiresome trials and remaining always faithful to her memory and to her heart. The glory of not following the path traced for her, of having continued fighting alone against everyone, facing them, even if trials were difficult. According to the definition
of Jean-Pierre Vernant:

L'héroïsme, c'est le fait qu'il y a dans la vie des actions qui dénotent
chez celui qui les accomplit une espèce de capacité de sortir du quo-
tidien, de sortir de la vie ordinaire, d'ouvrir une dimension qui est
une dimension héroïque, c'est à dire quasi divine parce que c'est
l'immortalité qui est là. L'immortalité ne consiste pas à avoir une
âme immortelle, elle consiste, de cette vie, à accomplir de telles actions, des exploits et surtout pas de bassesses, pas de choses pe-
tites, la générosité.[78]

---

75. Book XX, 79-90.
76. Nicole Loraux, *Les mères en deuil*, (Paris: Seuil, 1990), 74-75. "her incommensurable
   pain".
77. Papadopoulou-Belmehdi, *Le chant de Pénélope*, 156. "to bind herself to the status of
   spouse of Ulysses, Penelope has only one choice: to die".
78. Vernant, "Mythologie et citoyenneté", 51. "Heroism, is the fact that there are in life actions that denote in the one who accomplishes them a capability to get away from the
   daily routine, to escape from ordinary life, to open a dimension that is an heroic one,

Homer announces clearly that this honor given to Penelope will ensure her immortality in the glory. He expresses this through the words spoken by the shade of Agamemnon:

> You, Odysseus, man of many wiles, are blessed: the wife you won has every excellence. Her mind has understanding: she, unmatched Penelope, did not forget the man she wed. The daughter of Icárius will never lose the fame she has won; for your Penelope the deathless ones will shape a song to bring delight among all men on earth.[79]

Just as her spouse is the prototype of the hero, Penelope is the model of the exemplary woman. She is opposed to Clytemnestra, antagonist character who embodies the bad side of femininity. Papadopoulou-Belmehdi affirms that Penelope "représente le versant féminine des valeurs épiques".[80] She acquires "une gloire construite sur la communauté des épreuves"[81] in the sense that only the queen is worthy of being associated to the *kleos*, as only she talks of the heroic *kleos* of Ulysses in a town that has lost the memory.

Cunning

Women in the ancient Greek society had no right to take part in political matters as this is a privilege of men. It was also normal for political enemies to insult each other by using the term 'woman' to connote an enemy.[82] The same discrimination held for women in private affairs. For example, they had no rights to pursue sexual pleasure, which was a prerogative of men,[83] and likewise in marriage, they were generally offered to the highest bidder.

All this is valid also for Penelope. She cannot ignore the laws that regulate female existence, but she chooses to oppose them within her possibilities: "Car elle peut uniquement décider qui sera son nouveau mari, mais n'a aucun moyen de refuser le mariage. Il est clair que se marier e transmettre

---

that is to say almost divine because immortality is there. Immortality does not mean to have an immortal soul, it consists, in this life, to accomplish great actions, exploits and expecially not meaneses, or small things, generosity."

79. Book XXIV, 194-198.

80. Papadopoulou-Belmehdi, *Le chant de Pénélope*, 200. "represents the feminine side of epic values".

81. Papadopoulou-Belmehdi, *Le chant de Pénélope*, 201. "a glory built on the totality of her trials".

82. Loraux, *Les experiences de Tiresias*, 7-8.

83. Loraux, *Les experiences de Tiresias*, 16.

la royauté ne constituent pas pour elle une option mais une obligation."[84] She is a woman and does not have the power to act openly according to her wishes and her thoughts.

She finds ways to delay in her favor the decisions taken for her by using her cunning. Called *metis* in Greek, this way of getting what one wants in an indirect way is typical of the character of Penelope. Her cunning allows her to act, while at the same time keeping an appearance of inactivity, an artificial passivity. It is useful to the queen in two specific circumstances: to gain time in order to keep the throne of Ulysses vacant for the longest possible time and to ensure that she can give proof of her trustworthiness to her spouse should he return.

The stratagems of Penelope are inspired directly by the goddess Athena. According to Edouard Delebecque the different manifestations of the goddess that dispense advice and encourage the action "ne sont guère autre chose qu'une figure divine du libre arbitre humain".[85] The queen resorts to various subterfuges to maintain the vacuum of royal power and to keep the throne vacant in order to allow Ulysses to take back his place once he returns. They are useful to her to delay for the longest possible time the marriage imposed on her. Among these devices, one is most well known, practically the only one that is associated to her, without even knowing its exact meaning. It is the famous device of the shroud. The second device discussed here involves the bow. These two symbols, the loom and the bow, are directly connected to the pre-marital phase of the woman. A further device is linked to the nuptial bed that will sanction the final recognition of Ulysses by Penelope.

The shroud

The cunning linked to the weaving of the shroud is an episode chronologically anterior to the events related in the *Odyssey*. The explication of the subterfuge of the shroud is given in three occasions with the same words. It is narrated for the first time during an assembly by Antinous, one of the wooers, blaming the deceitful behavior of Penelope; a second time by the queen herself when she tells to Ulysses, disguised as a beggar, her way of "enrouler les ruses in pelotes"[86] to avoid the marriage; and finally by Amphimedon in Hades, the underworld, narrating to the shade of Agamemnon the misfortunes

---

84. Papadopoulou-Belmehdi, *Le chant de Pénélope*, 53. "As she can only decide who will be her new husband, but has no way to refuse the marriage. It is clear that to marry and transmit the royalty do not constitute an option but is an obligation."

85. Édouard Delebecque, *Télémaque et la structure de l'Odyssée*, (Aix: Ophrys, 1958), 37-38. "Are nothing else than a divine figure of man's free will."

86. "Weaving her cunnings".

that led the suitors to suffer the deadly revenge of Ulysses. The pretext utilized by Penelope to take time is the weaving of a shroud for Laertes, her fa-
ther-in-law. She invokes her duties as exemplary spouse and honorable Greek
woman: "Young men, since bright Odysseus now is dead, be patient; though
you're keen to marry me, wait till this cloth is done, lest any thread unravel.
This is lord Laertes' shroud — the robe he'll wear when dark death strikes him
down."[87] The words of the queen are well chosen. She adds a further trick with
the aim of making her demands accepted by the suitors: she assures them that
she believes in the death of her spouse while the real aim of her project is to
delay the deadline of the marriage and allow Ulysses time to return.

She states this only for the purpose of having her project endorsed and
so gain time. Moreover her acts contradict her words, as by declaring that
she does not want to waste the sewing thread she poses herself as a parsi-
monious wife. But reality produces a completely different result. During
the years that she has been weaving, the suitors have disposed freely of the
wealth of the palace. And this because "le premier souci de Penelope n'est
pas de préserver la fortune d'Ulysse mais sa mémoire".[88] This trickery is by
far the most effective in delaying the marriage imposed on Penelope. The
act of weaving in itself delays the decision, but this is not the full extent of
the trickery. Penelope has found a way to delay the marriage even further by
weaving during the day and unravelling each night what she has previously
woven. This is the most awesome of the queen's devices: she postpones the
wedding to a later, indefinite date that she can delay further and further, so
stopping in a way the flow of time.

Penelope has deceived the suitors but at the end of the third year one
of her maids betrays her. She is discovered and forced to stop the trickery.
However she needs to finish her shroud as she cannot bring to a halt a job already started. She has been able to "créer une inviolabilité rituelle aussi bien
dans le temps que dans l'espace".[89] We should recall the oath that Ulysses
asked her to take at his departure for Troy. It is at the origin of the queen's
wish to delay any re-marriage. The shroud allows her to keep a promise
made to Ulysses — of waiting until her son's maturity before re-marrying.
As long as she weaves, Penelope makes the others believe that she has accepted the death of her spouse, that nothing more connects her to Ulysses.
But the discovery of her trickery, at the beginning of the *Odyssey*, reveals

---

87. Book XXIV, 130-136.
88. Papadopoulou-Belmehdi, *Le chant de Pénélope*, 90. "the main concern of Penelope is
not to preserve the wealth of Ulysses but his memory".
89. Papadopoulou-Belmehdi, *Le chant de Pénélope*, 37. "create a ritual inviolability in
both time and space".

the motives hidden behind the initiative of the shroud. She delays the marriage but hides her categorical refusal by dissimulating her unfailing memory under an apparent conciliation.

The shroud has also the parallel role of keeping open, as long as possible, the possibility that Ulysses could still be alive. As long as the shroud is not finished, the throne belongs to an absent king; he can come back to take his place. The weaving is a struggle that allows Penelope to preserve her memory of the hero, her belief in the return of her spouse, her true vision of the world. Moreover, "en défaisant le tissue, elle défait aussi ce qui tend à devenir la réalité dominante à Ithaque: la mort et l'oubli du roi".[90] She prevents this lie from becoming a reality in the city.

Papadopoulou-Belmehdi provides a supplementary key to the issue of the shroud: by weaving a new tissue [fabric] in the palace, Penelope "introduit par le détournement des travaux de la laine l'état d'un arrêt ou d'une rupture".[91] Penelope by stopping the customary weaving of the wool and substituting it with the shroud introduces a new order of things. Papadopoulou-Belmehdi cites the Homer's interpretation of Penelope's weaving of the shroud: "Tant que le métier est dressée, il ne peut y avoir de fiançailles."[92]

In Homer's words Penelope's weaving of the shroud takes her back to the status of a maiden girl who cannot marry until the weaving is terminated. It as another way of: "caractériser la surdétermination de la figure d'Athéna, vierge tisserande, [dont les attributs] expriment l'idée d'une virginité inviolable, qui correspond à cet âge de la femme que la langue grecque qualifie d' 'indompté'".[93] According to this interpretation, the queen sitting in front of her weaving job acquires the status of *nymph*[94] "[nymph, νύμφη: bride, unmarried woman]"— not the status of a newly married young girl but of a young girl prior to the marriage, busy with virginal jobs. Weaving and the request to choose a new spouse reposition Penelope into circumstances that customarily precede a marriage. By weaving the shroud she takes refuge in

---

90. Papadopoulou-Belmehdi, *Le chant de Pénélope*, 180. "by unravelling the shroud, she undoes also what tends to become the dominant reality in Ithaca: the death and the oblivion of the king".

91. Papadopoulou-Belmehdi, *Le chant de Pénélope*, 35. "introduces by the diversion from the wool works a stop or a break".

92. Papadopoulou-Belmehdi, *Le chant de Pénélope*, 22. "As long as the weaving job is started there can be no marriage engagements".

93. Papadopoulou-Belmehdi, *Le chant de Pénélope*, 22. "characterizes the over determination of the figure of Athena, weaving virgin [whose attributes] express the idea of an inviolable virginity, that corresponds to the age of a woman that the Greek language qualifies as 'untamed'".

94. Papadopoulou-Belmehdi, *Le chant de Pénélope*, 96-126.

a traditional custom: before terminating the started cloths the weaver cannot be asked for marriage.

The suitors, however, continue to besiege the palace and to court the queen. Their abnormal behavior disrupts the rules of correct distance between the sexes that are part of the feminine ritual scheme; normally Artemis presides over the transition from nymph to married woman. Penelope's shroud stops time for an instant that lasts almost four years, during which time the suitors have occupied the palace. The completion of the shroud leads into the thematic of marriage. Before this, no weaving was really accomplished because the aim of Penelope was to maintain the symbolic incompatibility between weaving and marriage.

> Le mariage est un élément socialement stabilisateur, sa mise en cause menace des structures adjacentes.[95] [...] A Ithaque, le blocage du mariage provoque la désunion de la société. [...] La féminité insoumise est un élément de désordre. [...] La désunion des sexes, le mariage impossible apparait ici comme un indice de la désagrégation sociale.[96]

Penelope is thus at the same time nymph and spouse. In relation to Ulysses, she becomes a sort of spouse-nymph, one for whom he will have to fight to win for a second time. "Dans la littérature grecque, Penelope est le premier et le plus illustre exemple du détournement des travaux féminins."[97] During the four years in which she utilizes the stratagem of the shroud, Penelope sends messages to the suitors. Exchanging messages with the suitors could be seen as proof of the inconstancy of the queen, since she expresses doubts on Ulysses' being still alive and seems interested in re-marriage. But Papadopoulou-Belmehdi explains that this "ambiguïté des sentiments"[98] concerns the period of the trick of the shroud, itself part of a deceitful declamation. Penelope's messages have to be understood as part of a strategy for making the wooers wait.

95. Papadopoulou-Belmehdi, *Le chant de Pénélope*, 126. "Marriage is a socially stabilizing element, its indictment threatens the adjacent structures."

96. Papadopoulou-Belmehdi, *Le chant de Pénélope*, 132. "In Ithaca the block of the marriage provokes the disunity of the society (...) Rebellious femininity is an element of disorder. (...) The disunion of the sexes, the impossible marriage appears here as an index of social disintegration."

97. Papadopoulou-Belmehdi, *Le chant de Pénélope*, 30. "In Greek literature, Penelope is the first and the most illustrious example of diversion of feminine works."

98. Papadopoulou-Belmehdi, *Le chant de Pénélope,* 56."ambiguity of feelings".

The bow

The purpose of the trial of the bow is to decide among the suitors, designating one strong enough to equal Ulysses. This at least is what Penelope asserts when she faces them. It seems, however, that she brews another project: by being unable to choose one among them she gains still more time. As described earlier in the poem, only Ulysses is able to bend the bow and pass the twelve axes. The bow is the instrument by which Ulysses shows himself to the assembly before starting the slaughter of "cette foule éhontée".[99]

The bow is a pre-marriage symbol as it is an attribute of Artemis, who presides over the nymphs (maidens) before marriage and decides whether to entrust them to the sphere of Aphrodite. The bow is also often associated with the nightingale and to the swallow; its noise compared to the singing of these birds. Penelope refers indeed to the myth of Nightingale (Philomela) whose sister Swallow (Procne) killed her own son to revenge the rape committed by her husband. This reference "place l'épreuve sous un très mauvais augure".[100]

> Passer du métier à l'arc, répéter les phases de la parthenos et de la nymphe, tel sont les subterfuges rituels qui protègent – d'une façon purement symbolique – Penelope d'un mariage ressemblant par trop à un rapt.[101]

Edouard Delebecque[102] makes the conjecture that at this moment Penelope has already recognized her spouse in the person of the beggar, or at least she has some suspicions regarding his identity. The bow becomes for Penelope a way to test Ulysses, to verify if he is really her spouse hiding behind the rags. This trial will be then a trick that aims to recognize Ulysses.

The bed

At the end of the poem Penelope finds herself in front of the man she has been awaiting for twenty years; Ulysses has finally returned. He has slaughtered the suitors and stands in front of her. Yet she has difficulty in recognizing him and does not want to make mistakes. The bed plays a decisive role in the recognition of the hero. She has been waiting for so long her spouse,

---

99. Delebecque, *Telemaque et la structure de l'Odyssée*, 62. "this shameless crowd".

100. Papadopoulou-Belmehdi, *Le chant de Pénélope*, 142. "casts the trial in a bad light".

101. Papadopoulou-Belmehdi, *Le chant de Pénélope,* 126. "To move from the loom to the arc, repeating the phases of the parthenos and of the nymph, are the ritual tricks that protects – in a purely symbolic way – Penelope from a marriage that looks like an abduction".

102. Delebecque, *Telemaque et la structure de l'Odyssée*, 63.

and his return is so unexpected. At first Ulysses, disappointed by her refusal, asks for a bed to be prepared for him. Penelope then claims to have recognized her spouse and orders a servant to take their marital bed to the room where Ulysses has been settled. Outraged and surprised, he asks who has dared to move the bed he made with his own hands from the trunk of a living olive tree — one impossible to be displaced. Only by this explication is the queen finally convinced that the man facing her is Ulysses, returned after so many adventures.

Apparent inactivity

Penelope's cunning is extremely sharp. She acts for purposes that are different from those she states, but that's not all. Her actions are often the inverse of what they seem to do:

> Il s'agit d'un modèle très subtil d'action rusée: agir tout en semblant être dans la plus grande inactivité, ou ne rien produire en ayant l'air de s'activer. L'action ne sera perceptible qu'une fois obtenu son résultat irréversible.[103]

There is in Penelope a gap between being and seeming. The shroud is the most significant demonstration of it. She claims to be aware that Ulysses is dead and that she wants to weave a shroud for his father, but the truth is just the opposite. She does during the day a job that is undone in the night. She seems to progress in the realization of the shroud while she actually works towards its regression.

Conclusion

The theme of Penelope in the *Odyssey* is defined by a limited number of characteristics. This limited number is explained by the numerous contingent sub-categories they generate. I have focused on two fundamental notions: memory and cunning. The one being instrumental to the other. In the world of Ithaca, memory cannot perpetuate without the help of the cunning. In return, the trickeries have no reason to exist without the remarkable persistence of the memory of Penelope.

---

103. Papadopoulou-Belmehdi, *Le chant de Pénélope*, 42. "It is a very skilled form of crafty action: pretending to do nothing while being in full activity, or to not produce anything while giving the impression of acting. The action will be understood only once the result is irreversible."

To memory are attached various concepts that are consequences of this first characteristic: the queen as guarantor, defending the place, the memory and the honor of her spouse; the pulled-apart woman who chooses memory to the detriment of her own interests and of those of the ones near to her; isolation, the inevitable effect of perseverance when the others have left; pain, the sufferance of a woman that cannot forget the spouse who left twenty years earlier; and finally the *kleos,* honor and glory attributed to a woman out of the ordinary.

As for the cunning, it covers three areas: the preservation of the place of Ulysses and therefore of the royal power with the aid of the shroud and of the bow; the recognition of the spouse with the reference to the marital bed; and the appearances, the capability to hide the subterfuges under an apparent inactivity.

Penelope is a complex and essential character in the story of Homer. Without her, without her infallible memory and without her remarkable cunning, the very subject of the *Odyssey,* the return of Ulysses, would lose its meaning. "La mémoire d'Ulysse tient au fil de Penelope, véritable fil de destin d'une Ithaque devenue paysage irrationnel."[104]

---

104. Papadopoulou-Belmehdi, *Le chant de Pénélope,* p. "The memory of Ulysses is kept by thread of Penelope, real fate thread of a Ithaca that has become an irrational landscape."

PART II

PENELOPE IN THREE
(FEMINIST) REVISIONIST NOVELS

Gianni a Roma
1789

CHAPTER 3

ANNIE LECLERC: TOI, PÉNÉLOPE

(2001)

Si Ulysse était demeuré en Ithaque, pensais-tu alors, je n'aurais eu ni le temps ni la place de rêver, de changer de rêves, d'attendre, de craindre, de douter, de deviner, de croître en esprit, ce qui veut dire aussi, en liberté... bref, tu n'était pas aussi noir que tu le laissais entendre.[1]

Toi, Pénélope, published in 2001, is a novel by the French philosopher Annie Leclerc, who died 13 October 2006. Feminist writer and activist, she was born in 1940 and obtained a degree in philosophy at the University of Sorbonne. She contributed to various magazines, among them *Les Temps Modernes* of Jean Paul Sartre, there coming into contact with Simone De Beauvoir, with whom she collaborated in 1971 in signing the *Manifeste of the 343* published in *Le Nouvel Observateur* to demand the legalization of abortion.

Leclerc published her most famous book *Parole de femme* in 1974. There she lays down her particular feminism, focused not on equality between women and men but on the revaluation of feminine tasks to which she claims new value needs to be assigned.[2] In her opinion, women's traditional tasks as housewives and mothers need to be celebrated and rediscovered by women,

---

1. Annie Leclerc, *Toi, Pénélope*, (Aries: Actes Sud, 2001), 22. "If Ulysses had stayed in Ithaca, you thought, I would have had neither the time nor the place to dream, change my dreams, wait , fear, doubt, guess, to grow spiritually, which also means, in freedom ... well, you were not feeling as bad as you let others believe." My translation.

2. Annie Leclerc, *Parole de Femme*, (Paris: Grasset, 1974).

while the competition with men in the workplace should be abandoned. This position, in open opposition with the feminism of her time, resulted in the marginalization of the writer from the mainstream feminism of the 1970s and brought an end to her friendship with De Beauvoir. For more than fifteen years, until the 1990s, she moderated workshops in creative writing in the prisons, sharing Michel Foucault's criticism of the penitentiary system and denouncing its inhumanity and inefficiency.

In her work, reflection is never separated from autobiography. In *Toi, Pénélope* she places the reader at the heart of Penelope's thoughts in a revised version of the poem. This new version of the *Odyssey* is presented from the sole point of view of the queen as the story of a woman confronted with values that are not hers: the pride and the violence of men.

Plot

The novel opens with the solemn promise made by Penelope to Ulysses at his departure. It is followed by a short description of the consternations that the separation creates in the heart of the young spouse. Then come the years spent without him and the independence attained by Telemachus at adolescence. However the signs cannot be mistaken: Ulysses will be back soon. Penelope has no doubts as the prophecies, the flight of the birds and the dreams announce it. She waits for his arrival and imagines the subterfuges her spouse will use to enter into the palace without being recognized, as certainly this is his intention. Just then she learns about the arrival of a foreigner in Ithaca. He is with the loyal servants of Ulysses, too young to recognize their master in case he should come back. She is sure: he is her Ulysses who is finally back.

The foreigner comes to the palace and asks to be received. Telemachus gives him his protection and Penelope asks to meet him. She claims that this visitor could give her information regarding Ulysses and any news would be useful. The foreigner sets a late appointment in order to be alone with the queen. Penelope goes down to meet her son and give him some wise advice; but her real plan is to appear in front of the suitors hoping to catch a sight of Ulysses. There, advancing in front of the assembly of young people sitting to eat, she sees him at the bottom of the room, against the door. His dark and hard expression upsets her. It is him, but what rigidity is in his eyes. She understands then his desire for revenge and foresees the imminent slaughter.

The night arrives and the banqueting of the suitors is not finished yet. She has returned to her room. She tries to think of a way to avoid the massacre. Who then is this man? Certainly he is not the one she has been thinking about for the last twenty years. The man who came back bears the marks of the hardships he lived. A servant informs her of the insults that the maid Melantho has uttered towards the foreigner. Her blood freezes at the idea of the fate that Ulysses, the beggar, has adumbrated to the young maid in exchange. She could not bear anything bad happening to the girl that she has brought up as her own daughter. She thinks then about all the people she loves and who have helped her keep living and hoping for twenty years. Without them she would have never found the strength to resist.

The banquet finishes, and the young people return to their houses. Penelope goes down to speak to the foreigner. She is overwhelmed by the thought of Ulysses revealing his true identity to her. However nothing happens. The man affirms to be someone else and does not give in before the silent insistence of his spouse. The queen is terribly disappointed. He disclosed himself to his son but not to her. She leaves thinking about this man laying down on the ground in front of the fireplace who has refused to be given a bed in his own house. Feeling the pain of Ulysses, she understands that the deadly revenge will be not avoided, but she could not accept the death of Melantho, she would not bear it.

The morning arrives, Ulysses' bow is going to be offered to the suitors. Penelope hopes that this trial will force the foreigner to reveal himself to the assembly, as he is the only one who is able to bend it and avoid the massacre. Everyone tries his chance, Telemachus is the first; but no one is able to bend the bow of the king. Ulysses asks to try but the queen cannot see what happens next because her son sends her back to her rooms. She can listen, however, and the sounds that come to her ears are eloquent: the trap is set, the worst is to come. Taken by her sadness she falls asleep. Euryclea wakes her up, full of joy.

The suitors are dead, Ulysses is back! Penelope is not afraid anymore, everything is finished. She looks contented. Her spouse is waiting for her in the big hall, the same place where the massacre has taken place. She goes there, nervous. He is gorgeous, but she thinks that she needs more time as she cannot forget so easily the past twenty years. However she gives up. In his arms where happiness and sadness are mixed, she cries. He announces to her that he will have to leave again, face other trials to calm down the anger of the gods. The night is intense as are reunions. The universe joins their embrace. Ulysses tells her about all the adventures that he has lived since his departure, twenty years earlier.

As he recalls the young Nausicaa in the land of Pheacians, Penelope cannot restrain her jealousy: this is the only woman with whom he did not lay, the only one from whom he will have to escape or keep away. But as Ulysses has found back his kingdom of Ithaca, Penelope has found her ground, her divine spouse. With the morning reality comes back. He is already away from her. Their reunion has lasted only one night. Ithaca also awakens, and the news of the massacre spreads. A group of parents is coming to claim revenge for the killing of their dearest, but they are not taken into account. Of the companions of Ulysses none has returned, and all the youths have been killed the night before by the king. There are only children and old people, too weak to face him. That's why forgiveness is given. The story should stop there, but Penelope gives us more fragments of her life. Ulysses departed, as this is their destiny: eternal absence. She hopes for a better world for tomorrow, less violent. But for this we should never forget the young suitors scythed by a terrible death at the dawn of their life.

The Theme of Penelope

Leclerc definitely undertakes a metamorphosis of the theme of Penelope. This change is even more subtle since it recalls the same situations, almost with the same terms utilized by Homer. The reader finds again Penelope, queen of Ithaca, confronted after twenty years with the return of her spouse. S/he also finds all the characters of the *Odyssey*, no one is forgotten. But especially, all the important scenes are retold. The author retrieves all the key episodes of the poem with great accuracy, although she introduces some very personal modifications. She chooses a very particular style of writing: she mixes the modern plot with the ancient one. She retains the essential scenes that exemplify the theme of Penelope in the *Odyssey* and assigns to them a series of singular and intimate reflections, originated by the queen herself. In a familiar tone and in the second person singular, the reader gains access to the thoughts of a solitary woman. This new yet familiar environment gives the scenes a different meaning that influences the way we perceive the character of Penelope.

The novel takes place in the same epoch as the story by Homer, but there is only one location: the palace. Moreover, unlike the *Odyssey,* which retains the perspectives on the world of all the characters, the action here is perceived by one person only, the queen herself. While the *Odyssey* gives a multiple representation of the universe that surrounds it, here the reader has only one interpretation of reality. In *Toi, Pénélope* the queen of Ithaca is the same as in the *Odyssey*. There is no new symbolism nor any characteristic that could be associated with a modern heroine. Penelope is a woman of antiquity, though her thoughts are borrowed by the writer. Penelope is the main character of the novel. She is at the heart of the action and this makes a significant difference in relation to the Homeric epic. It is through her eyes and ears that the reader is put into contact with reality. The writer gives access to Penelope's intimate reflections, and in this the novel diverges from the *Odyssey* as the queen is no longer an enigmatic character. Interpretation is not necessary to define her role and her intentions. Light is shone on the smallest details of her reflections and offers in this way a clear access to her personality.

The queen is a woman of her time. Like the Penelope of Homer, she has not the power to contest freely the destiny that is imposed on her. She can only have recourse to cunning to escape to her obligations, and she uses it at her will. The trickeries that she "enroule en pelotes" are the same, but the plan behind them is not always alike. In the novel the mental process by which she arrives at her conclusions precedes all of her actions. So the reader learns at each new trick the exact goal that Penelope aims to attain. There are then no possible doubts regarding her intentions. The queen's ideas are clearly exposed. There is no trace here of a reserved or humble Penelope. She is not restrained. This can be remarked in the nature of her reflections. Annie Leclerc attributes to her very bold thoughts for a woman of antiquity. Her conception of her status exceeds the ancient social limits. The proximity of this story to the one by Homer allows a precise analysis of the character. All the characteristics of the theme can be found here but under another dimension: that of a woman who refuses her destiny, even more that in the *Odyssey*, and the destiny of men.

Memory

Penelope displays here the same infallible memory. She cannot forget the young spouse she lost twenty years earlier. Her spouse is "lost" as this new Ulysses is not the man who left for the war. The Ulysses the queen is thinking about is not the one that embarked with his men for Troy but the one who left her as he joined the other soldiers on the vessel. Waiting on the embankment with the other women, the man that Penelope saw climbing on the ship was not anymore the one that she had married:

> Il y a vingt ans qu'Ulysse s'est détaché de toi, que tu l'as vu, de tes yeux vu, se changer en un Ulysse que tu ne connaissais pas, en guerrier, en marin, en compagnon exclusif des hommes, en aventurier, en solitaire, en amoureux seulement de lui-même et de sa renommée.[3]

3. Annie Leclerc, *Toi, Pénélope*, (Aries: Actes Sud, 2001), 171. "It is twenty years that Ulysses has gone away from you, that you have seen him with your eyes muted in an Ulysses that you did not know, in a soldier, a mariner, a companion only of men, an adventurer, a recluse, a lover only of himself and of his reputation."

This information is offered towards the end of the novel, and it enables an explanation of the opinions of the young queen about the young and the old Ulysses. At the moment of this tearing departure, two groups have formed: the happy men on one side and the sombre women on the other. The ones happy to leave everything for the adventures expecting them, the others returning already to their new lives in which men will not take part. Women did not swear fidelity to them but to themselves, to the children and to their role as weavers. It is resentment that animates the hearts of the spouses abandoned for the pretext of a war, since they have left not to participate in the war but "pour courir les mers, les périls, les cités lointaines".[4] Penelope resents this war that drags men into its vortex of violence and death. In this context is resumed the episode of the refusal of the song by the bard: "Hier encore tu priais Phemios d'en finir avec ses récits de sang et de fureur rappelant sans cesse la triste destinée des héros d'une guerre que toujours tu avais maudite."[5]

The queen does not protest here in order to defend the memory and the heroic glory of her spouse; rather, she asks to the bard to stop celebrating a war that destroys men. She likes to listen to the songs celebrating Ulysses. To his name her thoughts ramble and join the wonderful man that he was at twenty. The queen keeps vacant the place of the absent king, but not for the same reasons. She resorts to trickeries to delay the moment when she will be forced to choose a new spouse, but her aim is not to preserve the throne. She does not know if Ulysses will come back one day. Moreover he will be not the same young man of former times, he will be the warrior returning from sinister struggles. She preserves his place, however, for two reasons. The first is to allow Telemachus to reach adulthood, as Ulysses has requested of her. Penelope had promised it, but it is to the man who was dying under her eyes that she swore it, to the man she loved, not to the man who was just leaving. The second reason is that she cannot decide too quickly since this would definitively eliminate him from the world of the living; he would be considered dead by her. Because of this promise made to the young Ulysses long before and because of her aversion to the idea that his death would be sanctioned by her, Penelope wishes to delay the marriage. The idea of a new marriage does not make her happy, but she still contemplates its possibility. Perhaps Ulysses will not come back. She appreciates the suitors, these carefree and lively young men, as they bring back life to the palace:

4. Leclerc, *Toi, Pénélope*, 169, "to sail the seas, the dangers, the faraway cities".
5. Leclerc, *Toi, Pénélope*, 37, "Just yesterday you prayed Phemios to stop with these stories of blood and rage, remembering incessantly the sad destiny of the war heroes that you had always cursed."

Ce n'est pas tant l'idée d'un nouvel époux que celle d'entériner à jamais la disparition d'Ulysse, qui te répugnait. Sinon, nulle horreur pour ces jeunes hommes pleins de vie, égayant de leur jeunesse et de leurs grâces l'enceinte si longtemps morose et attristée du roi absent.[6]

She loves to listen to them even if they feast shamelessly at the table of Ulysses, and she is delighted with this warm company for Telemachus and Melantho. She knows that soon a man will be near her, the reader finds her fantasizing, even if she prefers that this man would be Ulysses.

In her refusal to decide between a Ulysses alive or dead, Penelope allows the possibility that he is still alive. But she is not really the guarantor of his memory, or if she is, this is in spite of herself. Her aim is not to keep open his place nor to ensure his glory. The Ulysses of the old days, the one important to her eyes, is alive in her. Moreover, she does not have to oppose her memory to the collective oblivion. By desiring his woman, the suitors bear Ulysses with them. He is present in the memory of each of them, as they are greedy to seize his last treasure:

Ulysse sur le point de se voir effacé des vivants, remis à la légende, revenait hanter la mémoire, la crainte et le désir de chacun, tu le touchais dans leurs regards, tu le respirais au front de Télémaque, il était là, comme là, presque là.[7]

Penelope does not have the role of bringing the absent king back to the memory of Ithaca. The young people do it when they desire his treasures and his woman, the last treasure. Her refusal to re-marry and to choose prevents the memory of Ulysses from being transformed into a memory of the dead.

Telemachus shows more and more his desire to be the head of his house. The absence of the king has lasted too long, the young noblemen of Ithaca and of the surrounding regions push the queen to choose a new spouse from among them. Even the promise she made to Ulysses as he departed for Troy. Everything pushes her to remarry. But she cannot stand the idea of being held responsible for the proclamation of Ulysses' death. That is the reason

6. Leclerc, *Toi, Pénélope,* 39. "It is not so much the idea of a new spouse but that of never validating the disappearance of Ulysses, that repelled you. Otherwise no loathing for these young men full of life cheering up with their youth and their charm the gloomy enclosure, saddened by the absent king."

7. Leclerc, *Toi, Pénélope,* 31. "Ulysses on the point of being cancelled from the living beings, handed in to the legend, was coming back to haunt the memory, the fears and the desire of everyone, you could see this in their eyes, you could breath it facing Telemachus, he was there, as if there, almost there."

why she makes the waiting last. Only after the discovery of the trickery of the shroud she does not need other subterfuges to delay further the deadline of the marriage as she knows that Ulysses is coming back.

With her spouse away Penelope needs someone to listen to and with whom she can talk in strict confidence. So, often in the night, she speaks to her distant sister Iphtimé and acts as if she is actually answered. As Telemachus has grown up, he has begun to assert himself and to draw away from his mother. Melantho, brought up as her own child, reaches an age when young girls tend to turn towards men. Her entourage narrows.

A further feeling of solitude overcomes her when she learns that Ulysses is in Ithaca. Penelope is the only one aware of it, and she cannot reveal it to anyone at the risk of going against the will of her spouse. She has understood the stratagem he will adopt and foresees its consequences. The worst disappointment for the queen is the realization that the king is revealing little by little his identity to the ones who remained faithful to him, but not to her.

The pain over the loss of Ulysses is deep for Penelope. She has seen her man disappear, and he is no longer the young man of former days. Since his departure, she has sworn to live for herself and for her son. Suffering was too strong, a bond has been broken in an irreversible manner.

> Restais la douleur. Douleur de chair, douleur d'entrailles. Ulysse disparaissait, c'est toi Penelope qui était changée, déchirée au point de ne plus tout à fait te reconnaitre. Ulysse peut bien revenir, et ton cœur battre à se rompre a son approche, c'est un autre Ulysse qui s'en vient, une autre Penelope tremblante a sa venue. C'est à l'instant de votre séparation que cette métamorphose en chacun de vous s'était produite.[8]

As this deep pain passes, the queen finds something positive in the absence of her spouse. She even states that "longtemps ce ne fut pas difficile de vivre en Ithaque sans Ulysse".[9] This absence has allowed her to ponder on facts of life, to grow her spirit in freedom. She cries in front of the ones close to her, and her tears are sincere, but she is amazed by the pleasure she experiences in practicing her intellect, in strengthening it. All this is well worth

8. Leclerc, *Toi, Pénélope*, 170. "The pain remained. Pain in the body, pain deep inside. Ulysses disappeared, it was you Penelope who were changed, torn to the point of not recognizing yourself. Ulysses can come back at last and your heart beat up to breaking point as he approaches, it is another Ulysses that returns, another Penelope trembling at his arrival. It is at the moment of your separation that this metamorphosis in each of you has taken place."

9. Leclerc, *Toi, Pénélope*, 24. "For a long time now it has not been difficult to live in Ithaca without Ulysses."

the happiness that she has not lived. The absence of Ulysses has tested her heart, making it more fruitful. That's why she decided to take Melantho and bring her up as her own daughter; born from slaves, she has had the childhood of a princess. But it is above all else the memory of her native land that has forged Penelope in the way she is. It is the love she feels for life and for the ones close to her that allows her to endure:

> Si tu n'aimais pas Melantho, si tu n'aimais pas Dolios, si tu n'aimais pas ta sœur Ipthime [...] et si tu n'aimais pas aussi la troupe braillarde des prétendants [...], d'où tirerais-tu la force d'aimer un homme absent depuis vingt ans et qu'à peine tu connus? Si tu n'aimais pas l'aurore, si tu n'aimais pas les oliviers balbutiant de lumière, et surtout si tu n'aimais pas le chant de l'aède, comment pourrais-tu dire que tu aimes Ulysse? [10]

Moreover she suffers more for Telemachus than for Ulysses. The reader learns this when Penelope acknowledges that her son has gone looking for news of his father and has been threatened with death by the suitors. He is her child, more precious than the entire world, and during his absence she barely survives.

On the other hand, even if her loved ones have kept her alive, she comes near to wishing death. The author resumes the invocation to Artemis. Penelope is about to see Ulysses again, she is going to descend in the big hall to catch a glimpse of him. This prayer is unexpected at the point when she is finally going to see again the man about whom she has been thinking for so many long years. She asks the goddess for a gentle death in order to "ne plus consumer [sa] vie dans les sanglots à regretter l'époux dont nul en Achaïe ne pouvait égaler la valeur en tous genres".[11]

The key to this ambiguous section occurs towards the end of the story: the reader learns that the young Ulysses, the one whom Penelope continues dreaming about, even while awake, has disappeared a long time before to be replaced by a man thirsty for dangerous adventures. The foreigner, this disguised king hidden in the big hall in the shadow of the suitors, is not the man that she has been loving. He will never be what he once was. That

10. Leclerc, *Toi, Pénélope*, 102-103. "If you did not love Melantho, if you did not love Dolios, if you did not love your sister Ipthime [...] and if you did not also love the howler group of the suitors [...] where would you take the force to love a man absent for twenty years and that you have just met? If you did not love dawn, if you did not love the olive trees stammering of light and especially if you did not love the singing of the bard, how could you claim to love Ulysses?"

11. Leclerc, *Toi, Pénélope*, 86-87. "do not continue anymore wasting [her] life in tears, regretting the spouse that nothing in Achaea could emulate for valor in any field".

is why she fears being confronted by him and prefers death in order to rejoin the young man he once was. Later on, when she understands that she
cannot prevent the massacre from being perpetrated, she again invokes the
daughter of Zeus and prays her to penetrate her heart with one of her arrows. She would like to rejoin Ulysses as she has seen him in her dreams for
twenty years. As in death, spirits are glorified: "il faut bien que les âmes des
morts errantes au bord du Styx y soient au moins gardées dans leur forme
la plus belle, en leur âge le plus lumineux et accompli, leur âge sans âge qui
est celui des rêves".[12]

The only solution left is to find the young man of old times, "son Ulysse
bien-aimé que l'étranger chargé d'ans, d'épreuves et de fureur a vaincu".[13]
She cannot tolerate that the man just arrived is not her Ulysses and that he
means nothing to her. It is not the question of giving particular honors to Penelope. The story does not conclude with a hymn to her virtues or her glory.
The queen is a woman who endures the hardships of life. Ulysses has departed, life continues but without the youth that was making it less harsh.
Penelope has failed her enterprise. She wanted a peaceful son, nourished
with love and reflection, but the cruel acts of Telemachus are "une souillure
dont il ne sera pas lavé".[14] The more horrible part of the manslaughter de-
volves upon him: the hanging of the servants. The story finishes with the
hope that one day men and women will meet again to celebrate peace. But
for this to come about, it is necessary that the unfortunate suitors, victims
of the bloodshed, be never forgotten.

Cunning

Penelope often resorts to cunning. Her objectives are almost never the
same as those of the queen of the *Odyssey,* and she even introduces a new
one. Some episodes that in Homer had no trace of trickery acquire in Annie
Leclerc's telling the uncontestable mark of cunning. Every act of the queen
seems carefully calculated, and she continually keeps her plans concealed.
An important difference between Penelope in the *Odyssey* and in *Toi, Penelope* is that Leclerc's queen does not ignore the presence of Ulysses in the
palace. Her trickeries have different motives, and they hide a new meaning.

---

12. Leclerc, *Toi, Pénélope*, 140. "It is necessary that the souls of the dead wandering at the
    border of the Styx are at least kept in their best shape, in their more radiant and ac-
    complished age, their age without age that is the one of the dreams."
13. Leclerc, *Toi, Pénélope*, 140. "her beloved Ulysses that the foreigner loaded with years,
    trials and rage has substituted".
14. Leclerc, *Toi, Pénélope*, 141. "a stain that will be never washed away".

The shroud

Before she knows about the imminent return of her spouse, Penelope uses the shroud to protract time. She desires to delay a marriage for two main reasons. First of all, she keeps a promise made at Ulysses departure to wait for Telemachus to reach adulthood. The second reason is her unwillingness to take a stand in relation to the death of the king — she does not want to be the one to declare the end of the reign of her spouse.

When Penelope learns that Ulysses is in the palace, she is afraid for him, because she fears he will have to suffer the abuses of the suitors. She hears that the foreigner is badly hosted. She asks for a meeting with him to spare him the aggressiveness and scorn of the young men. For this she claims that he could have some news of the unfortunate Ulysses. She sends someone to look for him, but the beggar answers that he prefers to wait for the evening and the departure of the suitors. She deduces from this that he is going to reveal to her his true identity. Anticipating this, she wants to put an end to the fights that she hears from the ground floor, she knows he is involved in it. She covers her face with a radiant veil so that her face and her gaze cannot be seen. In this way she will be able to see Ulysses looking at her, without herself been seen. She goes down into the big hall and asks Telemachus to ensure the welfare of the foreigner according to the customs of hospitality. As Ulysses scrutinizes her from the back of the room, she realizes that this man is not the one who has haunted her dreams for twenty years. This Ulysses seems somber, irritated and smoldering.

The bow

During the meeting Ulysses does not want to reveal himself to her, preferring instead to lie. Initially, Penelope feels aggrieved and even resentful, but she realizes that Ulysses will not reveal himself before putting his plan into action. She notices his complicity with Telemachus, who is clearly aware of his father's real identity. With Ulysses' refusal to reveal himself, and looking at his darkened gaze, stiffened by hardships, Penelope guesses the terrible revenge that hangs over the suitors. She remembers a bad dream she had the previous night: her beautiful geese lazed around in the courtyard, suddenly an eagle appeared in the sky and struck upon them until none was left alive. The queen cannot accept this frightful threat and wishes to avoid seeing all these young people killed by the murderous madness of the returned king. She decides to force Ulysses to unmask under the eyes of everyone and to avoid the foretold slaughter, hoping that when the young men discover his real identity they will be cautious and will have a chance to defend themselves. Her plan is the following: she will propose the following day a trial to the suitors. The bow of Ulysses, that he is the only one able to use, will be employed in the choice of the new spouse: the queen will accept in marriage the one who is able to string the bow and shoot an arrow through twelve axe-heads. She hopes that only the king will be capable of such a feat and will be obliged to reveal his name to the assembly.

Melantho

Penelope believes that if she loses Melantho she will be unable to go on living; the pain would be too great:

> Melantho ne mourra pas, je le jure, je l'ai juré. Sinon ce sera moi. Tu dresses ton décret comme une hache de guerre entre Ulysse et toi. Puis tu refermes ton secret autour de toi, enceinte d'une résistance où nul ne pourra pénétrer.[15]

The death of the others upsets her, but she can put up with it, while the disappearance of the young girl would be unbearable. She would not survive the death of Melantho. The mother in her takes the precedence over the wife. Penelope opposes the will of Ulysses, without whom she could live twenty long years, for the sake of the love that she feels for the adopted child. " [...] le bébé s'est niché en toi, là où te faisait si mal l'absence d'Ulysse [...]. Et voilà aujourd'hui, vingt ans plus tard, ce serait Ulysse lui-même qui, sur Melantho, un bien aimée, ta vie continuée, appellerait la Parque de mort?"[16]

Penelope fears her adopted girl will be chosen for the revenge, "et plus ardemment que tout autre s'il se trouve menace".[17] She will not allow her spouse to get close to her, and she will hide her until his next departure. Although the reader learns all the other thoughts of the queen, the moment Melantho is secured is silenced; s/he does not know where the young girl is hidden. An single allusion allows one to locate her in the palace. Perhaps because her maid is the most precious thing in Penelope's world, even her thoughts cannot share so important a secret.

---

15. Leclerc, *Toi, Pénélope*, 142-143. "Melantho will not die, I swear it, I swore it. If not it will be me. You prepare your decree as a war declaration between Ulysses and yourself. Then you lock your secret within yourself, surrounded by a resistence wall within which nothing will be able to penetrate."

16. Leclerc, *Toi, Pénélope*, 150. "the baby has brooded in you, there where the absence of Ulysses was so painful [...]. And here it is, today, twenty years later, it would be Ulysses himself who, for Melantho, a loved being that kept you alive, would call the Fates of death?"

17. Leclerc, *Toi, Pénélope*, 104. "and more ardently than any other if he feels under threat".

The bed

Ulysses has bent the bow, his trap was set, he has massacred all the suitors. Everything is finished. Penelope has to surrender to the triumphant
Ulysses, but she does not yet want to go back to the bed of twenty years earlier, that cold grave left empty for so long. She tries to ignore him and asks
that a new marital bed be prepared. Ulysses does not understand the allusion and thinks that she means to displace the bed he built with his hands
upon the trunk of an olive tree. He is outraged: who could displace this bed
rooted in the ground? He insists, and Penelope gives in and throws herself
in his arms.

Double game

Penelope is known for weaving and unweaving the shroud, but here
she shows a new cunning: everyone thinks her unaware of Ulysses' return
and his deadly revenge, but she anticipates everything and is able to save
the essentials. Despite all appearances, she is "aussi rusée qu'Ulysse, sinon
advantage".[18]

Penelope is not a resigned woman whose days are spent waiting for a
spouse off on an adventure. Ulysses' absence does not condemn her to a life
without love. Her heart is big, for the whole world. She opens it to everyone.
The wound inflicted by the separation from Ulysses is healed by the adoption
of the little Melantho, a daughter of servants, brought up as a princess in the
palace. Solitude and sorrow have not disappeared, but she did not want to
give herself up to them. She has also promised fidelity to her children. The
memory of her native land, the laughs of the children, the olive tree in the
garden have kept her alive. It's her love for everything that hooked her up to
life. Above everything she loves her children. Ulysses comes after.

When Telemachus left Ithaca to seek news of his father, Penelope was
aware of the death threats that hung over his head. The anguish she felt was
immense: "C'est là, penses-tu, incapable de pire, un tourment passant en in-
tensité tous les tourments passés et à venir."[19] She feels the same for Melantho, whom she has been able to hide from the deadly madness of Ulysses.
In the novel, Penelope is more mother than spouse. This is one of the main
differences from the Homer's poem, where the queen places the interests
of the married couple before those of herself and the ones nearest to her.

Penelope here is not the exemplary woman described in the *Odyssey*.
She has very human — or better, feminine — defects. She is not content with

18. Leclerc, *Toi, Pénélope*, 14. "as cunning as Ulysses, if not more".
19. Leclerc, *Toi, Pénélope*, 53. "It is there, you think, it cannot be worst, an agony trespass-
    ing for intensity the past agonies and the ones to come."

being wise. Nor are her feelings so exemplary either. She is proud, a bit too much, thinking that she will surprise the returned king who failed to surprise her. She is jealous of the trust that her spouse shows in Telemachus but not in her, and of the young Nausicae whom Ulysses will never abandon, as she was the only woman he could not possess.

Resentment fills Penelope when she discovers what her young spouse of former times has become; the old Ulysses is not the one she has been dreaming about for twenty years. She feels disappointed by Ulysses' plans to deceive her and by his valuing his revenge more than her. She has many fears. She is frightened of not being recognized by Ulysses, she is worried for the lives of the ones she loves, and she fears returning to a bed abandoned for twenty years. She doubts the heroism of this man who is returned to spread death. She knows now that he is only a man: "Ulysse n'est pas Ulysse, mais un homme ordinaire."[20] Despite all this, she feels desire again for this man so heavily tried by his terrible hardships. As when the young suitors put their eyes on her, and she dreamt of a man at her side, it was not important which one, but she would have preferred Ulysses, of course.

Commentary

The author is a feminist, as is widely known. It is no accident that her choice has fallen on Penelope. The queen of Ithaca is an original feminine character of her time. In a way she risks becoming an anachronism, a feminist of Antiquity. In fact, Penelope does oppose her subordinate condition as woman and wishes to rise as far as she can in a world that is her own, despite the decisions that men take for her.

The philosophy of Annie Leclerc affirms that life has to be enjoyed, has to be fully felt. She advocates an ideal of non-violence based on the mutual respect between man and woman. Penelope's enterprise fails to create a better world. Telemachus disappoints her expectations, he remains tainted by the reckless violence of men.

Conclusion

Annie Leclerc recovers some fragments of the plot of the *Odyssey* that, placed in the context of her work, don't have the same meaning any more. She draws an Ithaca that is less hostile and a queen who is more human. She utilizes the French translation of the *Odyssey* by Victor Bérard, to which

---

20. Leclerc, *Toi, Pénélope*, 148. "Ulysses is not Ulysses but an ordinary man."

she refers in the preface, but she also quotes the text of Homer that she has known since infancy.

For this Penelope, the memory of Ulysses is not an aid to living. She feels that the man she loved died the moment he was replaced by the man going off to war. The young man of old times does not exist anymore, even though the tired-out king has returned to his kingdom. Penelope's love for the people and for the world are what have made her hold on to life and given her persistence to go forward, the loyalty to herself and to her children.

This queen also has recourse to the subterfuge of the shroud to delay the marriage. But it is through another plan that everything will be decided, as the deeper cunning revolves around Ulysses. She knows that he is coming back, she hopes to forestall his intentions and to unmask him on his arrival in Ithaca. Her stratagems aim to protect Ulysses, to persuade him to reveal his identity and avoid the slaughter.

Penelope is a mother before being a wife. This point is diametrically opposed to the Homeric poem, where the memory and love of the absent spouse go beyond everything, comprising even a death menace weighing upon her son. She has raised up another child, Melantho, daughter of servants, who has allowed her to fill the emotional vacuum left by the desertion of Ulysses. She perceives the hero's departure as an abandonment for which she feels a certain bitterness. She does not see the king crowned by glory, he is after all a man like the others, with his defects and his violence. Penelope herself is an ordinary woman, one who is not concerned with honors bestowed by her rank and condition. The author makes an eloquent reflection on this subject: "Que t'importe ta gloire quand tu n'es appelée qu'à te soumettre."[21]

In this work, Annie Leclerc shows her thought to be that of a moderate feminist who places women on a par with men, taking into account their respective differences. Her novel offers a hope of peace to generations to come and asks them to remember the horrors of violence, so that they will not be repeated. In this manner, Penelope represents her philosophical ideal.

---

21. Leclerc, *Toi, Pénélope*, 111. "What's the importance of your glory if you are only asked to submit."

CHAPTER 4

MARGARET ATWOOD: THE PENELOPIAD

(2005)

> He was always so plausible. Many people have believed that
> this version of events was the true one [...] I knew he was
> tricky and a liar [...] Hadn't I been faithful? Hadn't I waited,
> and waited, and waited, despite the temptation [...] And what
> did I amount to, once the official version gained ground? An
> edifying legend. A stick used to beat other women with.

The Penelopiad, 2

The Penelopiad is a novel published in 2005 by the Canadian writer Margaret Atwood, author of more than thirty-five works of fiction, poetry and critical essay. She was born in 1939 in Ottawa, Ontario, and graduated in 1962
from the University of Toronto, publishing in the same year her first book
of poems, *Double Persephone*. After receiving a master degree from Rad-
cliffe College, she began doctoral work at Harvard in 1961 but never completed her studies; her planned Ph.D. was on "Nature and Power in the English Metaphysical Romance of the 19th and 20th century".

Between 1966 and 1974 she published six volumes of verses as well as
two novels – *The Edible Woman* (1969) and *Surfacing* (1972) — while working in the English departments of several Canadian universities. In her first
works, as in the later ones, Atwood is concerned with the splitting up of the
self or with the 'power politics' between lovers, or with the need to revise
mythic stories, like those of Homer's Odysseus, to retell them from the silenced perspective of the female who has been seduced and abandoned. In
her first two novels — as in later ones like *Lady Oracle* (1976), *Life before
Man* (1979), *Bodily Harm* (1981), *Cat's Eye* (1988), *Alias Grace* (1996), and

The Blind Assassin (2000) for which she won the Booker Prize — she represents an individual questing for personal integrity and for a more harmonious relationship with the natural world.

Atwood's poetry and fiction is often a journey into the unconscious of her characters. Whether her central character is a pioneer woman or an author of Gothic romances, the character seeks some form of control over an environment that is seen as alien or alienating. A number of Atwood's characters refuse to be victims. In Atwood's view, Canadians have viewed themselves as victims of either English or American imperialism in the same way that women have perceived themselves as victims of masculine privilege. Atwood implies that cultural colonization and sexual subordination are parallel, if not identical, situations. Both the humor and the tenderness of her later works indicate how writing continues to empower Atwood to defy colonization.

In works such as *Bluebeard's Egg and Other Stories* (1986), *The Handmaid's Tale* (1987), *Good Bones* (1992) and *The Robber Bride* (1993), Atwood exploits fantastic, futuristic, and fairy-tale techniques to examine feminist ideology and women's biological, familial, and social experiences. After *The Penelopiad,* Atwood continued to produce novels situated in a futuristic dystopian society, 'speculative fiction' books, as she calls them. She has completed the dystopian trilogy started with *Oryx and Crake* (2003), followed by *The Year of the Flood* (2009), and *MaddAddam* (2013), and her last book, *The Heart Goes Last*, published in September 2015, is likewise set in a near future characterized by economic and environmental decline and a flawed humanity.

Atwood herself claims not to be a feminist, or perhaps more importantly, she claims a variety of stances towards feminism, including being belatedly embraced by the second-wave feminist movement. She challenges an easy equation of feminism and women, and she is as reluctant to be aligned with feminism as she is with any critical movement.[1]

Plot

The protagonist and first person narrator of *The Penelopiad* is Penelope. She is now dead, and after centuries languishing in Hades, the underworld, she has decided to tell everyone her version of the story because "many people have believed that his [Odysseus'] version of the events was the true one".[2] She is well aware of the legends surrounding her, "the official version" transmitted through the centuries celebrating her faithfulness.

1. Heidi Slettedahl Macpherson, *The Cambridge introduction to Margaret Atwood*, (Cambridge: Cambridge University Press, 2010), 60.

2. Margaret Atwood, *The Penelopiad. The myth of Penelope and Odysseus*, (Edinburgh: Canongate, 2005), 2.

From the beginning, however, her aim is clear: she will have nothing to do with the legend, and she has no intention of being a model for other women. Her waiting and her faithfulness have been transformed without her consent in an "edifying legend. A stick used to beat other women with."[3] She intends to distance herself from all this. The message is loud and clear: "Don't follow my example."[4] After centuries of silence it is now time "to do a little story-making".[5] Now that she is dead she has nothing to fear, she is no longer afraid of other people's criticism: "who cares about public opinion now".[6]

So chapter after chapter she recalls her life in a long flashback: her family life in Sparta, her marriage with Odysseus, his departure for Troy, her relation with the suitors up to the return of the king and the massacre of the young men and of the twelve maids. Her first-person narrative is interrupted now and then by the voices of the twelve dead maids, speaking via the Chorus as in Greek tragedy and becoming protagonists in ten of the twenty-nine chapters that comprise the text.

As Penelope recalls in the first chapters, her relation with the parents was quite difficult: the father had given orders to drown her in the sea, probably following the advice of an oracle, but her life was saved by a group of purple-striped ducks, and afterweards he had become excessively attached to her. Her mother, a Naiad – a water nymph – "preferred swimming in the river to the care of small children",[7] so Penelope could hardly count on her. At fifteen she was given as spouse to Odysseus, although he had not been considered by Penelope and her maids as a serious candidate for her hand, since "his father's palace was on Ithaca, a goat-strewn rock; his clothes were rustic; he had the manners of a small-town big shot, and had already expressed several complicated ideas the others considered peculiar".[8]

Odysseus was belittled by the maids and by Penelope's glamorous cousin Helen for his short legs. At the end, he was able to win the contest and marry her, thanks to a trick perpetrated with the help of Tyndareus, Penelope's uncle and the father of Helen: "he mixed the wine of the other contestants with a drug that slowed them down, though not so much as they would notice".[9] Tyndareus had promised Penelope to Odysseus "in return for assuring a peaceful and very profitable wedding for the radiant Helen".[10]

3. Atwood, *The Penelopiad*, 2.
4. Atwood, *The Penelopiad*, 2.
5. Atwood, *The Penelopiad*, 3.
6. Atwood, *The Penelopiad*, 4.
7. Atwood, *The Penelopiad*, 11.
8. Atwood, *The Penelopiad*, 31.
9. Atwood, *The Penelopiad*, 35-36.
10. Atwood, *The Penelopiad*, 37.

Breaking with tradition, Penelope followed her husband to Ithaca to start a new life. There she had to cope with the initial hesitations of her mother-in-law, Anticleia, and Odysseus's former nurse, Eurycleia. The first is described as a silent "prune-mouthed woman"[11]; while the second initially treated her like a child and patronized her with all sorts of directives, before finally accepting her and helping her enter into her role of wife and mother. A year after Telemachus was born, "disaster struck"[12] — Odysseus sailed away to Troy, leaving Penelope to look after their estate. Ten years passed. Her mother-in-law died; Laertes, Odysseus's father, left the palace for the countryside, Eurycleia got older. By now Penelope was running the estate, wisely and successfully. The Trojan War finished, but Odysseus still did not return, though news of him continued to arrive. More years passed, and no further news of him arrived anymore. "Odysseus seemed to have vanished from the face of the earth."[13]

When the king did not return to Ithaca the suitors started appearing on the scene "like vultures when they spot a dead cow".[14] At this point, to buy time and to postpone a decision concerning a new spouse, Penelope has the idea of weaving a shroud for Laertes. With the help of twelve maidservants she undoes during the night what she weaves during the day, until her trick is discovered and she is forced to decide on a new husband. At this point Odysseus returns to Ithaca. Penelope recognizes him immediately, though disguised as a beggar: "As soon as I saw that barrel chest and those short legs I had a deep suspicion, which became a certainty when I heard he'd broken the neck of a belligerent fellow panhandler."[15] She decides to keep her discovery to herself, since "it's always an imprudence to step between a man and the reflection of his own cleverness".[16]

Because she is well aware that only Odysseus can string his old bow, she proposes that the suitors hold a competition using the bow and the axes. While Penelope sleeps in her room, Odysseus kills all the suitors and then has Telemachus hang the twelve unfaithful maids, indicated as the disloyal ones by Eurycleia. Penelope is deeply sorry for her maids and decides to take her time before recognizing formally her husband. After her famous trick involving the nuptial bed, she consents to recognize him, claiming that "he'd passed the bedpost test, and that I was now convinced".[17] So finally the two

11. Atwood, *The Penelopiad*, 60.
12. Atwood, *The Penelopiad*, 76.
13. Atwood, *The Penelopiad*, 92.
14. Atwood, *The Penelopiad*, 103.
15. Atwood, *The Penelopiad*, 136.
16. Atwood, *The Penelopiad*, 137.
17. Atwood, *The Penelopiad*, 171.

spouses are reunited. Odysseus narrates to her all of his adventures – "the nobler versions"[18] – while Penelope recalls her "many tears" and "how tediously faithful"[19] she had been.

However, she instills some doubts on her own and on Odysseus's tale as she adds: "The two of us were – by our own admission – proficient and shameless liars of long standing. It's a wonder either one of us believed a word the other said. But we did. Or so we told each other."[20] Did she tell the truth to Odysseus? Is she telling the truth to us, her readers? No straightforward answer can be given, especially if we consider the narrative perspective of the twelve hanged maids, who blame both Odysseus and Penelope for their unjust deaths. In Hades, Odysseus is closely followed by the ghosts of the twelve dead maids whose systematic and eternal stalking reminds him his evil massacre.

The ghosts of the maids also accuse Penelope of passivity and complicity in their deaths, which was intended to cover her infidelities with the suitors by having the only witnesses killed. Theirs is the dissident voice that challenges the authenticity of Penelope's confession and contributes new light on the Odyssean myth.

The theme of Penelope

The author's introduction announces that *The Penelopiad* aims to offer a different version of Homer's *Odyssey* by giving "the telling of the story to Penelope and to the twelve hanged maids".[21] Atwood's retelling shifts the perspective from Penelope to the Chorus that personifies the voices of the maids. This shift in perspective has the effect of looking with new eyes not only at the figure of Penelope but also, more generally, at all the other mythical characters, as in Atwood's words: "Mythic material was originally oral, and also local – a myth would be told one way in one place and quite differently in another."[22]

The Odysseus described in Homer's poem — through the words of Nestor and Menelaus to Telemachus — is a straightforward hero fighting against monsters and seducing a goddess. However in Atwood's *The Penelopiad,* different and contradictory voices offer a more complex and less heroic picture of the man and his legendary adventures. While for some "Odysseus had been in a fight with a giant one-eyed Cyclops", for others "it was only a

18. Atwood, *The Penelopiad*, 172.
19. Atwood, *The Penelopiad*, 173.
20. Atwood, *The Penelopiad*, 173.
21. Atwood, *The Penelopiad*, xv.
22. Atwood, *The Penelopiad,* xv.

one-eyed tavern keeper, [...] and the fight was over non-payment of bill".[23] In the same way "the goddess on an enchanted isle" described by some, becomes for others only "an expensive whorehouse",[24] "the cannibals" and "the magic plant" only "a brawl of the usual kind"[25] and too much drinking.

In the same way Penelope feels the need to tell her own story because the portrait given by Homer or other writers of antiquity and transmitted through the centuries does not satisfy her. While on one hand she refuses the role of faithful wife given to her by Homer in opposition to unfaithful Clytemnestra, on the other she rejects the "slanderous gossip that has been going the rounds for the past two or three thousand years",[26] accusing her of sleeping with Amphinomus, or even with all of the suitors, and giving birth to the god Pan. Both roles are false, she affirms.

Penelope aims to show with her story that truth can be found exclusively neither in the mythical tales nor in the various subjective points of view, but only in a position that is in-between the two, and moreover, that this same 'truth' can vary according to the time in which the story is told. What was valid two thousand years ago cannot still be valid in our day. So the Penelope of *The Penelopiad* does not intend to subvert the events narrated in the Homeric poem but rather to reveal the other side of the docility and passivity she was forced to show, following the customs and the rules of her time. She recalls her imprisonment in a house where she was brought by her husband and where she was abandoned once he left for war; she recalls the difficulty of living in a house governed by her mother-in-law and her husband's old wet nurse, the same women who deprived her of the right to educate her son who, now grown, sees in her the cause of the loss of his inheritance; she recalls the deep solitude of the long years without her husband, mitigated only by the voices and laughs of the twelve maids that she has brought up almost as daughters; she recalls the arrogance of the suitors whom she could not reject and the lack of trust by her husband who revealed his true identity to their son but not to her; and finally she recalls his brutality in hanging the twelve maids.

Atwood's reading of the *Odyssey* switches between prose narration – the recollection by Penelope in Hades of the most important moments of her life – and other forms of writing that convey the voices of the twelve maids, represented as a Greek chorus. Their voices are heard through different narrative forms: in one chapter they declaim verses, in another they narrate stories or play the role of victims in a court proceeding against Odysseus; in another they discuss the anthropological meaning of their death or simply

23. Atwood, *The Penelopiad*, 83.
24. Atwood, *The Penelopiad*, 84.
25. Atwood, *The Penelopiad*, 83.
26. Atwood, *The Penelopiad*, 144.

dance and play. The objective is to emphasize their unnecessary death, for which Odysseus still stands unpunished — a death that their loving mistress was not able to prevent and that still causes her anguish and pain even in Hades. If on one side the author raises the character of Penelope and redeems the behavior of the maids towards the suitors, on the other she strongly criticizes the character of Helen, who is disapproved for her hollow vanity that caused the loss of so many lives and that still characterizes her in Hades.

Penelope has a strongly antagonistic relation with Helen who, by causing the Trojan War and the departure of Odysseus, has destroyed her life and initiated the deaths of many innocents. She becomes a sort of specular image of Penelope: the marital fidelity, cleverness and modesty of the queen of Ithaca stand in contradistinction to the unfaithfulness, beauty and glamour of the queen of Sparta. The "long-necked swan"[27] figure of Helen is contrasted to the "little ducky"[28] Penelope; the myth of the wise and thoughtful woman and wife transmitted by generations is in this sense continually confronted by the divine beauty and sex-appeal of Helen, whose sins of vanity and superficiality seem to be forgotten in virtue of her ascendancy over men. Even in the Hades, after more than two thousand years, she does not seem to have learned anything from her mistakes.

As asserted by Penelope: "She took their deaths [of the men who died in the war] as a tribute to herself."[29] Penelope is keenly aware of the vanity and superficiality of the cousin who has caused her so much pain, and she cannot contain her anger even in Hades: "Helen was never punished, not one bit. Why not, I'd like to know? Other people got strangled by sea serpents and drowned in storms and turned into serpents and shot with arrows for much smaller crimes."[30] By underlining her beautiful cousin's vacuity and lack of regret, Penelope intends to undermine the wrongly idealized image, transmitted through the *Odyssey*, of Helen as the archetype of femininity. Penelope is here giving her truth, her perspective to counterbalance a mythical truth that needs correction and amendment.

Memory

Memory, its relation with truth, its construction and de-construction are at the basis of the *The Penelopiad*. Penelope speaks to us from Hades, and her aim is to give to the modern-day audience her version of events. To do this she must rely on a memory that after thousands of years shows itself

27. Atwood, *The Penelopiad,* 33.
28. Atwood, *The Penelopiad, 33.*
29. Atwood, *The Penelopiad,* 75.
30. Atwood, *The Penelopiad,* 22.

to be still sharp and untarnished. As she explains in one of the last chapters of the book, she never drank from the "Waters of Forgetfulness" that enable the souls in Hades to wipe their past from memory and consent to "get [...] reborn and have another try at life".[31] Her narration's main reason is to change the perception that has been linked to her name for centuries. Through the use of her "infallible memory" she longs for the true story. She needs to look back in order to move forward.

Those who forget or deny the past are doomed to repeat the same mistakes, like Helen and Odysseus do. They have drunk the Waters, but "the Waters of Forgetfulness don't always work the way they're supposed to".[32] In their subsequent earthly "excursions" they have not modified their original nature or personality. Penelope finds Helen declaring on her return "how naughty she's been and how much uproar she's been causing and how many men she's ruined",[33] while concerning Odysseus she notes:

> He's been a French general, he's been a Mongolian invader, he's been a tycoon in America, and he's been a headhunter in Borneo. He's been a film star, an inventor, an advertising man. It's always ended badly, with a suicide or an accident or a death in battle or an assassination, and then he's back here again.[34]

Denying one's own memories also denies the possibility to change, to learn from previous mistakes, to become a better person. Penelope, on her side, did not want to drink the Waters. To remember, and most importantly to understand, the past can change the present. For her memory is a means of liberation. By recalling for the first time details that were not known before, she can free herself from an imprisoning history and give new meanings to her former actions. Moreover, Penelope does not want to forget the past, *and* she does not want to return among the living, since she has no hopes in a better future. Her past has taught her a hard lesson, one she cannot forget and has no intention to live again:

> My past life was fraught with many difficulties, but who's to say the next one wouldn't be worse? Even with my limited access I can see that the world is just as dangerous as it was in my day, except that the misery and suffering are on a much wider scale. As for human nature, it's as tawdry as ever.[35]

31. Atwood, *The Penelopiad,* 186.
32. Atwood, *The Penelopiad,* 186-7.
33. Atwood, *The Penelopiad,*187.
34. Atwood, *The Penelopiad,* 189-90.
35. Atwood, *The Penelopiad,* 188.

In *The Penelopiad* the memory of Penelope acquires new meanings; it is not limited to keeping alive the remembrance of Odysseus for twenty years, preserving the house and the throne of the hero. Instead, it spans over three thousand years, throwing new light on characters previously frozen within a mythical aura. Her memory no longer has the sole task of keeping alive the glory of Odysseus as the 'hero' depicted in the Homeric poem; on the contrary, she aims to recall him as a man with all his faults and defects. She was always aware of "his slipperiness, his wiliness, his foxiness, [...] his unscrupulousness",[36] but she never showed her true thoughts. As she tells us: "I kept my mouth shut; or if I opened it, I sang his praises. I didn't contradict, I didn't ask awkward questions, I didn't dig deep."[37] Penelope's memory is not only sharp but, more importantly, free from censure. She no longer wears the mask of the good and faithful wife. In Hades she has nothing to lose by revealing her truth. She is dead, as are all the members of her family and all the people who knew her: "who cares about public opinion now? The opinion of the people down here: the opinion of shadows, of echoes".[38]

The queen's infallible memory has ceased to be a tool to safeguard the *nostos* and the *kleos* of the hero; quite the opposite, it is used by the queen to subvert those roles. Odysseus is not more the brave and crafty hero described by Homer but instead an unscrupulous adventurers and a liar, perpetrator of the cruel slaughter of the young suitors and the unjust hanging of twelve innocent maids. By recalling the events, by giving her personal version, Penelope aims not to sing her husband's glory but to take her personal and patiently awaited revenge. The Odysseus she describes is completely deprived of glory, as is also the character of Helen. Both seem united by the same focus on themselves and on their own pleasures without any thought for the pain they give to the people around them.

The memory displayed by the queen in *The Penelopiad* is contrasted to the nostalgia (*nostos:* the return home), the longing to return home displayed by the Homeric Penelope. Nostalgia is the feeling that the good days are the bygone days. So nostalgia is the memory that comes from the desire to live again a happy and unrepeatable past. In *The Penelopiad*, however, Penelope has little to be nostalgic about; the time in which she lived is not one to which she wants to return. As described by the feminist critic Gayle Green:

> Nostalgia is not only a longing to return home; it is also a longing to return to the state of things in which woman keeps the home and in which she awaits, like Penelope, the return of her wandering

36. Atwood, *The Penelopiad*, 3.
37. Atwood, *The Penelopiad, 3.*
38. Atwood, *The Penelopiad*, 4.

Odysseus. But if going back is advantageous to those who have enjoyed power, it is dangerous to those who have not.[39]

The Penelope depicted by Atwood is still, as her Homeric equivalent, a wise woman, but she has lost her persistent and characteristic passivity and her enduring forgiveness towards the ones hurting her. She is now a woman who re-assembles her past through meditation and memory and tries to retrieve a new image of herself — not anymore so "considerate, trustworthy, all-suffering"[40] as she had been described. Penelope now shows openly her distrust and jealousy of Helen, her disappointment in the way Telemachus has been brought up and spoiled by Eurycleia, her disgust and hatred at Odysseus' killing of the suitors and maids. The new Penelope shows a stronger critical attitude toward every action and episode she recalls. Her past is remembered and re-analyzed with the aim of re-establishing justice, of re-creating a new, transformed version of the story. The passive nostalgia of the Homeric Penelope is replaced by the active memory of a woman determined to affirm her truth. As highlighted by Gayle Green:

> Nostalgia and remembering are in some sense antithetical, since nostalgia is a forgetting, merely regressive, whereas memory may look back in order to move forward and transform disabling fictions to enabling fictions, altering our relation to the present and future.[41]

Remembering in *The Penelopiad* is not left solely to Penelope but it is shared with the twelve hanged maids who are able to give their own version of the events in the first person, through the chorus. The hanging of the maids by Odysseus assumes here a new and unprecedented importance. This episode is at the heart of *The Penelopiad* while it is only superficially cited in Homer's version.

In her narration Penelope recalls how she decided to take twelve of her maidservants "the youngest ones, because these had been with me all their lives",[42] to help her with the weaving of the shroud for Laertes. She asked them secretly to be with the suitors and spy on them. Only now she realizes that keeping all this hidden from Eurycleia and from her husband was "ill-considered, and caused harm"[43] as, at the return of Odysseus, their relations with the suitors have been considered a betrayal and all of them have been killed as a consequence. She also recalls her dream in which her flock of lovely white

---

39. Gayle Greene, "Feminist Fiction and the uses of memory" in *Signs*, vol.16, no.2 (Winter, 1991): 290-321,296.

40. Atwood, *The Penelopiad*, 2.

41. Greene, "Feminist Fiction and the uses of memory", 298.

42. Atwood, *The Penelopiad*, 113.

43. Atwood, *The Penelopiad*, 118.

geese are killed by a huge eagle. Relating the dream to Odysseus-the-beggar, she is told that the eagle was her husband and the geese the suitors.

However, Penelope affirms: "Odysseus was wrong about the dream. He was indeed the eagle, but the geese were not the Suitors. The geese were my twelve maids, as I was soon to learn to my unending sorrow."[44] While Odysseus and Telemachus take their revenge on the suitors and maids, Penelope is in her room in a deep sleep. She does not realize anything until she is awakened by Eurycleia informing her of the brutal revenge of Odysseus and the killing of her maids. Penelope is shattered: "It was my fault! I hadn't told her of my scheme."[45] Penelope knows that the maids were innocent and were just following her orders but she cannot do anything now. "What could I do? Lamentation wouldn't bring my lovely girls back to life. [...] Dead is dead, I told myself. I'll say prayers and perform sacrifices for their souls. But I'll have to do it in secret, or Odysseus will suspect me, as well."[46]

The fear of coming herself under suspicion by Odysseus convinces Penelope to keep the secret for herself. However by not revealing the truth Penelope has doomed the young maids to an eternal unrest. In fact, since their death, they cannot find peace in Hades, where they seek justice and revenge from both Odysseus and herself. In *The Penelopiad*, the tale of Penelope is interspersed with the voice of the twelve hanged maids who speak through the chorus, utilizing various literary genres and forms. As acknowledged by Atwood's in the book's *Notes:* "The Chorus of Maids is a tribute to the use of such choruses in Greek drama."[47] The memory, and so the truth of the queen, finds a counterbalance in the memory of the maids who recall a different story in which they are the real victims and where Penelope is also implicated in their murder.

Two chapters in particular – among the ten that expose the perspective of the maids – are particularly interesting relating to Penelope's involvement in their death. Chapter XXI, entitled "The Chorus Line: The Perils of Penelope, A Drama", with the subtitle "Presented by: The Maids" and with a "Prologue: spoken by Melantho of the Pretty Cheeks" reproduces, in the form of a mini Greek drama, the dialogue between Eurycleia and Penelope, played by two maids, taking place in the moment they realize that Odysseus is back and is looking for revenge. This chapter is essentially an open accusation of Penelope for having demanded that Eurycleia point out to Odysseus the twelve maids to be killed, as they had been witnessing her numerous adulteries with the suitors and so constituted a

44. Atwood, *The Penelopiad*, 140.
45. Atwood, *The Penelopiad,* 160.
46. Atwood, *The Penelopiad*, 160.
47. Atwood, *The Penelopiad*, 198.

danger for the unfaithful queen. The Penelope of the Drama knows she is going to pay for her infidelities even if she affirms her right to pleasure as enjoyed by Odysseus:

> *Penelope:* And now, dear Nurse, the fat is in the fire –
>   He'll chop me up for tending my desire!
>   While he was pleasuring every nymph and beauty,
>   Did he think I'd do nothing but my duty?
>   While every girl and goddess he was praising,
>   Did he assume I'd dry up like a raisin?[48]

Eurycleia too is well aware of Penelope's lovers and reveals to Penelope that only the twelve maids are aware of her misconduct. At this point Penelope asks the old nurse to save her and Odysseus' honor:

> *Penelope*: Oh then, dear Nurse, it's really up to you
>   To save me, and Odysseus' honour too!
>   Because he sucked at your now-ancient bust,
>   You are the only one of us he'll trust.
>   Point out those maids as feckless and disloyal,
>   Snatched by the Suitors as unlawful spoil,
>   Polluted, shameless, and not fit to be
>   The doting slaves of such a Lord as he![49]

In this way the honor of Odysseus and the mythical faithfulness of the queen have been defended and propagated to the generations to come, building a myth on the basis of a lie: "Penelope: And I in fame a model wife shall rest – / All husbands will look on, and think him blessed!"[50] In the conclusion of the chapter "The Chorus line, in tap-dance shoes" comes on the scene and reminds the audience of the injustice they have been victims of :

> "Blame it on the maids!
>   Those naughty little jades!
>   Hang them high and don't ask why."[51]

Towards the end of the book we find another chapter relating the perspective of the maids and making reference to their deaths. The action of Chapter XXVI entitled "The Chorus Line: The Trial of Odysseus, as Videotaped by the Maids" takes place in a modern day court where Odysseus is on trial for manslaughter. After the closing speech of the defense attorney

---

48. Atwood, *The Penelopiad*, 149.
49. Atwood, *The Penelopiad*, 150.
50. Atwood, *The Penelopiad*, 151.
51. Atwood, *The Penelopiad*, 151.

who argues the right of Odysseus to kill the suitors as he was "merely acting on self-defense" and demands to "dismiss this case",[52] the maids from the back of the room ask to be heard, accusing Odysseus of massacring them in cold blood. The judge consents to listen to their accusations while the defense attorney rejects their claims on the basis of their implicated sex relations with the suitors, the "enemies"[53] of Odysseus. The judge refers to Book 22 of Homer's *Odyssey*, which he recognizes as being "a book we must needs consult, as it is the main authority on the subject".[54] There it is affirmed that the maids were raped and no one intervened to defend them. At this point Penelope is called as a witness. She seems sincerely sorry for the death of her maids and affirms while weeping:

> *Penelope*: I felt so sorry for them! But most maids got raped, sooner or later; a deplorable but common feature of palace life. It wasn't the fact of their being raped that told against them, in the mind of Odysseus. It's that they were raped without permission. [...]
> *Attorney for the Defense*: Without permission of their master, Your Honour.[55]

At the end of the scene the judge, talking to the attorney for the defense, decides to dismiss the case based on the fact that:

> Your client's [Odysseus'] times were not our times. Standards of behavior were different then. It would be unfortunate if this regrettable but minor incident were allowed to stand as a blot on an otherwise exceedingly distinguished career. Also I do not wish to be guilty of an anachronism. Therefore I must dismiss the case.[56]

To the maids, for whom justice has been refused again, it remains only to invoke the Erinyes, whom they implore to punish Odysseus and take vengeance on their behalf: "Oh Angry Ones, Oh Furies, you are our last hope! [...] Be our defenders, we who had none in life! Smell out Odysseus wherever he goes! [...] Let him never be at rest!"[57]

The maids' version of the events dismounts the mythical faithfulness of the queen, who deprived of her mythical fidelity aura shows the same desires and weaknesses as Odysseus, with whom she shares an equal capacity

---

52. Atwood, *The Penelopiad*, 177.
53. Atwood, *The Penelopiad*, 178.
54. Atwood, *The Penelopiad*, 179.
55. Atwood, *The Penelopiad*, 181-2.
56. Atwood, *The Penelopiad*, 182.
57. Atwood, *The Penelopiad*, 183.

for counterfeiting and forging the truth. A truth that is constructed and deconstructed continually showing us that we cannot yield to a single version of it. In a similar memory becomes a tool to justify one's own actions, and it is always, as Atwood shows us, a selective sort of memory that focuses on the issues most at heart for each character, justifying their actions and offering a version of events that changes according to the time and place of the recalling. Without the access to a singular and clear picture of the past, we need to distrust all ready-made myths and look between the lines for clues to their veracity.

Cunning

Atwood's Penelope is characterized by the same cunning and intelligence as Homer's. Additionally, her first person narration allows us to acknowledge the thinking behind her actions and words, revealing a more active and ironic character than the classic Penelope. Penelope of *The Penelopiad* is not only the object of the tale but the protagonist and narrating character. She narrates her life in flashback, in hindsight, with the knowledge and the maturity gained after living it. This gives her the option to explain but also to comment on the background of each of her actions, making us privy to her thoughts and plans. Her most famous trickeries – the shroud and the bed – are recalled and explained in greater detail, and others, unnoticed in Homer's version, are for the first time brought to light.

As in *Toi, Pénélope,* the queen of *The Penelopiad* identifies her husband immediately despite his disguise, and when, later on, she asks Eurycleia to wash his feet, she is quite conscious that this will lead to the recognition of Odysseus by the old nurse. Moreover, she reveals that her decision to propose the bow contest to the suitors had been a direct consequence of Odysseus' return, and that her testing him at the end with the bed was a calculated trick to make *him* wait, for once, and also to reassure him of her reliability and seriousness. We learn also of her decision to use the maids to spy on the suitors and of her being constantly informed by them, and so being aware of everything happening around her well before it was formally announced. However she had to show surprise, shed her tears, play her part following the customs and tradition of her time. Entering her thoughts, we discover that she considered Telemachus "a spoiled child", Helen the person who had ruined her life, Odysseus a liar and an unscrupulous man, and that she doubted the very existence of the gods and the truth of Odysseus' stories.

We discover from her recalling of her youth, how she had to learn very early to be self-sufficient, due to the absence of her mother – "My mother, like all Naiads, was beautiful but chilly at heart. [...] She preferred swimming

in the river to the care of small children, and I often slipped her mind"[58] —
and her father's attempt on her life: "I could see that I would have to look out
for myself in the world. I could hardly count on family support."[59] Though
not particularly beautiful she is singled out for her intelligence, a quality that
characterized her from an early age and seemed to be the main attribute bestowed on her by people: "I was smart, though: considering the times, very
smart. That seems to be what I was known for: being smart."[60] She was also
well aware that being smart was not the main attribute looked for by a husband in her time, though she could be chosen for her kindness:

> I was a kind girl [...]. I was clever [...] but cleverness is a quality a
> man likes to have in his wife as long as she is some distance away
> from him. Up close, he'll take kindness any day of the week, if there's
> nothing more alluring to be had.[61]

Once married to Odysseus and left alone in Ithaca she shows her skills by
becoming, without previous teaching or experience, a good manager of her
husband's estate and soon gaining the "reputation as a smart bargainer".[62]

The shroud

The scheme of the shroud is recalled by Penelope in one of the central
chapters. Here, as in Homer's version, Penelope tells the suitors that she will
decide on a new husband after having completed the weaving of a shroud
for Laertes, but secretly she unravels during the night the work done in the
day. Though the basic facts are the same, in *The Penelopiad* we learn some
details that are not disclosed or are only implied in Homer's version. By accessing Penelope's thoughts we have a more coherent portrait of the queen.
Her wisdom and her pragmatism are confirmed both in her scheme of the
shroud and in her attributing it to the goddess Athena, since "crediting some
god for one's inspiration was always a good way to avoid accusations of pride
should the scheme succeed, as well as the blame if it did not."[63] She shows
herself to be continuously aware of the gaze of others on her, and all of her
actions have two aims: the official and formal one and the hidden one.

So, she is aware that no one could oppose the weaving as "it was so extremely pious",[64] while building up her image as a serious and diligent wife

58. Atwood, *The Penelopiad*, 10-11.
59. Atwood, *The Penelopiad*, 11.
60. Atwood, *The Penelopiad*, 21.
61. Atwood, *The Penelopiad*, 29.
62. Atwood, *The Penelopiad*, 88.
63. Atwood, *The Penelopiad*, 112.
64. Atwood, *The Penelopiad*, 113.

"saying melancholy things like, 'This shroud would be a fitter garment for
me than for Laertes, wretched that I am, and doomed by the gods to a life
that is a living death' ".[65] Penelope plays with her image of faithful and passive wife and shows how this is intentionally constructed to convince the
suitors of her goodwill.

More information is disclosed here by the queen. On this occasion she
has chosen twelve maidservants that could help her with the task. She chose
from among the youngest ones, as they "had been with me all their lives".[66]
These were the only ones who knew about the unweaving of the shroud during the night. "It was they who helped me to pick away at my weaving, behind locked doors, at dead of night, and by torchlight, for more than three
years."[67] The atmosphere surrounding the three years is described by Penelope as full of "hilarity" and "complicity"; and she adds: "We were almost
like sisters."[68]

Even the secret's betrayal by one of the maids is considered an accident
by Penelope due to the young age of the maids: "I am sure it was an accident: the young are careless, and she must have let slip a hint or a word".[69]
The trickery of the shroud is doubled here by the revelation of another
stratagem conceived by the queen and undetected in Homer's version. Penelope had told the twelve maids to spy on the suitors "using whatever en-
ticing arts they could invent",[70] without revealing her plan to anyone, not
even Eurycleia. She even instructed them "to say rude and disrespectful
things about me and Telemachus, and about Odysseus as well, in order to
further the illusion".[71]

This information is central to the plot of *The Penelopiad* as it shows the
full innocence of the twelve maids, unjustly hanged by Odysseus on the basis of their supposed betrayal. Penelope, reconsidering her plan, realizes her
error and feels responsible for their death but, as she affirms, "I was running
out of time, and becoming desperate, and I had to use every ruse and stratagem at my command."[72] The scheme of the shroud was ultimately discovered, and the suitors "were very angry, not least because they'd been fooled
by a woman".[73] Penelope's plan fails, and her true aim is revealed.

65. Atwood, *The Penelopiad*, 113.
66. Atwood, *The Penelopiad*, 113.
67. Atwood, *The Penelopiad*, 114.
68. Atwood, *The Penelopiad*, 214.
69. Atwood, *The Penelopiad*, 115.
70. Atwood, *The Penelopiad*, 115.
71. Atwood, *The Penelopiad*, 117.
72. Atwood, *The Penelopiad*, 118.
73. Atwood, *The Penelopiad*, 118.

However, she is not overwhelmed by this defeat. She just needs to find new tricks, using the maids as sources of information, without exposing her cunning and continuing to maintain for the suitors her image of passive woman. Recalling her actions, the Penelope of today justifies her plan as the only way to defend herself. She does not agree with her name being attached to "Penelope's web" because "if the shroud was a web, then I was a spider. But I had not been attempting to catch men like flies: on the contrary, I'd merely been trying to avoid entanglement myself."[74] Atwood's object here is not only to illuminate the reasons for Penelope's actions but also to rectify interpretations that have long been given to these same actions, and so to dismantle all sorts of prejudice and bias that have been attached to the myth of Penelope over the centuries. By giving herself a voice, for the first time the queen can defend herself and explain her reasons, and lift the ambiguities and enigmas that have marked her as a character in Homer's poem.

The bow

The episode of the bow and axes takes new forms and meanings in *The Penelopiad*. The trial of the bow reenters here as part of a new plan devised by Penelope when she realizes that her husband is finally back, disguised as a beggar and looking for revenge. While in Homer's version Penelope is the last to recognize Odysseus, in Atwood's she is actually the first (if we do not consider Telemachus to whom Odysseus reveals his identity intentionally), though she keeps the secret to herself. His disguise comes as no surprise for her: "I would have expected no less of him",[75] she affirms in recalling the events.

She reads Odysseus' mind and knows that only his cunning can give him hope of taking back his throne: "He shouldn't simply march in and announce that he was Odysseus, and order them to vacate the premises. If he'd tried that he'd have been a dead man within minutes."[76] She also understands his decision to conceal his identity from her, and through her irony she shows her ability to take advantage of her husband's weaknesses: "If a man takes pride in his disguising skills, it would be a foolish wife who would claim to recognize him: it's always an imprudence to step between a man and the reflection of his own cleverness."[77] When beggar-Odysseus comes to see her in the evening she is well aware of his hidden identity. She has already decided to propose to the suitors the trial of the bow; she knows well that only

74. Atwood, *The Penelopiad*, 119.
75. Atwood, *The Penelopiad*, 136.
76. Atwood, *The Penelopiad*, 136.
77. Atwood, *The Penelopiad*, 137.

Odysseus can succeed in stringing it. She decides, however, to "flatter him by consulting him for advice".[78]

Her aim in recalling the events is to clarify that the arrival of Odysseus and the test of the bow were not a coincidence but were linked and intentionally crafted. In the same way she explains that the recognition of Odysseus by Eurycleia had also been set up by her, that she was not only aware of it but had deliberately planned it. "The songs say I didn't notice a thing because Athena had distracted me. If you believe that, you'll believe all sorts of nonsense. In reality I'd turned my back on the two of them to hide my silent laughter at the success of my little surprise."[79] The Penelope of *The Penelopiad* explains clearly what could only be inferred from Homer's version. She shows the perfect coherence between her cunning intelligence and her actions.

The bed

The queen's last trick also assumes a new meaning once we consider that she is aware of Odysseus' return. In her plan she could not forecast the slaughter of her twelve maids and this news sorrows her particularly. She needs time to disguise her true feelings from Odysseus, so she intentionally decides to tease him, refusing to recognize him immediately as he would have hoped, and instead making him wait, so taking a small revenge for the long years that she had been waiting for him. She acts the part of the faithful and serious wife, testing him in connection with the bed before finally deciding to "go through the business of recognizing him"[80] and accepting him as her spouse.

The events surrounding the return of Odysseus to Ithaca in *The Penelopiad* follow the same plot as Homer's poem. However here Penelope, unveiling in retrospective the hidden thoughts behind her actions is shown to have been a perfect master of disguise, capable of playing tricks on even the most skilled of the Greek heroes, Odysseus. Her husband is so much taken by himself and his plan for revenge that he does not consider the possibility of being recognized by his wife or revealing to her his identity. Penelope professes to understand the reasons behind his secrecy, but her teasing and testing him shows her desire to take her revenge.

Directness and Irony

One original characteristic of Atwood's novel in contrast to Homer's version is the use of irony and directness in the dialogues of the characters,

78. Atwood, *The Penelopiad,* 138.
79. Atwood, *The Penelopiad,* 140-141.
80. Atwood, *The Penelopiad,* 117.

which allows the reader to acknowledge their deeper thoughts and feelings and suffuses the plot with a new modernity. Penelope, for example, shows her cunning not only through her well-known tricks but also in the way she uses language, being frank and direct and at the same time turning the weapon of irony against her antagonists. This is shown in the chapters that describe her life in Hades, where her spirit, free from earthly conventions, displays openly her formerly hidden thoughts. An example is her meeting with the spirit of Antinous[81] whom she encounters while wandering in Hades. Antinous walks with "an arrow through his neck" in memory of the death he suffered by the hands of Odysseus. Penelope asks him to remove the arrow from his neck and to tell her the truth about the suitors' motives in wanting to marry her. So Antinous takes off his mask and reveals the plain truth: "We wanted the treasure trove, [...] not to mention the kingdom, [...] you weren't exactly a Helen, but we could have dealt with that [...]. All the better that you were twenty years older than us – you'd die first."[82] To the frank answer of Antinous Penelope responds with blunt directness: "'Thank you for your frankness' I said coldly. 'It must be a relief to you to express your real feeling for once. You can put the arrow back now. To tell you the truth, I feel a surge of joy every time I see it sticking through your lying, gluttonous neck.'"[83]

Penelope's relation with Helen is marked in the same way by caustic and sharp irony and the direct exchange of lines that find their apogee in one of the last chapters of the book entitled "Helen takes a bath".[84] In Hades, while wondering through the asphodel, Penelope sees Helen "followed by her customary horde of male spirits, all of them twittering with anticipation".[85] Helen tells Penelope that she is going to her bath and the large crowd is following her because "Desire does not die with the body [...] only the ability to satisfy it"[86]. The two women's antagonistic relation is expressed in a direct and witty interchange. Penelope accuses Helen of the men's deaths: "So you're washing their blood off your hands' [...] I hadn't realized you were capable of guilt." And Helen answers by the same tone: "Tell me, little duck – how many men did Odysseus butcher because of you? [...] I am sure you felt more important because of it. Maybe you even felt prettier."[87]

---

81. Atwood, *The Penelopiad,* 99-108.
82. Atwood, *The Penelopiad,* 102.
83. Atwood, *The Penelopiad,* 102-103.
84. Atwood, *The Penelopiad,* 153-156.
85. Atwood, *The Penelopiad,* 153.
86. Atwood, *The Penelopiad,* 155.
87. Atwood, *The Penelopiad,* 156.

The conventional and formal dialogues are replaced by a quick and frank exchange that gives a new modernity to the classical characterization of Helen and Penelope and amuses the readers.

Conclusion

Atwood's book has been called feminist by many critics, but Atwood has not agreed with that label; according to her, critics tend to call feminist all books narrated from the perspective of a woman, and this, like most of her books, has women as focal characters without aiming to convey a specific feminist message. Certainly Atwood's Penelope shows the characteristics of a strong and intelligent woman who had to play the part of a patient and faithful wife but who has always been in control of her actions.

On the opposite side is Helen, who plays the role of the antagonistic female character and represents a sort of negative of Penelope. Such antagonism between women is characteristic of other novels by Atwood (i.e. Elaine and Cordelia in *Cat's eye* and Iris and Laura in *The Blind Assassin*), and it follows the writer's doubts concerning a universal women sisterhood or even friendship. Penelope and Helen are two very different female characters at the heart of the plot whose lives are parallel and sometimes negatively intersect. Helen is described in very negative terms. Despite her beauty and attractiveness to men that have enshrined her as a mythical character for generations to come, she is described as a superficial and selfish woman who has no concern for others and who measures her own value by the number of men who have died for her sake. Her escape with Paris to Troy has been the first cause of the war and of the departure of Odysseus, changing forever the destiny of Penelope. In Homer's *Odyssey,* Penelope justifies Helen and is the only character sympathetic to her; but here Helen is considered the main cause of her troubles, which is made clear by the title of the chapter narrating the departure of Odysseus for war: "Helen ruins my life".[88]

While Homer's Penelope blames the gods for Helen's behavior, in *The Penelopiad* Helen's vanity alone is the cause of the war. Penelope intends to reestablish an historical truth, and her tale deconstructs the myths behind major characters like Helen and Odysseus, showing them with their ordinary weaknesses. Odysseus, in a similar way, loses in *The Penelopiad* the aura of mythical heroism and intelligence that has carried him to fame and is shown to be an arrogant and unscrupulous man, "a cheat and a thief",[89] who is rather easily tricked by his wife. Moreover, his double standard of

88. Atwood, *The Penelopiad*, 71-80.
89. Atwood, *The Penelopiad*, 31.

sexual conduct in relation to his wife and to the maids is denounced by Penelope, who displays in this respect an assertive stance in respect to marriage — showing her jealousy for his adulteries with Circe and Calypso while denouncing his expectations of faithfulness by her and by the maids.

One of the main differences from Homer's version is the introduction of the narrating voice of the twelve hanged maids. They provide a different version of events, offering the perspective of the slaves, a social class that has no voice in the Homeric poem. In both Penelope's and the maids' version, it appears clearly that they are victims of a deep injustice perpetrated by both Penelope and Odysseus. An injustice that is not recognized even by the modern court where the case is discussed[90] shows how justice and truth are relative concepts and are constrained by the ones who have the power and can decide what is right or wrong.

Penelope does not escape the accusation of being implicated in the death of the girls, and she is also shown to be part of the powerful elite who can decide on the life and death of others. The novel, by giving voice to different perspectives, implies that the truth is not unique and universally agreed upon. Even toward the end of the novel we cannot be certain of the truth of Penelope's version of events as Atwood's heroine continues to make new and surprising revelations.

The cunning but largely passive character of the *Odyssey* corresponds here to a very determined and unscrupulous woman who craftily plays her role and, in the same way as Odysseus, uses others for selfish ends. Along with the other female characters, she initiates the action while leaving male characters with the impression that they are directing events. Atwood's aim is to rewrite the myth of Penelope and the other characters transmitted to us by Homer — re-elaborating his figures through modern ideas of justice and gender equality. Like Northrop Frye in his *Anatomy of Criticism*,[91] she believes in the importance of archetypes and myths in the construction of our identity and in the use and re-use of them within literature. From this perspective, the myth of Penelope's passivity is challenged by the revelations made by Penelope herself and by the maids. For the epic's passive queen is substituted an astute and crafty woman who is not only aware of her role but extremely adept at disguising it.

90. See Atwood, *The Penelopiad*, ch. XXVI "The Chorus Line: The Trial of Odysseus, as Videotaped by the Maids", 175-184.

91. Northrop Frye, *Anatomy of Criticism: Four Essays*, (Princeton: Princeton University Press, 1957).

CHAPTER 5

SILVANA LA SPINA: PENELOPE (1998)

E in questi anni ho compreso che quando una donna è stata per un certo tempo realmente padrona della sua vita, non è più sposa di nessuno. E la sua casa non sarà più la casa dell'uomo che parte e ritorna a suo piacimento, ma ne cercherà qualcuna altrove – o forse nessuna.[1]

The novel *Penelope* by Silvana La Spina, published in 1998, is chronologically the first of the three novels analyzed here but certainly the least known internationally. The writer Silvana La Spina is considered by Italian critics one of the most interesting Italian writers of this generation. Born in Padoa, from a Venetian mother and Sicilian father, La Spina lives between Catania and Milan and is strongly linked to her Sicilian roots, which emerge in her language and in the plots of her novels.

She has published various kinds of novels, from historical novels to 'romanzo giallo' (police stories). Among her main works we can remember *Morte a Palermo* (1987), *L'ultimo treno da Catania* (1992), *Quando Marte è in Capricorno* (1994), *Un inganno dei sensi malizioso* (1995), *L'amante del paradiso* (1997), *La create Antonia* (2001). Three of her last novels, *Uno sbirro femmina* (2007), *La bambina pericolosa* (2008) and *Un cadavere eccellente* (2011), have as main protagonist a woman 'commissario', chief of police, Maria

---

1. Silvana La Spina, *Penelope*, (Milano: La Tartaruga, 1998), 136-7. "And over the years I realized that when a woman has been for a time actually in control of her life, she cannot be anymore somebody's wife. And her house will never be the house of the man that goes and returns to his liking, but she will look for another one somewhere else – or perhaps no."

Laura Gangemi, while her latest work *L'uomo che veniva da Messina* (2015) recalls the life of the Renaissance Sicilian painter Antonello da Messina.

With *Penelope*, as in *Toi, Pénélope* and *The Penelopiad*, La Spina re-interprets the Greek myth by giving the narrating voice and point of view to the queen. The novel, however, presents some characteristics that connect it strongly to the Italian feminist context. First of all, there is particular emphasis given to the violence and abuses that Penelope suffers from both her father Icarus and her husband Odysseus. Violence against women and the institutionalization of this violence within family and marital relations are at the heart of the novel, and these are certainly central issues in contemporary Italian feminism.

Another central issue in the novel is the rejection of a sacrificial notion of motherhood, so central to Catholicism, which is replaced by the search for a non-hierarchical relation between Penelope and Telemachus. One quite interesting and original aspect of the novel is the strong relations that Penelope has with other women, some of whom are absent from the Homeric version. With them she has a relation of "entrustment", similar to the Italian feminist concept of "affidamento".

Moreover La Spina introduces in her novel the archaic figure of the Great Mother, the primordial goddess whose rites are forbidden because they connect women with their own powerful selves. Penelope gives voice to all the women who have been humiliated, violated, or imprisoned for the sake of traditions and customs. She shows herself, however, to be a most exceptional woman; through violence and suffering she is able to choose the man she loves, Cleone di Lesbo, one of the suitors who will ultimately be killed by Odysseus in his final revenge. In the unpredictable final chapter Penelope decides to leave her husband and travel from court to court together with the least likely of friends, Euryclea, the old nurse of Odysseus. In fact, the two women, after a difficult relation marked by jealousy and lack of reciprocal trust, finally find support in each other's friendship and decide together to leave Ithaca, as friends, to enjoy their freedom.

La Spina's version of the Homeric myth draws largely from Greek mythology, blending well known myths and modern re-elaborations. Myths are central, but they are only the raw material on which the author skillfully embroiders her terribly modern story of women silenced by a destiny decided by others.

Plot

It is an autumn evening like many others in Ithaca. Ulysses has returned from Troy after twenty long years. He has accomplished his terrible revenge against the suitors and now, after retaking his place as king, is recalling his adventures to his drunken friends in the hall downstairs. He will go away again soon. Penelope is in her room, in the upper floor and hears his voice. She hears him saying that he does not want to leave his wife again but she knows he is lying. He is "Bugiardo. Menzognero."[2] Penelope recalls the night of the massacre and the strong desire she felt to kill him, but she did not want to antagonize the gods. He would have gone away soon anyway. She is known to be patient, "Penelope, la paziente."[3]

From this moment Penelope starts a long narrative flashback, recalling her life, her sufferings, the violence to which she had fallen victim since childhood adding grim and previously hidden details to her story. Her first memories go back to the sexual abuses she suffered from her own father, Icarius, who was secretly entering her bed when she was still a child. Having discovered her pregnancy, Icarius, to hide his wrong doings, offered her to the goddess Artemis as one of her priestesses. As priestess of Artemis during the festival dedicated to the goddess she had to lay with one of the men, covered by a mask, entering in the temple. Her sufferings, however, were not finished yet. Penelope is pregnant and on the point of giving birth when one night a soldier, Nauplio, sent by Icarius, comes to take her to Delphi under her father's order. During the sea voyage he tries to drown her, and in that moment Penelope gives birth to a monstrous child with two small horns on his head. She sees the child only for a moment before he disappears in the sea: "Un bambino. Bruno. Nero. Con due piccole corna sulla testa. Che si rotolò tra la schiuma, subito. E sparì nel mare."[4] In the meantime a group of wild ducks appears and takes her to safety after having skinned alive Nauplio. She is taken back to the temple of Artemis by the ducks, while the news of her rescue spreads in Sparta as a prodigy.

When her uncle, Tindarus, and her father come to visit her, she notices the presence of a beautiful girl, also a priestess living in the temple. Her name is Melissa. She is the daughter of a priest belonging to the Ioti, a people kept slave by the Spartans, and of a Spartan noblewoman. The Ioti had not always been slaves. They had been reduced to slavery by the Acheans. They had lost everything but not their religious belief in the goddess "la Magnifica",[5] or simply "la Dea",[6] 'the Goddess' as they called her. The worship of

---

2. Silvana La Spina, *Penelope*, (Milano: La Tartaruga, 1998), 9. "Liar. Mendacious". My translation.

3. La Spina, *Penelope*, 11. "Penelope, the patient".

4. La Spina, *Penelope*, 19."A child. Dark. Black. With two small horns on the head. Who rolled down in the foam, immediately. And disappeared in the sea".

5. La Spina, *Penelope*, 22.

6. La Spina, *Penelope*, 24.

the Goddess could be traced back to the island of Crete, as Samo, one of the priests of Artemis, reveals to Penelope. But the worship of the Goddess is forbidden and needs to be kept secret. Melissa, a worshipper of the Goddess, has the gift of prophecy. After one year as a priestess of Artemis, Penelope is permitted to leave the temple; in the meantime Melissa disappears. Penelope returns to the palace of Tindareus, and her cousin Clitemnestra is chosen as wife for Agamemnon. One day Melissa arrives at the palace and asks Penelope to follow her into the forest outside the walls of Sparta to assist in a celebration for the Goddess. Marfissa, the old priestess, confides that the Goddess was the first divinity, followed later by all the other gods. Penelope becomes a priestess of the Goddess and participates in ceremonies in the cave in the following months, always in secret. One day, however, Melissa is killed, and Penelope realizes that her father, Icarus, had ordered her murder. Penelope is devastated and starts mourning her friend.

Time passes, and it is now the turn of her cousin Helen, Tindareus' stepdaughter and Clitemnestra's sister, to be married. Suitors arrive at the palace, and Penelope hears for the first time the name of Odysseus, who has helped Tindareus avoid trouble once Menelaus was chosen as Helen's spouse. In exchange for his help, Odysseus had asked for Penelope to be his wife. The first time Penelope meets Odysseus she is not particularly impressed by him: "Niente di speciale, fu quello che pensai. Un furbetto dai capelli rossi e le gambe tozze, ancora troppo giovane per aver partecipato a tutte le imprese che di lui si raccontavano."[7] But she realizes that her father Icarius is jealous of Odysseus, and just for revenge she decides to become his wife. She elopes with him, and when Icarius follows them she covers her face with a veil, as required of her by Odysseus, to show that she is already his spouse. Penelope begins a new life in Ithaca. When she arrives, both Eurycleia, the old nurse of Odysseus, and Anticlea, his mother, are hostile to her. Odysseus leaves her alone to go hunting and disappears for months.

One day flooding endangers the lives of the people of Ithaca, and Penelope decides to shelter everyone in the palace. After this she is accepted as the new queen, and when Odysseus returns he reveals that he had left her alone to see how she would manage the palace without him. Penelope soon realizes she is pregnant. One day Eurycleia takes her to visit Ilizia, an old lady who can read the future. The old woman realizes upon her hands that Penelope is a priestess of the Goddess and says that she will protect her.

---

7. La Spina, *Penelope*, 47-48. "Nothing special, that's what I thought. A cheeky guy, with red hair and stubby legs, too young to have participated to all the ventures bestowed to him".

Penelope begins to discover the cruel side of Odysseus' character and starts hating him. One episode that she recalls involves Argo, Odysseus' dog, who ate the kittens of her cat Scilla. One day Agamennon and other kings arrive to Ithaca to take Odysseus to the war against Troy. At first, Odysseus makes a show of being insane by plowing his fields with salt, but when Palamede takes the infant Telemachus from Penelope's arms and puts him in front of the plow, Odysseus is forced to drop his pretense and follow them to war. However he will never forgive Palamede and will take his terrible revenge against him in Troy.

Odysseus leaves, and for many years there is no news. However there does arrive at the palace news of the sufferings of the women, Greek or Trojan, directly or indirectly involved in the war. Like Laodamia, wife of Protesilao, who committed suicide at the news of the death of her husband, or Andromaca who lost her husband, Hector, and saw her small child, Astianatte, killed in front of her eyes, or Cassandra taken as slave by Agamennon. And then Ifigenia, Criseide and Clitemnestra, this last the murderer of her husband Agamennon and killed in turn by her own son Oreste.

Eleven years have elapsed since the start of the war. Anticlea, Odysseus' old mother, dies without seeing her son, and Penelope knows that other women will die as well. One of the servants, Taminia, is seduced by a young noble man, Alcinoo, who together with others moved to the palace to convince the queen to remarry. Taminia, seduced and pregnant, hangs herself from a tree, as Peribea, the mother of Penelope, had done when Penelope was just a child. In the meantime more and more suitors arrive at the palace. Penelope cannot avoid them, and she cannot rely on anyone for help. When she feels the presence of her dead friend Melissa advising her to pray to the Goddess, Penelope begins to participate in the secret rituals to worship the Goddess even though Eurycleia tries to dissuade her. One of the suitors, Anfinomo, attracts her particular attention. He is the kindest of them all, and she begins to treat him with more familiarity than the others.

Her son Telemachus and Eurycleia, however, show their contrariety. Telemachus is sixteen and jealous of his mother. He cannot accept the idea of any other man being next to her. It is the same for Eurycleia, who rebukes Penelope for her intimacy with the suitors. In response Penelope sticks her hand with the needle she is using to sew, reminding the old nurse of her place. The queen's fancy is taken by Anfinomo, and she decides to invite him to her rooms. She prepares herself to receive him, but when he arrives she realizes that he is afraid of her and that he does not really love her as a woman but only as a queen. Later on, paying closer attention to details, she finally grasps that Anfinomo's interest is for someone else — not for one of the younger and more beautiful maids but in fact

for her son Telemachus who, conscious of being the object of desire, ex-
changes with his mother a satisfied smirk.

The time arrives for Telemachus to receive the traditional initiation into
manhood. Laertes informs Penelope that Mentor will kidnap him, as is the
custom, and will take him away to the mountains where through the rituals of Apollo he will become a man. Telemachus is gone for months; when
he comes back he is no longer a boy, now he is recognized as a man. Penelope enlists her nicest maid, Melantho, to separate Telemachus from Mentor, but after two days he throws the girl back at his mother's feet accusing
Melantho of being the lover of Alcinous.

Penelope knows that keeping the suitors in the palace will only create
troubles but she does not know what else to do. One day, while celebrating
the secret rituals of the Goddess, Melissa speaks to her through the voice
of Eurycleia and indicates a path to follow: she needs to gain time by telling the suitors she will choose the new spouse once the shroud for Laertes
is finished. All the suitors, and Antinous in particular, deplore the slow pace
of the queen's labor, but Telemachus refutes their accusations. One day Penelope realizes she has woven into the shroud the figure of a man: he is Cleone coming from Lesbos. She immediately unravels the work, but Melantho reveals it to Antinous, who accuses Penelope of unravelling in the night
the work done in the day. At that moment the herald announces the arrival
of a new suitor: Cleone of Lesbos. For Penelope it is love at first sight. Cleone is not like the other suitors. He is kind and handsome and of royal de-
scent. He does not stay in the palace, but prefers to rent a place for himself.
He comes more and more often to visit Penelope. He is able to write and Penelope orders that all the names of the people in the palace should be written on a cloth. Cleone is knowledgeable about the Goddess, and he tells Penelope that she is celebrated in Lesbos. Penelope then breaks her oath of
secrecy and reveals to Cleone that she is herself a priestess of the Goddess.
They then meet secretly in the cave where the ceremonies to the Goddess
take place, and they become lovers. Telemachus suspects something and decides to go to Sparta to seek news of his father. He leaves against the will of
Penelope, who has concerns for his life. She fears that he knows about her
relations with Cleone and that he is jealous.

Penelope also senses that Odysseus is coming back, and she asks to Cleone to leave Ithaca with her. The young man, however, refuses; he wants to
marry her and live in Ithaca lawfully. Telemachus returns from his journey
and informs Penelope that Odysseus is alive and will soon come back. He
also tells her of the arrival of a new guest, a beggar. Penelope immediately
senses danger; she runs to inform Cleone and ask him to leave Ithaca, but
she cannot find him and is told that he is away hunting. Back in the palace

Telemachus introduces her to the old beggar just arrived. She understands from his angry gaze that he is Odysseus. She decides to wait for the night to find Cleone and convince him to escape from Ithaca, but Odysseus stops her on the stairs and forces her back to her rooms. Penelope then asks Eurycleia to go to Cleone and command him to leave Ithaca as he is now in danger. The next day she finds out that Cleone is still there, at the dinner table. She goes looking for Eurycleia but cannot find her. All doors of the palace have been locked, and she cannot return to the salon where dinner is taking place. Penelope cannot do anything. She directs her anger at the maidens but she cannot leave her rooms. She hears Odysseus killing the suitors. Only Cleone is left, and it is Telemachus who asks his father to kill him. At that moment Penelope curses Telemachus and all of his descendents.

Everything is finished. Penelope is now in her rooms. It is autumn again. Penelope and Eurycleia are together. They hear the drunken Odysseus downstairs with his friends, recalling his adventures with Circe and Calypso. Eurycleia asks forgiveness of Penelope for failing to inform Cleone, and Penelope, remembering Eurycleia burying him out of piety, forgives her and decides that they will go away together as friends, leaving Ithaca forever. The last part of the story is narrated by Eurycleia. Years have passed and no one has ever found them. She also wished to leave Ithaca. She remembers the dead maidens, killed unjustly, and Anticlea who lived all her life with the guilt of a son, Odysseus, who was not Laertes'. Their departure has been kept secret by Odysseus. No one knows about them; in the closing words of Penelope, true freedom is silent: "La vera libertà è silenziosa."[8]

The theme of Penelope

A quick look at the plot of *Penelope* by La Spina reveals immediately how the author, playing with the material provided by Homer, has reread the myth of Penelope to show the human side of a women considered an archetype in Greek mythology. It is Penelope herself who narrates her story, a story that remained secret within the Homeric epics. It is the story of a woman who has been wounded, humiliated in her femininity but who still has been able to take back what men – her father, husband, son, suitors – had taken away: her freedom.

Penelope's story is conveyed through the memories and emotions of the past that she reveals to the old maid Eurycleia, while downstairs the drunken Odysseus narrates his adventures to his friends. Penelope as described by La

8. La Spina, *Penelope*, 138.

Spina is not the patient wife waiting for the return of her spouse, but rather a woman who has suffered abuse by her father, has been abandoned by her husband and has lived a prohibited love outside marriage. She is a woman who prays for the non-return of her husband, Odysseus, a cruel and violent man almost sadistic in his use of power over his wife and court. The Penelope who narrates the story is a disillusioned and bitter woman who has lost the only man she really loved, Cleone, and who no longer feels love for the other men of her life: Laertes, Telemachus and Odysseus.

They have all, with their selfishness, jealousy and cruelty, contributed to her sufferings. Penelope finds support over the years through the special bonds she develops with other women: first with Melissa, the priestess of the Goddess, who introduces her to the primordial and forbidden religion of the Great Mother, then with Anticlea and Eurycleia, the mother and old nurse of Odysseus, who distrust her initially but then discover they are united by a common destiny as women living in a world dominated by men. In the novel Penelope becomes the symbol of all the women oppressed by traditions, by patriarchal norms and violence who are yet somehow able to liberate themselves and to make their own decisions despite their oppression, and by virtue of a special bonding they are able to establish among themselves. The secret veneration of the Great Mother, the Goddess who existed before all other gods, witnesses the ancient power of women, denied by men through a strict prohibition of the cult.

The images of men in the novel completely overturn the heroic portrayals transmitted from Homer and Greek mythology. None of the male figures seems to correspond to their celebrated homonyms in the *Odyssey*. From Icarius to Laertes, from Odysseus to Telemachus, there is neither heroism nor humanity in the men who use power to subjugate the weak and in particular women. Icarius, the father of Penelope, is the first of these sad figures that Penelope describes. "L'Icario generoso con i poveri, i mendichi, le vedove e gli infanti derelitti. L'Icario comandante della fedelissima falange di spartiati, scorta privata del re suo fratello."[9]

A man renowned for his valor who within the walls of his house is raping his young daughter and driving his wife to suicide. Penelope remembers the day she found the dead body of her mother hanging from the fig tree the father had planted at Penelope's birth. "Avremmo dovuto leggervi un segno?"[10] she asks herself. Hanging herself on that particular tree seems

9. La Spina, *Penelope*, 13. "Icarius generous with the poors, the beggars, the widows and the orphans. Icarius the commander of the loyal private army escorting the king and his brother."
10. La Spina, *Penelope*, 38. "Should we consider it a sign?"

to be a clear signal that her mother knew one day Icarius would use violence on his daughter, this is the reason she killed herself on the tree that
had a special link to Penelope. In fact it was right after the death of her
mother that Icarius entered Penelope's bed and used violence on her. After
her pregnancy was revealed, Icarius forced her to serve in the temple of Artemis, where young girls had to sleep with men masked as gods. Then he
sent a young man, Nauplio, ostensibly to take her back to Sparta but actually to kill her at sea. She was saved by a flock of ducks who killed Nauplio,
and she gave birth to a dark boy-child with horns who immediately disappeared into the sea.

Penelope cannot forgive her father, and her decision to accept the pro-
posal of Odysseus is linked to her desire to escape from Icarius. When Odysseus leaves for the Trojan War, Penelope never considers going back to
Sparta because she does not want to see her father again. Still, she cannot
escape from the cruelty of men. When Odysseus, "un furbetto dai capelli
rossi"[11] asks for her as wife, Penelope looks at the face of her father and realizes "la rabbia. L'ira più tremenda."[12] She even suspects that Icarius might
order the murder of Odysseus, as he had done with Melissa. So, to take her
revenge on the father, Penelope decides to escape with Odysseus. She leaves
with him early in the morning, and when the father and a group of armed
men follow them to take Penelope back, Odysseus orders her to cover her
face with a veil to signify the fact that she is already his spouse. Penelope en-
joys her revenge: "Oh Dea, come fu dolce la tua vendetta."[13]

Her sufferings at men's hands do not end with her departure from Sparta.
As soon as they arrive in Ithaca, Odysseus leaves her alone in a new house
and with people that she does not know. Here Penelope will have to find her
own strength and demonstrate her value to the people of Ithaca, as well as
to Anticlea and Euryclea who try to patronize her. By taking the lead during
the flood and allowing all the people of Ithaca inside the security of the palace, she gains the respect of the people around her. When Odysseus comes
back and reveals that he knowingly put her to the test to see if she would be
able to confront his mother and old nurse, Penelope begins to resent his cruelty and feels the first signs of rage hardening her heart: "Non farlo mai più,
ti prego Odisseo. Già il mio amore per te è un poco morto, già sento mettere
radici al rancore e una rabbia quieta, ma costante mi indurisce il cuore."[14]

11. La Spina, *Penelope*, 48. "a red hair, foxy boy".
12. La Spina, *Penelope*, 48. "the anger. The most terrible rage".
13. La Spina, *Penelope*, 49. "Oh Goddess, how sweet it was the revenge you gave me."
14. La Spina, *Penelope*, 74. "Don't do it again, I beg you Odysseus. My love for you is al-
    ready partly dead, I already feel that resentment is putting down its roots and a calm
    but constant rage is hardening my heart."

Soon Penelope becomes pregnant, Telemachus is born, and Odysseus has to leave for the war. Long years of loneliness ensue, fifteen years pass, the war finishes, but Odysseus does not come back. Penelope feels the presence of her old friend Melissa who advises her to ask the Goddess for protection. From Ilizia, the old clairvoyant, she learns the site of the rituals and decides to observe them. During one celebration the voice of Melissa advises her to buy time by weaving a shroud for Laertes. Meanwhile Telemachus shows signs of jealousy towards the suitors that are arriving. He fears that the mother might choose the young Anfinomo, the kindest among them. Though Telemachus loves his mother, he cannot accept her sleeping with a man who is not Odysseus.

> Gelosia. Era questo il tarlo di Telemaco. Una gelosia furiosa, omicida, di chi teme la perdita del bene più caro. Gliel'avevo vista da qualche tempo nascere nello sguardo, gonfiare come un bubbone pestifero, e da lì germogliare fino a raggiungere i precordi. Gelosia. Il mostro dai mille occhi, la medusa che impietrisce l'animo e travisa ogni nostro gesto, atto, sospiro.[15]

As Telemachus becomes a man he internalizes the principles associated to manhood, the violence and cruelty that Odysseus and the other men embody. He ineluctably takes side with his father Odysseus, considering Penelope the property of her husband. Telemachus is not concerned with Penelope's happiness; he cares only about keeping his father's throne. When he realizes that Penelope has a relation with Cleone, he tries to prevent his mother from seeing him. The full dimension of Telemachus' hate for Cleone and his desire for revenge become clear in the final scene, when Odysseus has massacred all the other suitors and would perhaps have spared Cleone, had not Telemachus pushed him to kill: "No, padre, no. Non devi lasciare vivere proprio Cleone. Tu non sai ..."[16] This is the moment at which Penelope curses Telemachus and his descendents: "In quel momento ho maledetto Telemaco e tutta la sua stirpe."[17]

15. La Spina, *Penelope*, 94. "Jealousy. This was the obsession of Telemachus. A furious, murderous jealousy felt by the one who fears the loss of the dearest affection. I had seen it growing in the gaze, grow as a pestiferous swelling and from there sprout up to the heart. Jealousy. The monster of the thousand eyes, the medusa who hardens the soul and distorts each of our gesture, act, whisper".

16. La Spina, *Penelope*, 132. "No, father, no. You should not let Cleone live. You don't know...."

17. La Spina, *Penelope*, 132. "In that moment I have cursed Telemachus and all his descents."

Telemachus' desire for revenge towards the suitors, and towards Cleone in particular, associate him in Penelope's eyes with his father and his grand-father Icarius: "Lui, il figlio di Odisseo. Il nipote dell'osceno Icario."[18] As much as them he is cruel and brutal. He has instigated Odysseus to kill the only man that Penelope ever loved, thinking not of his mother's feelings but driven solely by the desire to take revenge. Icarius, Telemachus and Odys-seus are depicted by La Spina without the mythological and heroic aura we were accustomed to associate with them through the Greek epics. The phys-ical strength and bravery they show during the war conceal a dark and cruel side that is revealed in the personal and family relations. There is no love in their actions, only the desire to possess. This is even clearer in relation to the women nearest to them: mothers, wives, daughters. To be a man and a leader means to have no pity for the weakest and to be cruel. A man like Cle-one has no chance to impose his will on a world where only warriors can be-come leaders. This is clearly stated by Laertes when he confides to Penelope his thoughts about the young suitor, newly arrived in the palace: "Non è della pasta di Odisseo [...]. Non ha la forza di imporsi, non è un uomo di tempra, non è ...".[19] Before he terminates his sentence, Penelope completes it for him in her mind: ".... crudele, pensai, è questo che gli manca, la crudeltà. Come tutti voi, come Odisseo".[20]

Just before the arrival of Odysseus, Penelope reflects on the men in her life in a silent dialogue with her father, Icarius:

> [...] lui [Odisseo] in fondo non è diverso da te – è duro, violento, e, come te, mi ha sempre considerata una sua proprietà. Come Tele-maco mio figlio. Tutti uomini forti ma senza pietà, capaci di ucci-dere una giovane donna come Melissa, di condannare a morte un in-nocente come Palamede, di conservare il bisogno della vendetta nel cuore come Telemaco. Non siete come Cleone. Nessuno di voi lo è.[21]

Penelope is aware that Cleone is different from the other men and she loves him just for this reason. Moreover, this is the first time she could

---

18. La Spina, *Penelope*, 132. "He, the son of Odysseus. The nephew of the vile Icarius."

19. La Spina, *Penelope*, 107. "He does not have the temperament of Odysseus. He does not have the strength to impose himself, he is not a hard man, he is not..."

20. La Spina, *Penelope*, 107. " ...cruel, I thought, this is what he misses, cruelty. As all of you, as Odysseus."

21. La Spina, *Penelope*, 124. "Deep down he is not so different from you – he is hard, vio-lent, and, like you, has always considered me one of his properties. Just like Telema-chus my son. All strong men, but without pity, able to kill a young woman like Melissa, to send to death an innocent like Palamede, to keep the need for revenge in the heart like Telemachus. You are not like Cleone. None of you is like him."

choose her own lover: "E sono io che l'ho scelto."[22] The secret relations of Penelope with Cleone give a completely new perspective to her character. She is no more the faithful wife waiting for her spouse but a woman offended, violated and betrayed by the men nearest to her, one who finally finds happiness and freedom in a forbidden passion, outside marriage, with a man she has chosen for herself and who is the antithesis of the violent and cruel men who have made her suffer.

Memory

In this novel, even more than in the two previous ones, Penelope's memory is not an instrument to safeguard the *kleos* (the epic glory) of the hero, as in the Homeric original. Just the opposite, her memory draws a private and intimate portrait of the main characters, especially of the male heroes, exposing their most cruel and brutal sides. From Icarius to Odysseus and Telemachus, the memory of Penelope, through a simple and bare language, reconstructs the violence and suffering she has endured, showing the Homeric heroes as brutal and vile men not only towards their enemies but also, and especially, in their relation with women.

This is not, however, the only way memory is used in the novel. At a deeper layer the novel denounces the negation and willful obliteration of the feminine, through the prohibition on worshipping or even naming the Great Mother, the Goddess, described by Meso the royal bard from Crete as "una divinità antica come la terra. Essa è… Come dirti, la profondità immensa da cui tutti proveniamo."[23] This primordial female divinity was celebrated in Crete and is now worshipped secretly by the Iloti (helots), the people who lived in Sparta before the Acheans subjugated and reduced them to slavery.

Melissa, Penelope's first friend, daughter of a Spartan noblewoman and of the high priest of the Iloti, narrates the story of the Iloti, introducing her to the worship of the Goddess. The repossession of this female religious cult, deleted and negated by men and by the patriarchal systemin general, is the heart of the novel. It aims to foreground a 'symbolic' revolution through the repossession of the socio-symbolic structures on which the fundamental dissymmetry between the sexes is based.

In line with the Italian thought of sexual difference, La Spina declares the need for the re-appropriation of a female conceptual universe through

---

22. La Spina, *Penelope*, 124. "And it's I who have chosen him."

23. La Spina, *Penelope*, 26-27. "A divinity as ancient as earth. She is like… how to tell you, the immense depth from where we all come from."

the search for new symbolic roots that affirm the positivity of the difference of women. The feminist re-appropriation of female origin figures, such as the Goddess, questions a patriarchal order that defines the feminine as a site of male projections. Alternative figurations of female subjectivity are transformed into a foundational site for the empowerment of women.

One of the distinguishing features of patriarchy is the subordination of the mother with respect to the father. Though born of woman, man willfully obliterates the feminine, replacing the maternal origin with the abstract notion of man being at the origin of himself. "This re-appropriation of origin by man condemns the feminine to subsidiary position of necessarily silenced other."[24]

By giving back to women the originating cult of the Goddess, La Spina argues for a new symbolic foundation of difference, one where the feminine is not subaltern and inferior, but where this same dissymmetry becomes a factor of empowerment for women. Moreover, the cult of the Great Mother allows Penelope to create strong and lasting relations with other women who share her problems and sustain her in the moment of need. The relation she develops with Melissa has many of the characteristics of 'affidamento' ('entrustment') that characterize the relation between a young and older woman in the thought of sexual difference. In Melissa the young Penelope finds the only person she can count on. Through the secret cult of the Great Mother, the relation between the two women seems sealed by a superior power, one that gives to Penelope new hopes and energy.

Even after the death of Melissa, killed by order of Penelope's father, the relation between the two women does not terminate. In Ithaca, after the long absence of Odysseus, Penelope rediscovers the cult of the Goddess, and during one of the secret celebrations Melissa talks to Penelope through the voice of Eurycleia, advising her to weave a shroud for Laertes. The cult of the Goddess also seals another important relation: the one between Penelope and Cleone. It is in fact the revelation to the young suitor of her secret worship that ignites their reciprocal passion. Cleone, unlike other men, is knowledgeable about the cult of the Goddess, and he reveals to Penelope that the cult has never been prohibited in his homeland, the island of Lesbos:

---

24. Rosi Braidotti, "Foreword" in *In Spite of Plato. A Feminist Rewriting of Ancient Philosophy*, Adriana Cavarero, trans. Serena Anderlini D'Onofrio and Aine O'Healy, (Oxford: Routledge, 1995), xvii-xix, xvii.

> Da noi, a Lesbo, non c'è mai stato tale divieto, da noi tali dee sono
> state sempre potenti e venerate... E cos'altro è poi, regina, la divina
> Afrodite se non un'aspetto della medesima dea? La madre, la figlia,
> l'amante, come tutte le donne del mondo – oh quante cose sapevi,
> Cleone, quante.[25]

Since Cleone has participated in the celebrations of the Goddess, Penelope decides to share her secret with him, and in consequence they fix their first secret meeting in the cave where the Goddess reveals herself:

> "Io e Cleone, e tra noi quella promessa: la grotta oltre il boschetto
> di lauro, dove la Dea arcaica si rivela. Un appuntamento dunque, il
> primo – i tanti successivi non potrei più contarli."[26]

From the first moment, Cleone was distinguished from the other men by his gentleness and candor. Now, by sharing with Penelope the cult of the Goddess, he is further associated with feminine values, and his relation with Penelope seems to start under the good auspices and protection of the Goddess. Penelope, however, knows that Odysseus would never forgive her or Cleone should he come back one day and discover their relation. She even prays the Goddess to prevent or at least delay his return: "Sì, non c'è scampo per noi se ritorna Odisseo. – Oh Dea, fa che non ritorni. O almeno ritarda il suo cammino, perché io possa godere di questo amore. Ancora."[27]

Penelope by La Spina completely overturns the faithful and waiting spouse image drawn by Homer. Penelope is no more the keeper of the heroic memory of the hero or of the other male characters, but of their darker and somber sides. The violence and sufferings she has undergone, as well as the abuses endured by the women around her, are at the center of her tale. In this archaic patriarchal society where violence and cruelty reign, we discover through the eyes of Penelope how women recur to separatism as a political practice and try to recreate new spaces, rooted in the company of

---

25. La Spina, *Penelope*, 111. "In our place, in Lesbos, there has never been this prohibition, in our place these goddesses have always been venerated... and what else is then, my queen, the divine Afrodite if not a different aspect of the same goddess? The mother, the daughter, the lover, as all the women of the world – oh how many things you knew, Cleone, how many."

26. La Spina, *Penelope*, 113. "Me and Cleone and that promise between us: the cave beyond the laurel trees woods, where the archaic goddess reveals herself. An appointment, the first – the many more that followed I could not count anymore."

27. La Spina, *Penelope*, 119. "Yes, there is no escape for us if Odysseus comes back. – Oh, Goddess, let him not come back. Or, at least, delay his return, so that I can enjoy this love. Again."

other women and under the protection of the primordial divinity the Great Mother, the Goddess. Their secret cult provides them with a sense of self-belonging that eases the estrangement they feel towards patriarchal codes and creates a consciousness of new roots and spaces that are created by and for women.

The cunning

In La Spina's *Penelope* the queen is also characterized by a developed cunning that is equal or even superior to Odysseus'. Penelope is frequently alerted to the possibility of Odysseus' return, and she feels dread at the very thought of it. When she learns from Telemachus that an old beggar has arrived at the palace, she immediately grasps that Odysseus is back. Even before meeting him, she runs to inform Cleone, since she knows he will be the first victim of her husband's terrible revenge. She does not find him and she knows that this will cost him his life. Later on, during her first meeting with the beggar, she is well aware of Odysseus' disguise and she never lets her senses be fooled by her husband's shrewdness. So while the beggar talks to her she thinks to herself that she has to be careful, she does not have to trust him: "... in guardia, Penelope, in guardia. Sai bene di cos'era capace Odisseo."[28] Later on, to confirm her supposition, she also witnesses the reaction of the beggar to the death of the old dog, Argo:

> Argo è canuto, stanco, pieno di zecche [...] si accuccia ai piedi del mendico – un gemito ultimo e poi la fine. [...] E allora vidi le lacrime scendere lungo le tue guance luride, vidi come nascostamente le forbisti – cominci a soffrire anche tu, vero, Odisseo?[29]

Penelope knows that Odysseus is back and is purposely hiding his true identity from her, so she decides to play the same game. She wonders how he could have thought that she would not recognize him: "Come hai pensato di ingannare, me, Penelope, la donna che ti ha visto nei momenti di debolezza, o di furore? [...] Bene, continuiamo questa partita finché la notte arriva [...]".[30] She will lie to him as he lies to her, she will complain

---

28. La Spina, *Penelope*, 125. "...on guard, Penelope, on guard. You know well of what Odysseus was capable."

29. La Spina, *Penelope*, 126. "Argo is white haired, tired, full of ticks [...] kneeled to the beggar's feet. And then I have seen the tears falling down your dirty cheeks, I saw how you secretly concealed them – you are also starting to suffer, isn't it Odysseus?"

30. La Spina, *Penelope*, 127. "How could you think of deceiving, me, Penelope, the woman who has seen you in the moments of weakness, or of anger? [...] Well, let's continue playing this game until the night will come."

for the many years she has been waiting for him faithfully: "Oh come mi divertirò con te, Odysseus, una notte intera a disposizione a tessere inganni per te."[31]

Penelope plans to leave the palace during the night to warn Cleone, but she underestimates Odysseus' cruelty and desire for revenge. He blocks her on the stairs: "Torna subito a casa, signora, se non vuoi che un destino feroce si abbatta su di te."[32] It is no longer the beggar's voice speaking to her but Odysseus'. Penelope is once again forced into a passive and powerless position, no longer free to act. Later, she will try to send one of her maids to tell Cleone, but all the doors have been blocked. Even Eurycleia does not follow her orders, and Cleone will be killed by Odysseus along with the other suitors. Her cunning cannot help Penelope save the only man she loves. With the return of Odysseus she goes back to a position of subordination, and her cunning proves insufficient to modify the new order set up by the violence of Odysseus. Penelope's cunning cannot modify a system where all power rests in the hands of men.

The shroud, the bow and the bed

In her version of the *Odyssey*, La Spina does not give as much prominence to these three elements. The shroud is still present in the plot, though with different connotations, and the episodes of the bow and of the bed are completely omitted. Once Odysseus is back and has killed all of the suitors, Cleone included, Penelope is not interested in recalling the events that led to his victory. It is clear that she hates the man who is returned. There is no more life for her next to him. The episodes of the bow and of the bed, demonstrating the strength of the king and the cunning of the queen, lose their centrality once Penelope realizes she has lost the only one she loved, Cleone.

Even the episode of the shroud is linked to a prediction of the arrival of the young prince from Lesbos. Penelope follows the advice of Melissa and asks the suitors for more time to weave a shroud for Laertes. But unlike in the Homeric version, she unravels the shroud at night for a different reason. She realizes that on Laertes' shroud she has unintentionally woven the face of a man, Cleone, standing on his ship sailing towards Ithaca: "Si, Euriclea, fu in quella trama della tela da morto che io vidi Cleone, ritto sull'arco teso

---

31. La Spina, *Penelope*, 127. "How much fun I will have with you, Odysseus, a whole night at my disposal to weave tricks for you."

32. La Spina, *Penelope*, 129. "Go back home immediately, madam, if you don't want a terrible destiny striking down on you."

della nave proveniente da Lesbo."[33] In that moment she cannot know the identity of the man she has drawn. Frightened and perhaps aware that it is a message from the gods, she decides to unweave the shroud. It is then that Melantho betrays her and reveals her scheme to Antinous: "Ma quella notte stessa, alla luce delle lanterne subito sciolsi il ricamo. E Melantò ancella traditrice lo rivelò ad Antinoo."[34] Here the shroud assumes a different meaning. It is not a device conceived by the queen to keep alive the memory of Odysseus and allow him to come back, rather, it is a prediction of the arrival of Cleone, the man who will become Penelope's lover and change her life.

Cleone

Perhaps the most significant new element introduced in La Spina's novel is the adulterous affair that Penelope has with Cleone. Penelope is not anymore the faithful wife described by Homer; on the contrary, she despises her husband and chooses another man as her lover. Cleone is not a man like the others. He is different from Odysseus. He is neither violent nor cruel and he is younger than Penelope. All these are characteristics that do not make him a good choice for a new king, highlighted by Laertes' remark "Non è della stessa pasta di Odisseo."[35] However, it is just this difference that makes him special to the eyes of Penelope. He does not seem to share the same patriarchal value system — consisting of war, violence and cruelty — that unites the other men. He is also aware of the celebrations to the Goddess and does not endorse, like the others, the prohibition of her cult. Moreover he loves music and poetry and is able to write, a rare skill possessed in Sparta only by the scribes.

Cleone represents a new man — the opposite of the idealized hero of the Homeric epics. He shows a sensibility and candor which do not belong to Greek men. Moreover he is a prince and moves and talks with a royal elegance that strikes Penelope, accustomed to more rude and vulgar men. His arrival is surrounded by a divine aura. Penelope has seen his face on the shroud she was weaving for Laertes, in itself a prophecy of his death.

When the young prince arrives and introduces himself to the queen she immediately recognizes him and she is taken like in a magic spell. Later, recalling the event to Eurycleia, she cannot even remember what she did

33. La Spina, *Penelope*, 104." Yes, Euriclea, it was in the shroud that I have seen Cleone, standing on the ship coming from Lesbo."
34. La Spina, *Penelope*, 104. "But that same night, at the light of the lanterns, I immediately I loosened the embroidery. And Melanto treacherous maid revealed it to Antinous."
35. La Spina, *Penelope*, 107. "He doesn't have the temperament of Odysseus."

because she was so completely taken by him: "[...] cosa feci, quali furono i mie gesti? Nulla, nulla mi ricordo. [...] Tutti, dunque tutti presi da incantamento. E io più di tutti turbata. Ché mai avevo veduto simile eleganza di gesti, di parole."[36]

Through her love for Cleone Penelope discovers her physical desires; her love for him is passionate and erotic. She had suffered the violence of the father, and her husband had left her when she was still a young girl. She has never felt the same passion for any other man. After the first secret meeting in the cave of the Goddess, Penelope meets with Cleone many times. She asks him to run away with her, but Cleone refuses; he wants to marry her according to the rules of Ithaca.

Their relation cannot be kept secret for long. Penelope realizes that Telemachus has followed her to the cave and discovered them together. When he returns from Sparta he asks her arrogantly where her lover is: "Non vedo il tuo amante madre... dove l'hai nascosto, il nostro Cleone di Lesbo? – mi sussurra."[37] At the return of Odysseus it is Telemachus who encourages his father to kill Cleone. At the end of the novel, with Odyssues back and Cleone dead, Penelope realizes that she cannot live the same life with Odysseus anymore. He has killed the only man she loved; she cannot forget or forgive.

She knows now, however, that a different life is possible for her, and this transformation has been made possible by her love for Cleone. Penelope is transformed through her love, and she now becomes aware of her body, desires and needs. Cleone is at the heart of her deep transformation from a passive and subdued woman to one who takes destiny in her own hands. Her adulterous act represents for Penelope a re-birth to life through love and passion. The body is leading this transformation before the mind. She is taken by a passion that transforms the way she looks at life.

The faithful and passive wife gives place to a new woman who rejects the impositions and takes life in her hands by choosing for the first time the man she wants. Adultery in La Spina's novel becomes a symbol of freedom and liberation from the passivity and segregation in which women are enclosed, and it loses the negative connotations that characterize adulterous women in patriarchal societies. The consequence of adultery for Penelope is the awakening of her body and her mind to a new freedom. After her relation with

36. La Spina, *Penelope*, 106. "What did I do? How did I act? Nothing, nothing I remember. [...] Everyone was bewitched. And I was shaken more than anyone else. As I had never seen so much elegance in the movements and in the words."

37. La Spina, *Penelope*, 122. "I don't see your lover, mother... where have you hidden our Cleone of Lesbos? – he whispers to me."

Cleone, Penelope can no longer be the same woman. She cannot accept the abuse and tyranny of Odysseus, and the surprise ending of the novel is a direct consequence of this loss of adultery's shame.

A twist ending

Penelope by La Spina ends with a surprise, a real twist ending. Penelope does not go happily back to her married life, waiting for Odysseus to depart again for another of his adventures, as in the Homeric version. Instead, she decides to leave Ithaca. But surprises do not end there. She sails away with Eurycleia, the old nurse of Odysseus, the safeguard of Odysseus' honor, the woman who contributed to the death of Cleone by failing to inform him of Odysseus' arrival as Penelope had asked her to do.

What is the meaning of all this? What is the message the author aims to transmit? This ending is not historically and realistically credible, as it would have been impossible for a woman of Penelope's time to go away without the permission of her husband. Moreover Homer's audience would never have accepted the idea of a married woman abandoning her husband and taking her destiny in her hands, subverting the traditional woman's role.

The protagonist of *Penelope* does not belong to the Old Greek world. Penelope is the timeless and universal symbol of all battered, violated, abused women who decide to break the chains of passivity and self-victimization by which they are enclosed and to modify for themselves a destiny that had been set and imposed on them by others. But they cannot do this alone, and men are not really there to help them. The only solution is to rediscover a lost sisterhood, a network of assistance among women who share the same problems. Eurycleia has been listening to the story of Penelope. Now she finally realizes her own mistakes. The voice of the drunken Odysseus downstairs, recalling his sexual adventures to his friends, comes clearly to the ears of the two women and triggers Penelope's bitter comment: "Adesso guardami negli occhi, nutrice, e dimmi: per quest'uomo mi hai conservata? Per questo feroce tramatore di menzogne, per questo uomo violento, rude e così... estraneo?"[38] At this point Eurycleia understands her mistakes and asks for Penelope's forgiveness: "Perdono, Penelope, perdono, — singhiozza lei. E si getta ai miei piedi [...]".[39]

---

38. La Spina, *Penelope*, 134. "Now, look into my eyes, nurse, and tell me: for this man did you preserve me? For this cruel weaver of lies, for this violent and rough man, for this... stranger?"

39. La Spina, *Penelope*, 134. "Forgive me, Penelope, forgive me, – she weeps. And she threw herself at my feet."

Penelope's tale, the narration of her life and sufferings, shows the transformation of Penelope, but it is also an instrument of change for the old nurse. Through her new communion with Penelope the old nurse begins to see herself no longer as a slave but as a full human being with rights of her own. At the end of her narration Penelope decides she cannot remain in Ithaca and tells Eurycleia of her intention to leave. At this point Eurycleia begs Penelope to take also her in her journey: "[...] Eurycleia si getta in ginocchio: ti prego, Penelope, ti prego non lasciarmi qui ... con loro." [40]

Eurycleia has become aware for the first time of her individuality. Following Penelope's example she is also able to see herself as a free individual who can create her life and decide her destiny: "Io non ero nulla prima, dice, solo una schiava reietta dal letto di Laerte, ma adesso, con te... scrivimi il mio nome, signora, fammi sapere chi sono." [41] Through Penelope's friendship, Eurycleia starts redefining her identity. She asks Penelope to tell her who she is, to write down her name. When Cleone had arrived to the palace and Penelope had discovered that he was able to write she had asked him to write down everybody's name. The act of writing assumes for Penelope and Eurycleia a special meaning: by identifying people and things with specific signs, the act of writing provides a special identity, affirms the current existence and secures the memory of people and things to future generations. For Eurycleia to have her name written down means to define clearly her being as unique. Penelope listens to her requests and gives her an identity: "Tu sei Euriclea, le dico, la nutrice. E non sei più una schiava. (...) tra poco – forse – non saremo più Penelope e Eurclea, ma due amiche sul piatto specchio del mare. Due naviganti, forse persino due raminghe, che andranno di corte in corte... senza mai fermarsi." [42]

The last pages of the novel conclude with the narrating voice of Eurycleia. Some years have passed and Odysseus has never found them. Eurycleia is a different woman now. Her journey with Penelope has opened new horizons not only geographically – "l'immenso regno del divino Poseidone" [43] but, more importantly, inside herself:

40. La Spina, *Penelope*, 134-5. "Euriclea falls on her knees: I implore you, Penelope, please don't leave me here... with them."
41. La Spina, *Penelope*, 135. "I was no one before, she says, only a slave rejected from the bed of Laertes, but now, with you... write my name, my Lady, let me know who I am".
42. La Spina, *Penelope*, 135. "You are Eurycleia, I tell her, the nurse. And you are not a slave anymore. [...] soon – perhaps – we won't be anymore Penelope and Eurycleia, but two friends on the flat glass-like sea. Two sailors, perhaps even two wanderers, who will go from one court to the other... without ever stopping."
43. La Spina, *Penelope*, 136. "the huge kingdom of divine Poseidon".

E in questi anni ho compreso che quando una donna è stata per un certo tempo realmente padrona della sua vita, non è più sposa di nessuno. E la sua casa non sarà più la casa dell'uomo che parte e ritorna a suo piacimento, ma ne cercherà qualcuna altrove – o forse nessuna.[44]

Eurycleia's has been an internal journey that has matured and transformed her. During their journey they have heard about Odysseus and his adventures, with his name associated to ideas of freedom. For Eurycleia this is unjust: "What about us?" she asks to Penelope in the last lines of the novel: "E di noi? Di noi nulla? No, nulla, ha risposto Penelope. La vera libertà è silenziosa. E stranamente ha riso."[45] Penelope and Euriclea are finally free. They have won their freedom. No one has given it to them. They can be themselves without following the orders of others. Theirs is a freedom that comes from inside and that no one will take away from them. It is a freedom that does not need to be shouted but lived.

Conclusion

The novel by La Spina is certainly the harshest and roughest of the three novels analyzed here. In sharp and bare language, often bitter and merciless in recalling the violence experienced by the female protagonists, La Spina takes us backstage of the heroic epics where no male character shows any real sign of heroism.

The narration by Penelope is heart-wrenching, direct and almost brutal. There is no irony or sentimentality displayed. Even the relation with Cleone is from the beginning associated with death. The young man is destined to die. His values and attitudes are completely different from the ones that kings and heroes need to be able to seize the power. There is no mercy or pity for the weak, and women certainly are the ones paying the highest price. Mothers, daughters, wives are cloistered within their houses, used and exchanged as objects, violated or killed without any possibility of freedom except suicide.

The picture of the Homeric world drawn by La Spina is intentionally disturbing and provoking. The novel has the clear objective of denouncing

---

44. La Spina, *Penelope*, 136-7. "During these years I have understood that when a woman has been for a certain time master of her life, she cannot be anymore somebody's wife. And her house will not anymore be the house of the man who goes and comes back at his liking, but she will look for another one somewhere else – or perhaps no one."

45. La Spina, *Penelope*, 138. "And about us? Nothing about us? No, nothing, answered Penelope. True freedom is silent. And unexpectedly she laughed."

the social mechanisms of oppression of women and the acritical acceptance of internalized traditional models of womanhood — such as the division of roles, the physical and psychological violence on women, the different meanings given to male and female adultery. Penelope and Eurycleia are not only women of the past. They represent a universally and timelessly degraded and humiliated womanhood. How can woman escape from this patriarchal cage, find a freedom that seems to be denied? One answer the novel gives is through narrating their lives, recalling their stories, sharing their sufferings, transmitting their experiences orally or by writing.

And it is, in fact, through disclosing her version of the story, by recalling the terrible events of her life that first Penelope and later Eurycleia show their resistance and opposition to any form of dominion. The act of narrating gives back to the female protagonists their identities by plumbing the depths of their own existence in relation to the others. By narrating her story Penelope re-emerges physically and spiritually from a condition of numbness, melancholy and depression into which she had fallen after the return of Odysseus and the death of Cleone. Not only narrating one's own story but also listening to someone else's tale can change one's life, as is the case for Eurycleia. Penelope narrating her life to Eurycleia creates a new bond between the two women, and this special relation, this friendship, will be the foundation of a new life for them both. This special bonding among women is another step towards the conquest of individual freedom offered by the author. The relations with Melissa and later with Eurycleia can be interpreted within the Italian concept of sexual difference as the practice of entrustment "la pratica dell'affidamento", in which one woman recognizes that another has more competence and enters in a relation of trust with her, so she can be helped to realize her full potential. We can witness this relation between Melissa and Penelope when Melissa introduces Penelope to the cult of the Goddess and transmits knowledge that will help Penelope access to a new mode of existence. In the last part of the book, it is Eurycleia who entrusts herself to Penelope and through their friendship is able to re-define her identity and her place within society.

The rediscovery of the cult of the Goddess is an important element; it grounds the relations among women in connection to a higher figure who represents and protects them. By bringing to light the old myths of the Great Mother, La Spina follows the path of French feminists such as Luce Irigaray, Julia Kristeva and Hélène Cixous and of Italian feminist philosophers such as Adriana Cavarero and Luisa Muraro, who aim to lay the foundation for the creation of a new symbolic order through the relation with the mother and with an archaic, primordial mother, the Goddess. The value given to this elevated religious figure allows women to find a new strength and arrive at their own sense of worth. Within this re-established mother's genealogy a new symbolic order in her name can be envisioned. The novel seems to show that through this renewed relation and entrustment women can find new identities and challenge the norms established by patriarchal society. The novel by La Spina most definitely re-interprets the archetype of Penelope within a feminist perspective and completely transforms the figure of the queen, refuting the passive and faithful image of mother and wife, making Penelope the archetype of a new female subjectivity, and laying the foundation of a potentially new socio-symbolic order.

CONCLUSION

Life is like an echo: if you do not like what you see,
you need to change the message that you send.

James Joyce

Analyzing the theme of Penelope from Homer's *Odyssey* to La Spina's *Penelope*, Leclerc's *Toi, Pénélope* and Atwood's *The Penelopiad*, the multiple facets that compose the prismatic figure of the queen of Ithaca have been brought to light and given new life.

The analyses and interpretations of recent critics, like Papadopoulou-Belmehdi in particular as analyzed in the second chapter, have shown that the character of Penelope drawn by Homer in the *Odyssey* is a rich and complex figure, going far beyond the simplistic aspects of fidelity and patience for which she is most generally renowned. Far from being an inactive, submissive and subdued woman, the queen of Ithaca is continually acting in the shadows — as she is well aware that the rules of Greek society do not allow her to openly refuse to re-marry. She displays an interesting array of trickeries, fine-tuned in line with her infallible memory. Moreover she is a central character of the epic; in the words of Papadopoulou-Belmehdi "she is the key not only of his *nostos* (return) but also of his *kleos* (glory)". Without Penelope and her matchless memory Ulysses would have been unable to regain his place as king of Ithaca. It is her memory and not the collective one that allows him to regain a throne that no one had yet been able to seize.

Next to 'memory' the other step on the thematic path of this study has been Penelope's 'cunning' or *metis* in Greek. Like Ulysses, Penelope continuously shows "an astute kind of intelligence that understands the situation and keeps it under control."[1] Her device of weaving during the day and unweaving during the night to gain time with the suitors and her organization of the trial of the bow have been transmitted to us by tradition. Less well-known is the ruse of the bed that she uses to test Ulysses/the beggar on the veracity of his claims. One further element of her cunning is the apparent inactivity under which she hides a continuous action.

Penelope s presented by Homer as a model to follow, in direct contrast with Clytemnestra, wife and murderess of Agamemnon, both for her faithfulness to the live memory she keeps of her far-away spouse and for the capability to use her *metis*, showing her equality and even superiority to her husband in weaving trickeries.

Though interesting and enlightening, the picture drawn by anthropologists and critics of ancient Greece, as discussed in the second chapter, is nonetheless based on the figure of woman constructed by a man according to the values and principles of an ancient society. To illustrate to a really revolutionary re-vision of the character of Penelope we turned to contemporary novels and in particular to revisionist novels written by women who, projecting their feminist concerns, aim to create new representations of female subjectivities for an outright re-definition of femininity.

The three contemporary novels analyzed here were written at short intervals and with no direct or clear influence among them, and they show evident differences in style, plot and character development. The order in which they have been analyzed in this book has been set intentionally, according to their degree of conformity to the plot and the portrayal of the characters to the original version by Homer.

Toi, Pénélope (2001) by Annie Leclerc is certainly the nearest to the *Odyssey*. As claimed by the author in her preface to the novel, no modifications to the plot of the poem have been made: "J'ai répris le recit d'Homère sans en rien modifier."[2] Within the novel are constantly cited and intermingled with the narration the original verses of the Homeric poem, extracted from the 1942 French translation by Victor Bérard.[3] As demonstrated by the title, the narrative is centered on the perspective of Penelope with the utilization

1. Adriana Cavarero, *In Spite of Plato. A Feminist Rewriting of Ancient Philosophy*, trans. Serena Anderlini D'Onofrio and Aine O'Healy, (Oxford: Routledge, 1995), 18.

2. Leclerc, *Toi, Pénélope*, 16. "I have followed the tale by Homer without modifying anything."

3. Homère, *Odyssée*, trans. in French by Victor Bérard, (Paris: Armand Colin, 1942).

of an original second person narration ("tu"/"toi") to refer to the main character, Penelope. This narrative technique, utilized mainly in modern and post-modern novels and in the French 'Nouveau Roman' ,[4] puts the reader immediately at the center of the story and seems to question not only Penelope but each of the readers accessing the text. The style is also very similar to the epic poem in its use of polished and lyrical language that takes the readers back to the atmosphere of the *Odyssey*.

Likewise, the plot does not offer any particular surprise. As in the *Odyssey*, Penelope is a wife, but she is first of all a mother. She shows her feelings for Telemachus whom she loves deeply, and she is aware that by growing he is becoming more distant from her. When he decides to leave Ithaca to seek news of his father, the narrator affirms: "Ulysse, en s'en allant, n'avait pas emporté le monde avec lui. Télémaque, si."[5] Penelope feels a similar love for Melantho, the young servant she has brought up as her daughter. She could not have endured her death. Penelope is able to hide her before the massacre of the suitors and the disloyal servants. No details are given in the novel, but we understand that the young girl has been taken to a safe place.

In her relation with Ulysses, Penelope shows a more intimate and feminine side. She is jealous of her husband. After the massacre of the suitors, Ulysses narrates his adventures, his capture by Circe and Calypso, and his meeting with Nausicaa, the only woman who did not force him to lay with her. As a mature woman and wife, Penelope ponders that since he could not have her, he would always keep this young princess' memory intact: "C'est ainsi que pour ne l'avoir pas possédée, il la gardera à jamais, unique, incomparable, levée en son berceau de brume, telle qu'elle lui apparut."[6] She becomes jealous of her because she fears that it will be Nausicaa, the inaccessible virgin, and not herself, Penelope the wife, who will be remembered by Ulysses in the other life. So Nausicaa's place is preferable to her own : "S'il en est une à envier ce ne peut être que Nausicaa."[7]

In Penelope's eyes Ulysses is not a hero but just an ordinary man. She suffers for his hiding from her behind the mask of a beggar, his revealing his identity to Telemachus and to the old nurse Eurycleia and not to her. One of the main difference, in fact, from the Homeric version – that we find in all

---

4. One of the most interesting examples of Nouveau Roman written in second person narration is *La Modification*, Michel Butor (Paris: Édition de Minuit, 1957).

5. Leclerc, *Toi, Pénélope*, 56. "Ulysses when he left did not take the world with him. Telemachus did."

6. Leclerc, *Toi, Pénélope*, 201. "For not having possessed her, he will remember her forever, unique, incomparable, standing up in her cradle of mist, as she appeared to him."

7. Leclerc, *Toi, Pénélope*, 202. "If there is someone to be envied it can be only Nausicaa."

three novels analyzed here – is Penelope immediate recognition of Ulysses even disguised under the clothes of a beggar. While Homer keeps Penelope in the dark about the real identity of the beggar, Leclerc shows how Penelope is aware of his identity even before seeing him and how her actions following his arrival are influenced by this knowledge.

Another important difference from the Homeric version is the strong criticism of violence and aggression expressed by Penelope, who considers them primary male values. When she is sent to her rooms by Telemachus just before the trial of the bow, she considers how men are just using women as pretexts to embark in wars: "Les hommes ne cessent de prendre prétexte des femmes pour se faire la guerre. Mais c'est la guerre qu'ils veulent, bien plus que les femme."[8] She remembers the day all the men left for the Trojan War — how they were shouting and laughing while the women were closed in their silence. The women were building their fortresses to which men had no access: "Ce que vous pensiez vous ne le diriez pas. Vous garderiez tout pour vous."[9] By creating their own interior worlds, women could hide their feelings, as Penelope herself has been doing during the absence of her husband.

On the other side, Penelope is well aware that the world of men is linked to war and violence. Even Telemachus, the son so loved and brought up by women, has been transformed by the arrival of Ulysses. Penelope learns from Eurycleia that Ulysses had ordered Telemachus to kill the traitor maidens with the sword but that Telemachus decided it would be a too honorable death and instead has hanged them. Penelope is initially shocked by the behavior of her son but then she understands: Ulysses had not allowed him to draw the bow and Telemachus had directed his repressed anger against the young servants: "Quel ouragan furieux a retourné le fils humilié en homme impitoyable, transgressant l'ordre sacrée du père, serrant la corde autour du tender cou des servants!"[10] Otherwise, how could someone like Telemachus be responsible for a so terrible killing? She cannot avoid the thought that the real cause is Ulysses and his urge for revenge that has spread the violence in her house. And this violence is not finished. The parents of the young princes killed by Ulysses are now seeking their revenge. Again Penelope cannot do anything to avoid the violence. She, like the other women, has no voice. She can just wait in her room for news of the battle.

8. Leclerc, *Toi, Pénélope*, 164. "Men use women as a pretext to make war to each other. But it is war that they want, much more than women."

9. Leclerc, *Toi, Pénélope*, 169. "You would not say what you thought. You would keep everything for yourselves."

10. Leclerc, *Toi, Pénélope*, 214. "What a furious hurricane has transformed the humiliated son in a pitiless man, disobeying the sacred order of the father, tightening the rope around the neck of the servants."

Penelope cannot accept violence and war and, unlike Ulysses, she does not justify the massacre in name of a "juste vengeance".[11] War is the worst thing that men can do. In the final pages of the novel the writer reflects on the causes of war; she suggests that women should not be the only ones left to mourn the lives lost but that they should instead share this pain with men, demanding them to stop the killing. Her novel ends with the old Penelope and Ulysses embracing each other and crying together.

The second novel, *The Penelopiad* (2005) is the most recent and popular of the three. Penelope relates her story in a first-person narration from Hades, the underworld, more than two thousand years after the events. The tone of this novel is much lighter than the others; there is a suffused irony that makes readers laugh and reflect at the same time. Penelope here is a more ambiguous character. Her narration is accompanied by a contrasting version offered by the hanged maidens, introduced as a Greek chorus, who instill continuous doubts on the veracity of her tale and on her faithfulness in general. The original plot is generally followed, and all the main events related in the *Odyssey* are here re-called. However the description of the characters is decisively different. Both Odysseus and Penelope are very different from the original version. Odysseus is a plain liar with little of the heroic man transmitted from tradition. Penelope, on her side, is a woman who just wants revenge on both her husband and her cousin Helen. She is not the faithful and passive character we have been accustomed to but a modern and angry wife who expresses her anger at having being transformed through time into an "edifying legend. A stick used to beat other women with."[12] Her message is clear from the first pages: "Don't follow my example."[13]

Penelope's relation with Telemachus is also quite conflictual. She clearly considers him a spoiled child, and her relation with Melantho is not as central as in the previous novel. More space is given to Penelope's youth by recalling events transmitted by oral tradition which do not appear in the *Odyssey*: the attempted murder by her father and being saved by a group of ducks; the early memories of her mother, a Naiad, who preferred swimming to staying with her; the ironic and negative comments of Helen and her maids on Odysseus when he came to ask for her in marriage; her antagonistic relation with her cousin Helen.

The Penelope drawn by Atwood offers a very different representation of the myth. Penelope is as astute and canny as Ulysses, and like him she is also

11. Leclerc, *Toi, Pénélope*, 229. "right revenge".
12. Atwood, *The Penelopiad*, 2.
13. Atwood, *The Penelopiad*, 2.

a very good dissimulator or even an outright liar. The existence of natural masculine and feminine qualities is completely overturned in this novel; it is clearly shown that both men and women play parts according to their role and gender that most of the time do not correspond to their real thoughts. In this novel, as in the previous one, Penelope also recognizes Ulysses immediately when he returns. Moreover, she uses the maids to spy on the suitors so she is fully aware of everything happening in the palace though hiding her thoughts.

By placing all the main characters in Hades centuries after the events, Atwood allows them to be blunt in their recounting of events; their stories become almost confessions. So Helen, Antinous, the maidens, Eurycleia reveal to the readers their hidden thoughts and their own versions of facts since now they are free to speak with nothing to lose. The result is a very intriguing tale where different perspectives interlace and give us multiple and sometimes opposing truths. The real victims, however, appear to be the twelve maidens, hanged by Ulysses, forgotten by tradition or remembered only as traitors. The same Penelope honored by tradition for her constancy is accused by the maidens of complicity in their murder to prevent their possible revelations of her unfaithfulness.

Another interesting difference from the *Odyssey* is the language. There is nothing lyric or classic in the dialogues or in the tale recalled by Penelope. The language is frank and direct with a edge of sarcasm characterizing the speeches of the main characters. The novel is constructed like a piece of theatre where the reader's interest is held by shifting perspectives and the irony that characterize the different scenes. It is not surprising that shortly after publication the book was adapted into a theatrical version and performed in England and Canada in 2007.

The third novel here analyzed has been *Penelope* (1998) by Silvana La Spina, chronologically the first published but certainly the farthest and most original in respect to the Homeric plot. La Spina's novel has neither the lyrical nor ironic tone displayed by the previous texts but is characterized instead by strong realism and crude language. Penelope recounts her life to Eurycleia, while Ulysses is downstairs, drunk, recalling his sexual adventures to his friends. Penelope denounces the violence that men use on women and in recalling her life she reveals very brutal details relating to the relation with her father, the suicide of her mother, the selfishness of her husband and son. No man seems to avoid a generally pitiless and almost sadistic behavior towards women. The only one who will turn out to be different and who does not share the "manly" values of violence and oppression of the weak is Cleone of Lesbos — the only man whom she herself has selected but whom Ulysses will kill in his final revenge.

Penelope is not only a clear denunciation of patriarchy, it is also a hymn to a mythical sisterhood among women rooted in the archaic cult of the Great Mother, la "Dea", the Goddess. By destroying and prohibiting this cult, men have wiped out the foundational site for the empowerment of woman, denying the authority of the mother as public function and in symbolic terms. In line with the Italian concept of sexual difference, La Spina focuses her novel on the re-discovery of maternal authority through the re-evaluation of this ancient cult. Melissa, the priestess of the Goddess and friend of Penelope, is in this perspective a central character. She will help Penelope in her self-development and even after death will be able to guide and advise her. This relation can be read through the lens of sexual difference as "affidamento" or "entrustment". According to this "pratica dell'affidamento" a woman recognizes that another woman has something more and can help her to realize her full potential.[14] This is not a relation based on equality but on "un di più", something more that the entrusted woman possesses in respect to the less experienced one. In the words of Luisa Muraro: "dall'essere in relazione con lei ti viene un di più di esistenza".[15]

Penelope learns from Melissa the worship of the Goddess and with it re-discovers her body, her femininity and her strength. The novel is rooted in a clear-cut difference between the world of men and that of women. Telemachus by growing into a man through the rite of passage from childhood to manhood becomes alienated from his mother as he assimilates the values shared by men and associated in the novel with violence, arrogance and subjugation.

Cleone, the only man loved by Penelope, has been chosen by the queen because he is different from the other men. He is a poet, he likes music, he can write, and he shares with Penelope the cult of the Goddess. None of the men Penelope met before are in any way similar to him. However he is considered by Laertes not apt for ruling because he does not share the values of violence and cruelty that a king or commander needs to be respected. Penelope is an adulteress in this version of the story and loses her conventional role of faithful wife. Circumstances however seem fully to justify the queen. She has never been loved by any man. From father to husband and son, no one has shown any care for her. With Cleone she discovers that she can love with passion and that she can be loved and respected by a man.

14. Milan Women's Bookstore Collective, *Sexual Difference: A Theory of Social-Symbolic Practice*, trans. Teresa de Lauretis and Patricia Cicogna, (Bloomington: Indiana University Press, 1990).

15. Luisa Muraro, "In the name of the Mother. Sexual Difference and the Practice of 'Entrustment' " in *Cultural Studies Review*, vol. 11, no. 2, (Sept. 2005): 36-48, 42. "By being in a relationship with her you acquire something more–un di più–of existence, life."

A further difference from the Homeric version is the surprise ending that sees Penelope and Eurycleia leave Ithaca and gain their freedom by travelling anonymously in unknown lands. This relation between the two women is also surprising, since through the Homeric poem we have learned to regard Eurycleia as quite suspicious of Penelope and almost competing with her for Ulysses' recognition. However it is Eurycleia who, after listening to Penelope's story, realizes that she has more in common with her than with the men and asks to join her in the journey. While in the first part of the book it is Penelope who enters into a relation of entrustment with Melissa, at the end of the novel it is Eurycleia, though older than Penelope, who realizes she needs her help to discover who she really is. She has no separate identity; she is just one of the slaves. With Penelope she becomes a person, an individuality who discovers herself to have her own will and desires. By asking Penelope to write her name, Eurycleia is metaphorically born again to a new life. In consequence, she cannot remain where she is. She asks Penelope to take her on the journey on which she is about to embark, a journey that expresses a deep transformation for both women from subjugation to freedom.

The analysis of these three novels has shown how in the last decades the traditional representation of Penelope as myth of true womanhood based on faithfulness and patience has been challenged. This current revision of the myth is also, and especially, the consequence of a new feminist sensibility that has been developing since the late 1970s and that has called into question the gendered hierarchy of society, exploring cultural understandings of what it means to be a woman.

These revisionist novels give new life and voice to Penelope, a classic literary figure created by a male writer, Homer, within a patriarchal social structure. They offer challenging re-readings and re-interpretations by women writers of a traditional model of woman. The three novels differ in tone and style but share the same criticism of patriarchal values via a first-person female perspective. In all three novels the main hero Ulysses becomes representative of male values, consisting fundamentally in the celebration of violence and war and indifference to the sufferings of the weak. In *Toi, Pénélope* and in *Penelope* this difference between men's and women's spheres of action is clearly gendered, while in *The Penelopiad* the difference is more suffused as Penelope is accused by the maidens of being as much a liar and cheater as her husband.

Masculinity and femininity — and characteristics assumed to be naturally linked to women, such as passivity, naivety, innocence — are revealed as disguises intentionally chosen by women for their own defense. In all three novels Penelope reveals herself to be very aware of the things happening around her. Unlike the Homeric version, she recognizes Ulysses when he arrives in the palace and proposes the trial of his bow knowing that he is the only one able to string and draw it.

In all three novels Penelope criticizes the violence of Ulysses against the suitors and the maidens; and especially in *The Penelopiad* and *Penelope* she considers the suitors and the maidens as innocents killed unjustly. Ulysses could have taken back his throne while sparing the lives of so many young people, and his action is considered in a negative light in all three novels.

If we consider the mythical faithfulness of the queen, this is read differently in each of the three versions. While *Toi, Pénélope* adheres to the Homeric version, in *The Penelopiad* the revelations of the maidens seem to instill doubts on the queen's faithfulness. The novel *Penelope* clearly portrays an adulterous relation of Penelope with Cleone of Lesbos, whom the queen has willingly chosen as her lover. All three novels, however, make clear that the relation between Penelope and Ulysses is not a match of two similar souls as suggested from the Homeric poem and that the principal thing both spouses have in common is their cunning and ability to concealing their real thoughts. In this sense, Penelope appears to be much more actively involved in the political life of Ithaca, where she uses her shrewdness and acumen to manage the palace and the island once Ulysses is gone to war. In *The Penelopiad* moreover she uses the maidens as spies on the suitors. In *Toi, Pénélope* she is able to save the life of Melantho, the young servant she loves as a daughter, hiding her from the fury of Ulysses. Penelope's relation with Telemachus is not read in the same way in the three novels. In *Toi, Pénélope* the queen keeps her son in the highest consideration while planning her actions and is more a mother than a wife. In both *The Penelopiad* and *Penelope* the son is seen as a spoiled and selfish young man who has many of the characteristics of his father and feels no real love or respect for his mother.

It is not surprising that in all three novels men in general do not enjoy the particular respect of Penelope. In a patriarchal society such as ancient Greece men were certainly the masters of their houses. However, men appear not only to control their women but also to use violence on them. In both *The Penelopiad* and *Penelope* the attempt by Icarius, the father of Penelope, to kill his daughter is recalled. The more explicit in this direction, however, is *Penelope,* which focuses most strongly on domestic violence. In this novel, Icarius is accused of raping his daughter and causing the death of his wife. He also kills Melissa, the friend of Penelope. Ulysses also is a violent and almost sadistic man, and his presence will also draw Telemachus into this spiral of violence.

To conclude, we can say that the three novels are clear denunciations of patriarchal society, but their final messages and solutions differ quite significantly.

Toi, Pénélope focuses on a strong repudiation of war and on the need for men and women to come together so that men, listening to the demands of women, can learn to avoid violence. The feminist perspective expressed here represents the concern of the author, Annie Leclerc, who gives women a special role in guiding men towards the creation of a better world.

In *The Penelopiad,* the post-modern approach of Margaret Atwood directs our attention to how subjectivity is not fixed and coherent but contradictory and constantly being reconstituted in discourse every time we think or speak. Truth and knowledge are not objective, but constructed through discourse, reflecting relations of power. There is no single truth in the novel, with Penelope showing herself to be a master of disguise as much as Ulysses. She is accused by the maidens who cannot obtain justice for their deaths even in Hades. The novel seems to show that between women and men there is not a difference given by nature, but only differences due to their respective social and gender positions in society and the expectations others have of them. So both Ulysses and Penelope are skilled liars; and there is no sisterhood possible among women. Penelope is strongly critical of her cousin Helen while the maidens take every possible occasion to accuse Penelope. Atwood's feminist approach is clearly post-modern in that it denies speaking for a universal 'woman' while giving multiple voices to women from the margins.

The last novel, *Penelope* by Silvana La Spina, is imbued with concepts drawn from the Italian feminist thought of sexual difference: sisterhood among women based on entrustment and the figure/cult of the mother/goddess. The issue of domestic violence is also at the center of the novel, highlighting the need to oppose any form of socio-symbolic and physical violence and domination imposed on women within the 'cage' of patriarchy. This is the only novel offering a different ending, which can be metaphorically read as the journey that every woman needs to take to find in herself the freedom to be the kind of woman she chooses, without being caught in pre-fixed gendered models of womanhood.

By deconstructing the character of Penelope, new and unexpected representations of womanhood have been brought to light, offering new models and shaping new patterns of womanhood. One of the most familiar slogans of Western feminism has been 'the personal is political', showing how gender relations within the domestic realm are strongly connected to the same relations in government policy, laws, social relations, job market, etc. Traditions, values, customary ways of doing things have been frequently detrimental to women's interests and have been underpinned by unspoken assumptions about sex roles, about how it is proper for them to behave.

Changing these assumption is one of the political concerns of feminism in general. Within the specific field of literature this task has been translated into a revisionist examination of classic representations of women and into the creation of new and challenging female characters able to represent the multiplicity of womanhood.

Women are not a homogenous group, and in the same way, feminist modes of theorizing and narrating are not all alike. However what these writers share is the criticism of androcentric (male-centered) ways of knowing, challenging much of what has passed for objective knowledge but instead has been produced by men. Women, living in male-dominated societies, have more often been the objects of knowledge than the producers of it. Feminist theory in general and feminist criticism and literature in particular aim to give voice to women, to make women generate knowledge about women.

Within this path, a feminist revision of myths of womanhood and a re-writing of female archetypes from a feminist perspective, as of Penelope in this case, are inevitable because they can help broaden the definition of femininity to include new possibilities and more inclusive representations of female identity.

BIBLIOGRAPHY

Anderson, Linda. *Plotting Change: Contemporary Women's Fiction*, (London: Edward Arnold, 1990).

Anzaldúa, Gloria Evangelina. *Borderlands/La Frontera: The New Mestiza*, (San Francisco: Spinsters/Aunt Lute, 1987).

Anzaldúa, Gloria and Cherríe Moraga eds., *This Bridge Called my Back: Writings by Radical Women of Color*, (New York, 1981).

Arthur-Katz, Marylin. *Penelope's Renown. Meaning and Indeterminacy in the Odyssey,* (Princeton N.J.: Princeton University Press, 1991).

Atwood, Margaret. *The Penelopiad. The Myth of Penelope and Odysseus*, (Edinburgh: Canongate, 2005).

Benni, Stefano. *Achille piè veloce,* (Milano: Feltrinelli, 2003).

Berard, Victor. *L'Odyssée d'Homère, étude et analyse*, (Paris: Mellottée, 1934).

Bertoletti, Isabella. "Feminist Theory: Italy" in *The Feminist Encyclopedia of Italian literature*, Rinaldina Russell ed., (Westport-Connecticut, London: Greenwood Press): 113-116.

Blau DuPlessis, Rachel. W*riting Beyond the Ending: Narrative Strategies of Twentieth-Century Women Writers*, (Bloomington: Indiana University Press, 1985).

Bono, Paola and Sandra Kemp, eds. *Italian Feminist Thought. A Reader*, (Oxford: Basil Blackwell, 1991).

Braidotti, Rosi. "Commento alla relazione di Adriana Cavarero" in Cristina Marcuzzo and Rossi Doria Anna eds., *La ricerca delle donne. Studi femministi in Italia*, (Torino: Rosenberg & Sellier, 1987), 188-202.

———. *Nomadic Subjects: Embodiment and Sexual Difference in Contemporary Feminist Theory,* (New York: Columbia University Press, 1994).

———. "Foreword" in *In Spite of Plato. A Feminist Rewriting of Ancient Philosophy*, Adriana Cavarero, trans. Serena Anderlini D'Onofrio and Aine O'Healy, (Oxford: Routledge, 1995), xvii-xix.

Brunel, Pierre. *Homère. VIII siècle av.J.-C.*, (Paris : SEM, 2009).

Buffière, Félix. *Les mythes d'Homère et la pensée grecque* (Paris: Les Belles Lettres, Collection d'études anciennes, 1956).

Butler, Judith. *Gender Trouble: Feminism and the Subversion of Identity* (London: Routledge, 1990).

Butor, Michel. *La Modification,* (Paris: Édition de Minuit, 1957).

Cade Bambara, Toni ed., *The Black Woman: An Anthology* (New York, 1970).

Cantarella, Eva. *Storie di dei ed eroi,* (Milano: Mondadori Scuola, 2010).

Carby, Hazel V., "White Woman Listen! Black Feminism and the Boundaries of Sisterhood," in *The Empire Strikes Back: Race and Racism in 70s Britain,* ed. Centre for Contemporary Cultural Studies (London: Taylor & Francis, 1982), 211-234.

Cavarero, Adriana. "The Need for a Sexed Thought" in P. Bono and S. Kemp eds., *Italian Feminist Thought. A reader,* (Oxford: Basil Blackwell, 1991), 181-185.

———. *In Spite of Plato. A Feminist Rewriting of Ancient Philosophy,* trans. Serena Anderlini D'Onofrio and Aine O'Healy, (Oxford: Routledge, 1995).

Christian, Barbara. *Black Women Novelists: The Development of a Tradition, 1892-1976* (Westport, Conn: Greenwood, 1980).

Cixous, Hélène. "The Laugh of the Medusa", trans. Keith Cohen and Paula Cohen, *Signs* vol.1, no. 4, (Summer 1976): 875-893.

———. "Sorties", trans. Ann Liddle, in *New French Feminisms: An Anthology,* ed. Elaine Marks and Isabelle de Coutivron, (New York: Schocken, 1981), 90-98.

Citati, Pietro. *La lumière de la nuit,* trad. Tristan Macé et Brigitte Pérol, (Paris: Gallimard, 1999).

Claudel, Paul. *Œevres en prose,* (Paris: Gallimard, Biblioteque de la Pleiade, 1965).

Clayton, Barbara. *A Penelopean Poetics. Reweaving the Feminine in Homer's Odyssey,* (Lanham: Lexington Books, 2004).

Cruik-shank, Margaret, ed., *Lesbian Studies: Present and Future* (Old Westbury, New York: Feminist Press, 1982).

Dante, Alighieri. *La Divina Commedia,* Vol. 1 Inferno, ed. by Natalino Sapegno (Firenze: La Nuova Italia, 1955).

Delebecque, Eduard. *Télémaque et la structure de l'Odyssée,* (Aix: Éditions Ophrys, 1958).

———. *Construction de l'Odyssée,* (Paris: Les Belles Lettres, 1980).

De Beauvoir, Simone. *Le deuxième sexe* (Paris: Gallimard, 1949).

Dell'Abate-Çelebi, Barbara. "Italian Feminist Thought at the Periphery of the Empire", *LITERA, Journal of Western Languages and Literatures,* vol. 22, no. 1 (2009): 17-35.

———. *L'alieno dentro. Percorso semiotico alle origini del romanzo femminista italiano,* (Bruxelles: Peter Lang, 2011).

Derrida, Jacques. "Structure, Sign and Play" in *Writing and Difference,* trans. Alan Bass, (London: Routledge, 2005), 278-294.

Eisenstein Hester and Alice Jardin eds., *The Future of Difference,* (New Brunswick, NJ: Rutgers University Press, 1980).

Ellmann, Mary. *Thinking about women,* (New York: MacMillan, 1968).

Estévez, Carmen ed., *Ni Ariadnas ni Penélopes: Quince escritoras espanolas para el siglo veintiuno,* (Madrid: Castalia, 2002).

Faderman, Lillian. *Surpassing the Love of Men: Romantic Friendship and Love between Women from Renaissance to the Present* (New York: Morrow, 1981).

Felson-Rubin, Nancy. *Regarding Penelope: From Character to Poetics* (Princeton: Princeton University Press, 1994).

Fetterly, Judith. *The Resisting Reader. A Feminist Approach to American Fiction,* (Bloomington: Indiana University Press, 1978).

Friedan, Betty. *The Feminine Mystique,* (New York: W. W. Norton, 1963).

Frye, Northrop. *Anatomy of Criticism: Four Essays,* (Princeton: Princeton University Press, 1957).

Fuss, Diana ed., *Inside/Out: Lesbian Theories, Gay Theories,* (New York: Routledge, 1991).

Gallop, Jane. *Around 1981: Academic Feminist Literary Theory,* (New York/London: Routledge, 1992).

Gilbert, Sandra M. and Susan Gubar eds., *The Madwoman in the Attic. The Woman Writer and the Nineteenth-Century Literary Imagination,* 2nd ed. (Yale: Yale University Press, 2000), 1st ed. Yale University, 1976.

————. *The Norton Anthology of Literature by Women. The Traditions in English,* vol. 1, 3rd ed. (New York: W. W. Norton, 2007).

Greer, Germaine. "Flying Pigs and Double Standards", *Times Literary Supplement,* (July 26, 1974), 784-787.

Greene, Gayle. *Changing the Story: Feminist Fiction and the Tradition,* (Bloomington: Indiana University Press, 1991).

————, "Feminist Fiction and the uses of memory" in *Signs,* vol.16, no. 2 (Winter, 1991): 290-321.

Gubar, Susan. "What Ails Feminist Criticism?", *Critical Inquiry,* vol. 24, no. 1 (Summer, 1998): 878-902.

Haraway, Donna. "A Manifesto for Cyborgs: Science, Technology, and Socialist Feminism in the 1980s," in *Feminism/Postmodernism,* ed. Linda J. Nicholson (New York: Routledge, 1990).

Haste, Helen. "Sexual Metaphors and Current Feminisms" in Anna Bull, Hanna Diamond, and Rosalind Marsh eds., *Feminisms and Women's Movements in Contemporary Europe,* (New York: St. Martin's Press, 2000): 21-34.

Heitman, Richard. *Taking her seriously. Penelope and the plot of Homer's Odyssey* (Ann Arbor: The University of Michigan Press: 2005).

Hite, Molly. *The Other Side of the Story: Structures and Strategies of Contemporary Feminist Narrative.* (Ithaca, NY: Cornell University Press, 1989).

Homer, *Odyssey,* trans. Allen Mandelbaum, (New York: Bantam, 1991).

Homère, *Odyssée,* trans. in French by Victor Bérard, (Paris: Armand Colin, 1942).

Hooks, bell. *Ain't I a Woman: Black Women and Feminism* (Boston: South End Press, 1981).

Irigaray, Luce. *This Sex Which Is Not One*, trans. Catherine Porter and Carolyn Burke (Ithaca, N.Y.: Cornell University Press, 1985).

—————. *Speculum of the Other Woman*, trans. Gillian C. Gill (Ithaca, N.Y.: Cornell University Press, 1985).

Jardin, Alice. "Prelude: The future of Difference" in *The Future of Difference*, Hester Eisenstein and Alice Jardine eds. (New Brunswick, NJ: Rutgers University Press, 1980), xxv-xxvii.

Keating, AnaLouise ed., *EntreMundos/Among Worlds: New Perpectives on Gloria E. Anzaldúa*, (New York: Palgrave Macmillan, 2005).

Kolodny, Annette. "Dancing through the Minefield: Some Observations on the Theory, Practice and Politics of a Feminist Literary Criticism", *Feminist Studies*, vol. 6, no. 1 (Spring 1989): 1-20.

—————. "A Map for Rereading: Or, Gender and the Interpretation of Literary Texts", *New Literary History,* vol.11, no. 3, On Narrative and Narratives: II (Spring, 1980): 451-467.

Koppelman Cornillon, Susan. *Images of women in fiction, Feminist perspectives* ed., (Ohio: Bowling Green University Popular Press, 1973).

Kristeva, Julia. "Talking about *Polylogue*", trans. Seán Hand, in *French Feminist Thought. A reader*, Toril Moi (Oxford: Blackwell, 1987), 110-117.

Lambin, Gérard. *Homère le compagnon*, (Paris: CNRS, 1995).

La Spina, Silvana. *Penelope*, (Milano: La Tartaruga, 1998).

Lauter, Estella. *Women as Mythmakers. Poetry and Visual Art by Twentieth-Century Women*, (Bloomington: Indiana UP, 1984).

Lazzaro-Weis, Carol. "The Concept of Difference in Italian Feminist Thought: Mothers, Daughters, Heretics", in Graziella Parati, Rebecca J. West, *Italian Feminist Theory and Practice: Equality and Sexual Difference*, (Madison, Teaneck: Fairleigh Dickinson University Press, 2002), 31-49.

Leclerc, Annie. *Parole de Femme*, (Paris: Grasset, 1974).

—————. *Toi, Pénélope*, (Aries: Actes Sud, 2001).

Lévêque, Pierre. *L'Aventure grecque*, (Paris: Armand Colin, 1964).

Loraux, Nicole. *Les experiences de Tiresias. Le feminin et l'homme grec*, (Paris: Gallimard, 1989).

—————. *Les mères en deuil*, (Paris: Seuil, 1990).

Lorde, Audre. *Sister Outsider,* (New York: Trumansburg, 1984).

Mactoux, Marie Madeleine. *Penelope. Legende et mythe* (Paris: Les Belles Lettres, 1975).

Magli, Patrizia ed., *Le donne e i segni: scrittura, linguaggio, identità nel segno della differenza femminile*, (Ancona: Il lavoro editoriale, 1988).

Malerba, Luigi. *Itaca per sempre,* (Milano: Mondadori,1997).

Manganelli, Giorgio. "Di Circe e di Penelope", in *Ti ucciderò mia capitale,* (Milano: Adelphi, 2011).

Marks, Elaine and Isabelle de Courtivron eds., *New French Feminisms. An Anthology*, (Amherst: University of Massachusetts Press, 1980).

Milan Women's Bookstore Collective, *Sexual Difference: A Theory of Social-Symbolic Practice,* trans. Teresa de Lauretis and Patricia Cicogna, (Bloomington: Indiana University Press, 1990).

Millet, Kate. *Sexual Politics*, (New York: Doubleday, 1969).

Miller, Nancy. *Subject to Change*, (New York: Columbia University Press, 1988).

Moers, Ellen. *Literary Women*, (London: The Women's Press,1986). 1st ed. New York: Doubleday, 1976.

Mohanty, Chandra Talpade. "Under Western Eyes: Feminist Scholarship and Colonial Discourses", in *Contemporary Postcolonial Theory: A Reader*, ed. Padmini Mongia (London: Arnold, 1996), 172-197.

Moi, Toril. *Sexual/Textual Politics: Feminist Literary Theory*, (New York: Methuen, 1985).

————— ed., *French Feminist Thought: A Reader* (Oxford: Blackwell, 1987).

Muraro, Luisa. *L'ordine simbolico della madre*, (Roma: Editori Riuniti, 1991).

—————. "The Passion of Feminine Difference beyond Equality", in Graziella Parati and Rebecca West, eds., *Italian Feminist Theory and Practice. Equality and Sexual Difference*, (Madison, Teaneck: Fairleigh Dickinson University Press, 2002), 77-87, 79.

—————. "In the name of the Mother. Sexual Difference and the Practice of 'Entrustment'" in *Cultural Studies Review*, vol. 11, no. 2, (Sept. 2005): 36-48.

Nagy, Gregory. *The best of the Achaeans.Concepts of the Hero in Archaic Greek poetry*, (Baltimora: The Johns Hopkins University Press, 1999), 2nd revised edition.

Nerlius, Bernardus and Demetrius Chalcondyles, eds., Homerus, *Editio Princeps* (Homer, Works), (Florence, Italy: 1488), Greek.

O'Connor, Erin. "Preface for a Postcolonial Criticism", *Victorian Studies*, vol. 45, no.2, (Winter 2002): 217-46.

Olsen, Tillie. "Silences: When Writers Don't Write" in Susan Koppelman Cornillon, ed., *Images of Women in Fiction. Feminist Perspectives*, (Ohio: Bowling Green University Popular Press, 1973), 97-112. Republished in *Silences*, (New York: Delacorte Press/Seymour Lawrence, 1978).

Papadopoulou-Belmehdi, Ioanna. *Le chant de Pénélope. Poétique du tissage féminin dans L'Odyssée*, (Paris: Belin, 1994).

Parati, Graziella and Rebecca J. West, eds., *Italian Feminist Theory and Practice: Equality and Sexual Difference,* (Madison: Fairleigh Dickinson University Press, 2002).

Planté, Christine. *La petite soeur de Balzac. Essai sur la femme auteur*, (Paris: Seuil, 1989).

Plato, *Phaedo*, tr. David Gallop (Oxford: Clarendon Press, 1975).

Pucci, Pietro. *Ulysse polutropos*, (Lille: Presses Universitaires du Septentrion, 1995).

Rasy, Elisabetta. *La lingua della nutrice. Percorsi e tracce dell'espressione femminile*, (Roma: Edizioni delle donne, 1978).

Rich, Adrienne. "When We Dead Awaken: Writing as Re-Vision" in *College English*, vol. 34, n.1, (1972): 18-30. Republished in *On Lies, Secrets and Silence: Selected Prose, 1966-1978* (New York: Norton, 1979).

Robert, Fernand. *Homère*, (Paris: Presses Universitaires de France, 1950).

Rosenfelt, Deborah. "Feminism, 'Post-feminism', and Contemporary Women's Fiction", in Florence Howe, ed., *Tradition and the Talents of Women* (Urbana: University of Illinois Press, 1991), 268-91.

Russ, Joanna. "What can a Heroine Do? Or Why Women Can't Write" in Susan Koppelman Cornillon, *Images of Women in Fiction. Feminist Perspectives*, (Ohio: Bowling Green University Popular Press, 1973), 3-20.

Russell, Danielle. "Revisiting the Attic. Recognizing the Shared Spaces of *Jane Eyre* and *Beloved*", in Federico, Annette R. ed., *Gilbert and Gubar's The Madwoman in the Attic After Thirty Years,* (Missouri: University of Missouri Press, 2009*)*, 127-148.

Russell, Rinaldina, ed., *The Feminist Encyclopedia of Italian Literature*, (Westport, Connecticut: Greenwood Press, 1997).

Saldivar-Hull, Sonia. *Feminism on the Border: Chicana Gender Politics and Literature* (Berkley: University of California Press, 2000).

Scarparo, Susanna. "Feminist Intellectuals as Public Figures in Contemporary Italy", *Australian Feminist Studies*, vol. 19, no. 44 (July 2004): 201-212.

Showalter, Elaine. *A Literature of Their Own: British Women Novelists from Brontë to Lessing* (Princeton, New Jersey: Princeton University Press, 1977).

———. "A Criticism of Our Own: Autonomy and Assimilation in Afro-American and Feminist Literary Theory" in Sandra Kemp & Judith Squires eds., *Feminisms*, (Oxford-New York: Oxford University Press, 1997), 58-69.

Slettedahl Macpherson, Heidi. *The Cambridge introduction to Margaret Atwood*, (Cambridge: Cambridge University Press, 2010).

Smith, Barbara. "Toward a Black Feminist Criticism", *The New Feminist Criticism: Essays on Women, Literature, and Theory*, ed. Elaine Showalter (New York: Pantheon Books, 1985), 125-143.

Spacks, Patricia Meyer. *The Female Imagination. A Literary and Psychological Investigation of Women's Writing*, (London: Allen & Unwin, 1976).

Spivak, Gayatri Chakavortry and Harasym Sarah eds., *The Post-Colonial Critic: Interviews, Strategies, Dialogues,* (New York: Routledge, 1990).

Stanton, Domna C. "Language and Revolution: The Franco-American Dis-Connection", in Eisenstein Hester and Alice Jardin, eds., *The Future of Difference,* (New Brunswick, NJ: Rutgers University Press, 1980), 73-87.

Stendhal, *De l'amour*, (Paris: 1822).

Stimpson, Catherine R., "Zero Degree Deviancy: The Lesbian Novel in English", *Critical Inquiry*, vol. 8, no. 2 (Winter 1981): 363-379.

Suleri, Sara. "Woman Skin Deep: Feminism and the Postcolonial Condition," *Critical Inquiry*, vol. 18, no. 4 (Summer 1992): 756-769.

Tarozzi, Bianca. "Variazioni sul tema di Penelope" in *Nessuno vince il leone: variazioni e racconti in versi*, (Venice: Arsenale, 1989).

Trousson, Raymond. *Thèmes et mythes. Questions de méthode*, (Bruxelles: Editions de l'Université de Bruxelles, 1981).

Vallvey Angela. *Los estados carenciales*, (Barcelona: Destino, 2002).

Vernant Jean-Pierre, *Mythe et pensée chez les Grecs. Études de psychologie historique*, (Paris: Maspero, 1965).

———. "Mythologie et citoyennete" in *Democratie, citoyennete, et heritage greco-romain*, Pierre Vidal-Naquet, Jean-Pierre Vernant and Jean-Paul Brisson, (Paris: Liris, 2004), 41-72.

Violi, Patrizia. *L'infinito singolare. Considerazioni sulla differenza sessuale del linguaggio*, (Verona: Essedue edizioni, 1986).

Walker, Alice. *In Search of Our Mothers' Gardens*, (New York: Harcourt, 1983).

Wallace, Michele. "For Whom the Bell Tolls: Why America Can't Deal with Black Feminist Intellectuals", *Voice Literary Supplement*, no. 140 (Nov. 1995), 19-24.

Widdowson, Peter. "Writing back: Contemporary Re-Visionary Fiction", *Textual Practice*, vol. 20, n.3, (2006): 491-507.

Woodhouse, William John. *The composition of Homer's Odyssey*, (Oxford: Clarendon, 1930).

Woolf, Virginia. "A Room of One's Own", in *Selected Works of Virginia Woolf*, (Ware, Hertfordshire: Wordsworth, 2005).

Zamboni, Chiara. 'Ordine simbolico e ordine sociale' in Diotima, *Oltre l'uguaglianza: le radici femminili dell'autorità*, (Napoli: Liguori, 1995), 33-51.

Zancan, Marina. *Il doppio itinerario della scrittura. La donna nella tradizione letteraria italiana*, (Torino: Einaudi, 1998).

FIGURE CREDITS